THE
NEW ABC OF
SHOOTING

By the same author

THE
NEW ABC OF
SHOOTING

*A fully revised and updated
guide to game and rough shooting,
pigeon shooting, wildfowling, deer-stalking
and clay pigeon shooting*

Edited by Colin Willock

Illustrated by Rodger McPhail

ANDRE DEUTSCH

The original *ABC of Shooting* first published 1975 by
André Deutsch Limited
105 Great Russell Street London WC1

Second impression 1980
Third impression 1985

The New ABC of Shooting first published in 1994 by
André Deutsch Limited
106 Great Russell Street London WC1B 3LJ

CIP data for this title is available from The British Library

ISBN 0 233 98854 8

Printed in Finland
by WSOY

94 - 78857

Contents

CONTENTS

A Note
on the Contributors

THE LATE TERENCE BLANK, BSc joined the research staff of the ICI Game Research Station in 1948. Until 1959 he worked mainly on wild partridges and published a number of scientific and popular articles. Later, he was concerned with problems of the managed pheasant and was Research Director of the Game Conservancy. He died in 1984. His contribution has been brought up to date by Mike Swan of the Game Conservancy Advisory Service.

GEOFFREY BOOTHROYD has at one time or another been involved in game shooting, wildfowling, clay bird shooting, full and small-bore target shooting and deer stalking. A restriction on outdoor activities, allied to an increasing interest in the history and development of firearms, resulted in an attachment to pistol shooting. He is the author of many books and writes for magazines in the UK and USA as well as being a regular contributor to *Shooting Times*.

W. A. CADMAN, BA, OBE is a retired officer of the Forestry Commission who served in East Anglia, Wales and the New Forest (as Deputy Surveyor), for thirty-four years. He is a keen naturalist, sportsman and author of books on wildfowling (*Tales of a Wildfowler*) and deer (*Dawn, Dusk and Deer* and *Fallow Deer*, an FC publication). He served on the committee which advised the Secretary of State for Scotland on the 1954 Bird Act (and previously served on the similar English committee). He served on the Management Committee of the BASC (British Association for Shooting and Conservation) for seventeen years. His OBE was given for voluntary work in wildlife conservation. He has just completed a book of tales of sporting dogs.

CHARLES COLES was born in Australia. From boyhood he was a keen shot and naturalist. He spent his professional life in the Game Conservancy and its antecedents, joining in 1937. He became Director in 1960, retiring in 1981. His main objective has

1

always been to initiate practical research into the urgent game problems of the day, and inform the shooting and farming public how the information can be applied.

He has made several documentary films on keepering, game management and shooting subjects and presented regular BBC radio and TV programmes on wildlife conservation. He has published six books as well as English edition works on game by German and Spanish authors.

C. L. Coles has carried out consultant work on game management in nearly all European countries – including the former Soviet-bloc states – as well as in the USA, Japan, and North and West Africa. In 1984 he was awarded the OBE for conservation work, and the CIC Gold Medal in 1990.

DAVID GARRARD was born in Surrey in 1914, and began home-loading while an impecunious student at Wye College in the early 1930s. After a period as a farm manager he became an advisor with the Ministry of Agriculture, a post he held for thirty years and described as not without its advantages when it comes to combining business with pleasure. A lifelong wildfowler, a member of BASC since 1949 and a founder member of the South Lincolnshire Wildfowlers Club, he has found home-loading to be the answer to many of the wildfowler's problems.

JEFFERY HARRISON, OBE, MA, FLS, FZI (Sci), MBOU, was Honorary Director, Conservation and Research, of BASC, a council member of the Wildfowl Trust, former Chairman of the Wildfowl Conservation Committee of the Nature Conservancy and the UK Representative on the International Waterfowl Research Bureau. He was an enthusiastic wildfowler and the pioneer of the BASC/ Wildfowl Trust gravel pit reserve near his home in Sevenoaks, which is his best memorial. As well as numerous articles in the scientific press, Wildfowl Trust publications and *Shooting Times*, he wrote several books including *Estuary Saga*, *Pastures New* and *A Wealth of Wildfowl*. He died several years ago, shortly after shooting a right and left of duck on opening day.

TONY JACKSON, born in 1937, started his sporting career on the mudflats of Chichester harbour. Formerly Editor of *Shooting Times*, he has spent the greater part of his life with gun, rifle

2

and horse. He has shot and stalked throughout Britain, hunted big game in Africa, Europe and North America, and is a keen foxhunter. Now living in West Dorset, in ideal shooting and stalking country, he considers himself extremely fortunate to have enjoyed such a wide variety of sporting opportunities.

ALAN JARRETT, who has revised the clay pigeon shooting section, lives in Chatham, Kent, close to the Medway Estuary and the Isle of Sheppey. He works in the plastics industry. He started wildfowling in 1968 at eighteen years of age and began writing professionally on shooting in 1975. Since then he has written almost five hundred articles for the shooting press and two books: *Wildfowling – One Winter's Tale* and *Shooting at Clays*. He has been chairman of the Kent WCA for the last ten years. Alan Jarrett is a member of BASC's Council, Chairman of the BASC Wildfowling Liaison Committee and a member of BASC's Conservation and Research Committee.

LEA MACNALLY, who died in 1993, was born 1926 in Fort Augustus, Invernesshire. He stalked, studied and photographed deer since his late teens and was for many years deerstalker on Culachy estate, Fort Augustus. He was employed as warden-naturalist with the National Trust for Scotland at Torredon, Ross-shire. A council member, in Scotland, of the British Deer Society, he was presented in 1971 with the Balfour Brown Trophy 'for significant contribution to the conservation of deer in Britain'. Lea MacNally lectured on Highland wildlife, contributed to *Shooting Times*, *The Field*, *Scots Magazine* and *Scottish Field*. His books include *Highland Year*, *Highland Deer Forest*, *Wild Highlands* and *The Year of the Red Deer*.

RODGER MCPHAIL (illustrator) was born in Lancashire in 1953, and studied for three years at the Liverpool School of Art. Shortly afterwards he received commissions to paint a series of partridge shooting scenes in Spain. He held his first one-man exhibition at the Tryon Gallery in 1977 and has exhibited there ever since. He was brought up wildfowling on the Dee estuary, is a keen and expert shot, fisherman, stalker and naturalist and has become, without doubt, the country's leading sporting painter. His work has often been compared to that of Archibald Thorburn. His two illustrated books *Open Season* and *Fishing Season* show the wide range of his work. Married, he lives with his family in Lancashire.

WILLY NEWLANDS wrote the Game Conservancy's books in the days when that organisation was still the Eley Game Advisory Station. He also bred many unusual gamebirds at Fordingbridge, from capercaillie to Reeves pheasants and prairie chickens. After a Churchill Fellowship in wildlife management took him to the United States, he worked for international conservation organisations in the Himalayas and Mauritius before returning to game farming in the UK. Aged fifty-eight, he is now a freelance journalist (Travel Writer of the Year, 1983 and 1987) and TV presenter. Willy lives with his computer-executive wife, Dorothy, in Chelsea and Kincardineshire, where they are restoring Lauriston Castle, home to her family for 450 years.

DEREK PARTRIDGE was Vice Chairman of the Executive Council of the Clay Pigeon Shooting Association and Chairman of the CPSA's British International Board. He competed at all forms of the sport (DTL, double-rise, handicap, skeet, sporting, ISU skeet, FITASC sporting) and competed internationally around the world at Olympic Trench, Universal Trench and Automatic Ball Trap. He has shot for the England DTL Team, the Great Britain Olympic Trench and Automatic Ball Trap Teams. He won a Silver Medal at the 1969 US World Moving Target Finals (Olympic Trench); and Gold Medals at the 1972 Paris Grand Prix (OT) and the 1973 Nordic Championships (Ball Trap), also shooting the world's first 100 straight at this new form of international competition during this event. His valuable contribution has been revised by Alan Jarrett (see note).

JOHN PHILLIPS was born in Largs, Ayrshire, in 1934, was educated at Harrow and Cambridge where he got a BA in Agriculture. He was a farm manager and feed salesman before farming his own 110 arable acres in Fife. In 1965 he became a game advisor with the Eley Game Advisory Service, forerunner of the Game Conservancy. Later he became game advisor to the Economic Forestry Group in Edinburgh. He is a freelance consultant on wildlife management and founded the Reconciliation Project, now the Joseph Nickerson Reconciliation Project, to further the cause of the joint management of grouse and grazing animals.

RICHARD PRIOR is one of those happy people who have managed to turn their hobby into their profession. From the lowly grade of Trapper (Third Class) he rose in sixteen years to Head Ranger in the Forestry Commission. He moved to the Game Conservancy for five years before launching out as an independent Deer Consultant. He has written many books on deer, and is Consultant to both the Game Conservancy and the British Deer Society. He is a keen game shot and fisherman.

JEAN SKINNER is Information Officer for the BASC, married with three children and living on the outskirts of Chester. Joining the BASC staff in October 1974 as a secretary, she worked with the then Director-Development for the first ten years. She has helped the Association's Director Firearms & External Services with firearms department work and was particularly involved during the progress of the Firearms (Amendment) Bill – attending Committee stages and Readings in both Houses. Since implementation of the 1988 Act she has continued to provide help and advice to many BASC members as part of the BASC Firearms Department team.

MIKE SWAN is the Game Conservancy's advisor for the south-east of England. He has been part of the Game Conservancy's advisory team since 1982. Mike is a keen all-round sportsman, with particular interests in wildfowling, rough shooting, woodland stalking and fishing. He writes regularly for the sporting press on most aspects of game managment, including a weekly rough shooters column in *Shooting Times*. He is the author of two books, *Fowling for Duck* and *Rough Shooting*, as well as being involved in the production of the Game Conservancy's well known green guides.

PETER TURNER was born in 1934, educated at King Edward's School, Birmingham, and Pembroke College, Oxford, and qualified as a solicitor in 1961. He was introduced to shooting by his father who took him out on some of his rough shooting and wildfowling expeditions when he was at home on leave during the Second

World War. He shot his first pheasant at the age of ten and his first duck one year later. In conjunction with a friend, he built a gunning punt which is in regular use. When the shooting season is over he goes fishing and deer stalking. The law has changed considerably since he wrote his contribution. At his suggestion it has been updated by Jean Skinner, Information Officer of BASC (see note).

COLIN WILLOCK, born 1919, spent the war in the Royal Marines and the first twenty years of his career in Fleet Street editing magazines, including *Lilliput*. He was assistant editor of *Picture Post* and became the first editor of *The Angling Times*. He went into television in the late fifties, becoming deputy editor of *This Week* current affairs programme. He transferred to Anglia Television to start a new wildlife programme called *Survival* in 1961, was creative head and producer of same, writing and producing around four hundred programmes until his retirement in 1989. Colin Willock has written over thirty books including best-selling novels, thrillers, humour, travel, field sports, wildlife, biography and autobiography. Most relevantly to this book he has for twenty-five years contributed a weekly page to *Shooting Times* called 'Town Gun'.

Introduction

Since this book first appeared in 1975 a great deal has changed in the shooting field and not all of it for the better. As predicted in the introduction to the first edition, shooting has grown enormously in popularity as more and more urban dwellers have discovered the pleasures of the countryside, including field sports.

On game shooting, at least, this had two immediate and obvious results. The first appears, mercifully, to be on the wane, namely the influx of shooters who really had little desire other than to fire lots of cartridges at poorly shown pheasants. Numbers slain on the day were what mattered, not the height, speed and quality of the birds driven over the guns. Many so-called commercial shoots cashed in on this with disastrous results for the sport. Firms sometimes bought days as 'corporate entertaining' for clients who knew or cared little about the niceties or etiquette of shooting. Perhaps the only good result of the recession was that it very largely knocked this development on the head. Some commercial shoots, run on excellent lines, still exist, of course, but the opportunist shoots which specialised in 'the numbers game' have, thank heavens, mainly sunk without trace. Some of the novice guns who were initiated into shooting in this way found their way into game shooting of higher quality and developed their skills and knowledge. It is hoped that this new edition of the ABC will help them and many other newcomers to widen their interests. There is much more to shooting than just letting your gun off and taking home a brace at the end of the day!

The other inevitable result of the increased popularity of shooting has been the escalation of costs, particularly where game shooting is concerned. The individual contributors to this book have, of course, covered this when updating their own chapters but some horrifying generalisations are perhaps appropriate in this introduction. At the moment of writing, the Game Conservancy Trust – the invaluable organisation that carries out scientific research on behalf of the sport – reckons the cost of rearing a single pheasant and putting it in the bag at between £15 and £17. To buy a first-class, 200—250 bird, driven pheasant day, is likely to set an individual gun back between £400 and £500. The bill for a day's driven grouse shooting might, on some moors, be double that. And people complain about the cost of their annual golf club subscriptions!

It is not, thank heavens, all like that. Friends can still run their own small shoots reasonably cheaply by doing the rearing and feeding themselves. Pigeon shooting is usually free, though some farmers are even starting to charge for that. Wildfowling, in my view the cream of shooting sport — though pigeon decoying runs it a very close second — is, apart from club subscriptions, virtually free. It is still possible for young people to find their way into the sport, often through beating on shooting days and building up good relations with farmers and keepers. Shooting is not yet, I am happy to say, entirely ruled by the cheque book.

Shooting men at all levels should not, however, feel complacent about the future of their sport. The hunt saboteurs have been remarkably successful in their virulent and sometimes violent campaign against fox hunting. Shooting is already in their sights. And yet, I find many shooting people who believe it can't happen to them. Believe me, it can and it will.

Nor should anyone forget that EC regulations, formulated in Brussels, pose continual threats to the sport of shooting. A year or so ago, it seemed that Britain would lose its right to shoot wood pigeons outside a very short (non-nesting) season. Brussels proposed to protect our number one agricultural pest for about nine months of the year, along with — can you imagine? — crows and magpies. Britain very rightly told Brussels what to do with the suggestion, although it was flouting EC law in so doing. There are many other possible EC regulations that could adversely affect our sport. At the moment of writing a proposal is still hanging around by which game would have to be inspected on the shoot by a vet and chilled — chilled! — if it was subsequently to be sold. Such regulations coming from a community in which many countries catch and kill millions of migrant songbirds a year are plainly ludicrous. For all these and many more reasons, the sport of shooting in Britain needs its watchdogs and not only watchdog organisations but, even more important, the support and interest of all shooting men.

Now for the ABC: in planning this book, my objective was to cover all aspects of shooting fully enough to satisfy both beginner and expert and yet not at encyclopaedic length.

How is such a book to be organised? First of all it has to be a reference book and one that supplies bedrock information. The basic requirement, therefore, is that it falls into main sections − Game Shooting, Stalking, Pigeons, Clay Pigeons, Wildfowling and so on. It would be too much to ask that all readers are vitally interested in *all* sections, yet I hope very much that there will be sufficient common ground for the reader to wish to visit the other man's moor, heath, marsh or covert − to use but a few of the volume titles from the long defunct, but unsurpassed, Badminton Library series. Incidentally, it occurred to me as editor that some element of that great Edwardian work would not come amiss herein and that the element an editor should seek to recapture is the highly personal and sometimes idiosyncratic flavour that the Badminton Library volumes contained. They weren't, for example, ashamed of a personal or racy anecdote or two. And so, in this book, I have assembled the sort of contributors who, born half a century earlier, would undoubtedly have sired at least part of the Badminton Library. They not only know their stuff but can put it across in their own highly individual way. All I have done as editor has been to brief them and ensure that their contributions conform to a basically uniform pattern so that readers can find their way about the book with ease.

As a naturalist cum shooting man, I feel very strongly that sportsmen should not shoot, or for that matter fish, without knowledge and appreciation of their quarry. The most obvious argument for this is that by understanding their quarry they stand the best chance of coming to terms with it successfully. This applies in all departments of shooting, but especially so in wild-fowling, pigeon shooting and stalking. But far beyond this, I honestly don't feel much sympathy with guns who just go out and shoot things in order to see them fall down. If that is the way you feel, then take up clay-busting to the exclusion of all else. As a sport on its own, of Olympic status no less, it has a section to itself in this book.

On many big continental shoots the slain are laid out at the end of the day and the keepers blow a salute to the fallen. This, to the undemonstrative British, may seem to be going a little far.

9

Nevertheless, the principal is an admirable one: respect for the quarry. There exists this undeniably strong tie between hunter and hunted which the anti-sport faction can never understand or appreciate. To me it is unarguable that when this tie exists the sportsman feels a keener joy and satisfaction in his hunting. I believe that knowledge of the natural history of the quarry is a vital element in the complete shooting man's make-up, leaving aside how such knowledge may influence the size of the bag on any given day. So I have asked distinguished naturalist sportsmen to set the scene for each main section of this book with a chapter that deals fully with the natural history of the quarry concerned.

The problem about a book that covers such a wide field is to know where the boundaries to that field should be drawn. I thought for a long while about gundogs. To my way of thinking, shooting is only half a sport without a dog. Wildfowling should not even be attempted without a good water dog to retrieve one's birds. Dogs are an integral part of shooting and therefore of a shooting book. But if dogs, why not dog training? It was tempting, but I decided that this was ranging out too far. Dogs, therefore, appear, but only where relevant and essential to the branch of the sport under discussion.

On the subject of weapons I had few problems. The right gun is at least as important as the right fishing rod. So is the right ammunition. And if foreign guns – and there are several very good ones – are still reasonably cheap, ammunition most certainly is not, hence a section for would-be home-loaders. Choice of the correct weapon is fully dealt with for each department of the sport.

Few shoots these days would be as good as they are but for the rearing techniques developed in the first place by the experts of ICI, later IMI, and now the Game Conservancy Trust. With a bit of common sense and access to the expertise that has built up on the subject, almost anyone can rear his own birds and put them to covert. So rearing and game preservation deserves a substantial section.

All this assumes that you have somewhere to shoot. This is a problem that this book cannot solve for you although it can give pointers in the right direction. Shooting can always be found at a price, an increasingly large one, through advertisements in the sporting press. It is not so easy for the young gun or the newcomer, however. Mercifully, free or virtually free pigeon shooting can still be found — provided you can persuade the farmer or landowner that you are competent, safe and trustworthy. Wildfowling clubs are often keen to take on young members and teach them the right way to approach their sport on the foreshore where, of course, shooting is free.

However, before thinking about finding shooting, the novice should consider the basics of learning to shoot and above all learning to shoot safely. Shooting schools are the place to go. Instructors will not only get the novice breaking clays in a surprisingly short time (like golf lessons the magic doesn't always follow you into the field!) but will measure the pupil for gunfit. It is amazing how many experienced shooters have never bothered to have their gun fitted to their own physique. Guns can be lengthened, shortened, given 'cast-on' or 'cast-off' (a right or left off-setting of the stock) by any good gunsmith. Gunfit is an absolute 'must' for successful shooting. Why spend a lot of money on a gun if it doesn't point in the right direction when you put it to your shoulder?

Another equally important aspect for the novice, indeed for the experienced gun too, is the law as it affects shooting and the ownership of weapons. The original contribution on this complicated subject was by Peter Turner, who was then the legal expert for The Wildfowlers' Association of Great Britain (WAGBI). Peter suggested that I should have his chapter updated by WAGBI's successor, the British Association for Shooting and Conservation (BASC). It is a successor only in so far as the organisation has changed its name to embrace wider objectives including conservation and game shooting. Jean Skinner of BASC kindly made the quite substantial modifications needed.

Finally, I would urge anyone interested in the sport of shooting, and, more important, in its continuance, to support the organisations that do represent it and battle for it. I am constantly appalled by the number of game guns I meet who are not members of any of the organisations that fight their corner in the media, at Westminster and, increasingly, in Brussels. I give details of these organisations at the end of the section on the law.

I am sure that this book has a long life ahead of it. This, its fourth edition, has been modernised and revised almost from first

11

page to last. Despite this there are bound to be things I have omitted which readers would like to see included. I shall always be delighted to receive suggestions in the hope that I can incorporate them next time round.

Colin Willock

I
GUNS

I
Guns

I have owned a good many guns and will probably own one or two more before I finally hang them up. My personal armoury has included everything from a half-pound punt gun, a double 4-bore, single 4-bore, muzzleloading 10- and 8-bores, twelves, it goes without saying, of many styles and actions, down to a single and double 20-bore which my sons long ago took unto themselves. The one thing I have never possessed and do truly covet is a really superb game gun. The way prices are today I doubt whether I ever shall. I shoot game with the nearest I can get to this, a Spanish AYA no. 1 which is a joy to handle. For wildfowl and pigeons I use a Greener box-lock non-ejector. It's chambered for three-inch cartridges which I seldom use or need, except on rare grouse-shooting expeditions. From a fairly lengthy career of sometimes fickle gun ownership, I have come up with only one conclusion. The gun and, indeed, the cartridge with which you shoot best is the one that you believe in most. Guns are like certain golf clubs. Have confidence in them and you can hit impossible shots with them.

Best guns are often made as numbered 'pairs'. I never shoot in situations where I need two guns and a loader. Should this happen to you, I recommend that you go to a shooting school to perfect the necessary loading and change-over drills!

In terms of how it throws the pattern, a 'best London gun' will perform demonstrably better than the foreigner you buy for a tenth of the price. It will not, however, shoot ten times as well. Both will kill birds if held straight. The 'best' gun, or even merely a side-by-side with a good name on its action, will look better and feel better and, because of this, may shoot better for you. It will certainly hold, and almost certainly increase its price better. This may be reason enough for buying it in the first place. To a large extent, the gun you purchase will depend on the use to which you intend to put it. I have briefed my contributors to deal separately with guns for different branches of the sport. But first I asked Geoffrey Boothroyd to explain how we have got the guns most of us use today.

C. W.

15

Shotguns

Geoffrey Boothroyd

The gun you shoot with today has not changed much in over a century, that is if you use a side-by-side double. In fact, many of the guns at present in use are over one hundred years old and still giving good service.

Such longevity is unusual in this age of planned obsolescence. It isn't accidental. There is a very good reason why both the designs and the guns based on these designs have stood the test of time. The reason in one word is quality.

The foundations upon which this appreciation of quality was built were laid in the opening years of the nineteenth century, in the days of flintlock muzzleloading guns. An improvement in speed of ignition and quickness of loading came with the introduction of percussion ignition. This swept away the tyranny of flint and steel and substituted the little copper cap, a cap that is still with us in the base of a modern cartridge.

It would be easy to describe the modern shotgun in its variant forms but a better understanding and appreciation can be obtained if the improvements that we, today, take for granted are described in an historical context. Let's trace the development of the shotgun from just over a century ago, from the time when loading at the breech end of the barrels became both practical and acceptable.

Modern shooters understandably accept that this is the best way to load a shotgun. But, in 1851, when the first successful breechloader was exhibited by the famous Paris gunmakers Lefaucheux at the Great Exhibition in London, there were many who thought the breechloading pinfire was a 'specious pretence'. This comment was made by no less a personage than W. Greener, a staunch advocate of the muzzleloader and a man who stated that 'no fear need be entertained that the use of breechloaders will become general....'

It is, of course, easy to smile, but Greener did have a formidable list of faults to back his prejudice. What was not appreciated was

17

that these faults would, in time, be eradicated and the virtues of quickness and ease of loading would triumph.

One of the fundamental problems was the pinfire cartridge itself. An accidental knock on the pin could cause the cartridge to ignite. Although I have never heard of this happening the hazard was appreciated. Pinfire gun cases were made with special safety provision for the cartridges.

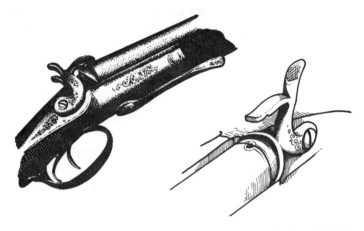

The first British breechloader, the Joseph Lang pinfire of 1852. Note (*right*) that provision has to be made at the breech end of the barrels for the pins of the cartridges.

Ten years after the Great Exhibition, George Daw, the London gunmaker, introduced the centrefire sporting cartridge which, in all essentials, is the same as that used today. The cartridge came from France and was Schneider's variant of the cartridge invented by Pottet of Paris. Daw was unsuccessful in endeavouring to restrict manufacture. His efforts to do so were defeated in a celebrated court case before Vice-Chancellor Sir W. P. Wood in 1867 brought by the famous firm of Eley Bros. Although unsuccessful in this direction, Daw's centrefire shotgun, first introduced in 1861, was a success and the brief reign of the pinfire was brought to a sudden conclusion. Unlike the muzzleloader, the pinfire had very few adherents. Once the centrefire gun was established, the pace of invention and improvement went at a truly fantastic rate.

There had been other centrefire guns before the Daw, the

Needham and the Lancaster, but neither were on the main stream of development and need not be considered here. The type of gun which was to emerge was the centrefire, hammered, under-lever, with extractors. Fitted with either back action or bar action lockwork, little changed from the day of the flintlock, this type of gun was to reign supreme for many years and countless numbers are still in use today. Pinfire guns had no extractors since the cartridge could be removed by 'the touch of a finger'. This was not always so and the sportsman was provided with a special tool which slipped over the protruding pin and so saved the finger nails. The centrefire cartridge had no pin so an extractor was developed by Charles Lancaster. Variants of this system were used until the introduction of ejectors. Lancaster's gun was very expensive and so were the special cartridges, so that its use was limited. The simple single 'tooth' of the Lefaucheux barrel locking system with the forward lever under the fore-end lacked strength and was not easy to operate. This system was modified by Henry Jones, a Birmingham gunmaker (who unfortunately did not renew his patent) into what we today call the rotary double-bite grip. Guns employing this type of breech closure were still being made thirty years ago and many are still in service since this method of locking has the merit of great strength.

REBOUNDING LOCKS

The lines on which development was to run in the second half of the nineteenth century can be summed up simply: speed and ease of operation. One of the earliest inventions which met these criteria was the rebounding lock which first appeared in the 1860s. The pinfire gun, which used the same lockwork as both the flint and percussion guns, had to have the hammers drawn back to half-cock before the gun could be opened. This was due to the overhang of the hammer nose. Even when centrefire guns came into use, this was still a necessary operation because the striker tended to remain impressed into the indent in the cap. If the hammers could be made to rebound to the half-cock position automatically, then this would save one operation in the reloading cycle and speed up the operation. Stanton, the celebrated lock-maker of Wolverhampton, patented the best of his rebounding locks in 1867 and contemporary opinion held 'that the plan was exceedingly simple, ingenious and efficacious'. The sportsman certainly thought so. This invention was so rapidly adopted that gun catalogues ceased to comment on the fact that rebounding locks were fitted.

Automatic retraction of the strikers was a subject which produced a number of ingenious solutions. A simple coil spring was the eventual answer. The complicated cams and mechanical systems of retraction survive to mystify those who encounter such a gun in their search for a bargain.

BOLTS AND LEVERS

Perhaps the next most important development was the Purdey bolt. The Daw gun had employed an underlever that was pushed forward instead of rotated. Purdey's improvement on the Schneider and Daw patents was to employ a flat bolt locking into two bites or notches in the lumps, those pieces of metal that can be seen under the barrel of most double shotguns. The flat bolt travels in grooves in the bar of the action. Originally the bolt was drawn to the rear to unlock by means of an underlever in front of the trigger. This lever was pushed forward by placing the thumb through a convenient hole in the trigger guard.

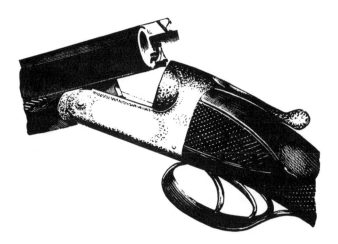

The doll's head extension,
also showing the absence of underbolts.

Most of the locking systems which are operated by underlevers require the hand to be removed from the stock. This is not so with the top lever which can be pushed across by the thumb without the hand losing contact with the small of the grip. The first of these lever systems to gain popularity was invented by Westley Richards in 1858. The locking system was based on an extension of the top rib, which lies between the two barrels of a double gun. This extension hooked into the standing breech and was held in position by the top lever. Westley Richards further improved this system in 1862 and a great number of guns have been built employing the Westley Richards 'doll's head extension' as the only means of bolting the barrels. When the Purdey bolt is combined with the Westley Richards top lever and doll's head extension (even when the latter is not bolted) an extremely strong breech closure results. An alternative to the Westley Richards doll's head extension is the Greener 'crossbolt'. Variations of this will be found on guns of German origin or design.

COCKING SYSTEMS

Although great strides had taken place in securing the barrels to the action, little work had been done on the firing mechanism. Smoothness and ease of operation had been improved but there was no fundamental change until the appearance of the hammerless, self-cocking action of two Birmingham gunmakers, W. Anson and J. Deeley. Hammerless guns had appeared before the A & D but, without doubt, this was the most important.

The first guns with Anson & Deeley lockwork were manufactured by Westley Richards in 1875. To keep matters in the family, the barrels were secured to the action by the WR top doll's head extension and toplever. Like most truly great inventions, the A & D action had the merit of simplicity. No fewer than fifteen parts were eliminated from the normal sidelock mechanism. No greater praise can be given than that this mechanism is still in use and, of even greater importance, is still being manufactured.

With the elimination of the external hammers some means of cocking the mechanism other than drawing back on the hammer 'ears' had to be found. The earliest systems used a modification of the lever which operated the breech-locking mechanism. But this made the movement of the lever rather hard, since the lever had to cock one or two mainsprings in addition to any other work it was called upon to do. In order to ease the strain on the sportsman's thumb, the tendency was to make the lever

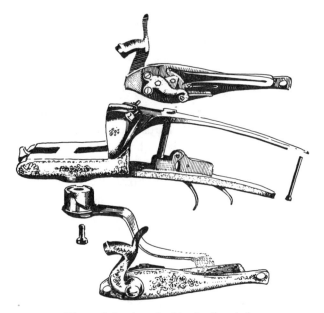

Dismantled action of a 'standard' underlever,
centrefire sporting shotgun.

longer and longer. This was self-defeating since it then had to be moved further and this took time. A very long lever was already available, the barrels! In the A & D mechanisms, it was the fall of the barrels that cocked the internal tumblers or hammers. The makers of sidelock guns also employed barrel cocking, the internal tumblers being rotated by either rods or levers put in motion by the rotation of the barrels and fore-end around the action knuckle. All that was now necessary was for the top lever to be pushed over, the barrels opened, the cartridges introduced and when the barrels were closed the gun was cocked and ready to fire.

Now that there were no external hammers, it was difficult to see if the gun was cocked. Several ingenious safety schemes were introduced. As familiarity with the action increased, most people

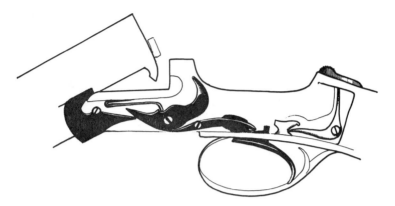

The Anson and Deeley action,
showing how the fall of the barrels cocks the gun.

knew that if you opened the gun, you cocked it. The option no longer rested with the shooter as it had done in the days of the hammer gun. Safeties appeared which blocked the triggers. These were made automatic so that, as the gun was opened, the safety was automatically applied. Blocking the triggers prevented them from being pulled, but it did not prevent the gun from being fired if the sear was jarred out of the notch or bent in the tumbler. This could happen as a result of wear, a distortion of the wood in the area where the lock was inletted, by an accumulation of dried oil or by a severe jar. Accidents of this nature did happen. To eliminate them, a more efficient safety system appeared known as the intercepting safety. This system introduces an additional limb which prevents the tumbler from fully falling unless the

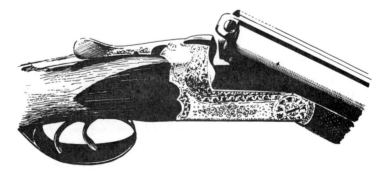

The Greener 'crossbolt' fitted to a pre-war German boxlock 12-bore.

trigger has been pulled. It is easier to fit such safeties on to sidelocks than boxlocks or A & D type actions and in general A & D actions lack intercepting safeties.

Irrespective of the type of mechanism employed, the gunmaker was trying to provide his customer with an action that was strong, easy to cock and which ensured that the cartridges did not misfire due to mechanical faults. In addition, the lock had to be 'quick' to ensure that the shortest possible time elapsed between the trigger being pressed and the gun firing. The mechanism had to be safe and also made from proper materials so that it had a long and useful life. Wear, all too often, also meant reduction in the safety margin. The mechanism had to be easy to operate without harsh action and give a crisp, smooth trigger pull, of equal weight for both locks.

SELECTIVE EJECTORS

Only two further improvements saw effective use. The first was the selective ejector. Extractors had been fitted to the earliest of centrefire guns and these withdrew both the fired and unfired cases partially from the chambers so that the head could be grasped and the case withdrawn. This, of course, took time. What the Victorian sportsman wanted was for the fired cases to be expelled from his gun without any effort on his part. Not only that, but the mechanism had to tell the difference between the fired and unfired case, hence the term 'selective ejectors'. Out went the empty case but the unfired cartridge remained in the gun, head protruding from the chamber in case the cartridge had to be withdrawn to unload. The first effecitve system was invented by Needham in 1874. This was further perfected by J. Deeley who improved the A & D action by adding his ejector mechanism. The ejector mechanism is, in reality, another gunlock. The Deeley ejector is cocked by the closing of the gun. Although in the 1880s and 1890s over twenty patents were taken out for ejector systems, only two main types have enjoyed widespread adoption – the Deeley and the Southgate.

The second improvement was the single trigger. The systems which have appeared can be classified simply into three; pull systems, delay systems and pendulum or inertia systems. All

A best London gun, a modern Holland & Holland sidelock.

are either selective or non-selective. The non-selective system deprives the user of the greatest single merit of a double gun, the instant choice of open or choke boring. Selective systems to some extent reduce the claimed advantage of the single trigger − speed − since time has to be spent in operating the selector. They are expensive, complicated and can get out of adjustment, but once you have used a single trigger gun there is a great reluctance to return to a double trigger gun, particularly when one has to shoot under really cold conditions.

OVER-AND-UNDER

One other important development in gun design occurred, the reappearance of the over-and-under gun. The word 'reappearance' is used because the over-and-under was not invented at the turn of the century. Barrels placed one on top of another had been used almost from the beginning of multi-barrelled weapons. What was new was the breechloading over-and-under. In Britain many of our early attempts at this design failed because the guns concerned lacked grace and style. Two models surmounted this difficulty. The first was the Boss, the original patents for which were obtained in 1909; the second, the Woodward. One of the problems with over-and-unders had been the retention of bottom lumps and the Purdey bolt which had made the gun extremely deep and consequently ungainly. Both the Boss and Woodward designs discarded the bottom lumps. Locking was achieved by bites located towards the centre of the barrel group. With 'lumps' located on each side of the barrels, rather than underneath, the depth of the action could be kept within reason. Neither of these guns was cheap. It was left to the genius of an American designer, John Moses Browning, and to the ingenuity of the Belgian firm of Fabrique Nationale to produce an over-and-under which could be built by modern production methods and sold at a reasonable price. The Browning 'Superpose' was introduced in 1926 and coincided with the death of the inventor. Still in production, the Browning is kept up to date in styling and can be bought with ventilated rib, single trigger and automatic safety. A very wide range of finishes is also available and like many British designs,

A typical modern over-and-under, in this case of German manufacture.

the Browning is now very widely copied. Although widely sold in America, the Browning was never made there and indeed the manufacture of high quality US shotguns has always presented problems. The only American-made over-and-under was the Remington Model 32 which employed top bolting and, as the name implies, was introduced in 1932. High manufacturing costs resulted in the gun being discontinued after ten years. However, a similar locking system is employed by the 'Lion' manufactured by Valmet Oy of Finland. In Germany, the over-and-under or *Bock-Doppelflinte* has long enjoyed popularity and is available from a number of makers, with sidelocks, A & D type actions, Blitz triggerplate actions and locking systems based on the Kersten crossbolt.

The oldest firearm manufacturing company in the world, Pietro Beretta of Gardone, Italy, build an unusual over-and-under where the locking is achieved by two small cylindrical bolts which protrude from the breech face. Other Italian guns such as the Franchi Model 63 and the Breda 'Sirio' employ the Browning type of bolt.

REPEATERS

If side-by-side or over-and-under guns do not suit, then two other types of shotgun are available which offer more than one shot, the pump and the automatic. Both are American inventions and have been brought to perfection today by up-to-date production methods.

Repeating shotguns have been made which have employed most of the available systems, revolving, bolt action, slide action, lever action and automatic. The earliest repeating shotgun to achieve commercial success was the Spencer. The cartridges were contained in a tubular magazine under the barrel and the mechanism was operated by a sliding 'hand piece', or movable fore-end. As such, this gun was the father of the many slide action or 'trombone' repeating shotguns which have appeared since.

The first of the repeating Winchester shotguns was, as one might have expected, a lever action . This was the Model 1887. With a later variant, this type continued in production until 1920.

The Winchester Model 12 slide action repeater.

In 1890, Winchester bought a patent for a slide action shotgun from Browning Bros of Ogden, Utah. Their first slide action shotgun was the Model 1893. This gun was not successful, but an improved version, the Model of 1897, became one of the most popular shotguns ever made. Countless numbers are still in use. Enjoying equal popularity was the Winchester Model 12 developed by Thomas C. Johnson and first sold in 1912. By 1943, one million had been made. It was later replaced by the Model 1200 slide action. Winchester's great rivals, Remington, entered the repeating shotgun field slightly later. Their first repeater was a hammerless gun with the popular slide action. This appeared in 1907 as the Model 10. All of the early Remington slide action guns featured bottom ejection of the empty case. Today, the

Ithaca Model 37 is representative of this type of solid action shotgun.

The self-loading or 'automatic' shotgun was also an American invention, the first commercially successful example being the Remington Model 11 Autoloader based on John M. Browning's patent of 1900. The design was offered to Winchester who turned it down owing to a disagreement over terms. Remington acquired the design and manufacture commenced in 1905. Two years earlier, Fabrique Nationale manufactured the Browning design under licence. As the Browning Automatic Shotgun, it is still in production. This 1900 vintage design has been very widely copied and 'improved'. FN continue to manufacture it as originally designed and the outline of the action body is as distinctive as a Rolls-Royce radiator.

The traditional Browning design is of the long recoil type where the barrel slides back and forth. The barrel and breech, locked together, recoil for about three inches, the breech is unlocked and latched in the rear position, the barrel moves forward, unlatches the breech which then moves forward under the drive of the recoil spring chambering a new cartridge before being locked to the barrel ready for firing.

The FN Browning five-shot automatic.

The first successful fundamental design change came in 1954 when Winchester brought out their Model 50 Autoloader. This relies on a different principle, the 'Williams Floating Chamber', with which the barrel remains stationary. The Model 50 was the forerunner of the next generation of autoloaders, the gas-operated rather than the recoil-operated guns. Here Remington were the first with their Model 58. Gas-operation appears to be steadily gaining ground and invention in this field has certainly not been exhausted by any means.

FOREIGN GUNS

Along with the greater variety of types of sporting shotgun, single barrel, double barrel, over-and-under, slide repeater, autoloader, the shooting man of today also has a wider choice of country of origin. The traditional areas of manufacture still produce shotguns. For example, guns of the very highest quality possible are still made by the London trade to standards established a century ago. Birmingham still makes guns of extremely high quality though, alas, not in the numbers of yesteryear. Britain no longer boasts of the number of 'provincial' makers many of whom such as John Dickson of Edinburgh manufactured firearms of a quality unequalled anywhere. Few of these makers are left. Fortunately, Dicksons of Edinburgh are still with us.

In Belgium, the picture is similar, except that the Belgian trade has the enormous advantage of the giant firm of Fabrique Nationale. FN can produce guns of high quality and then leave the option open to the purchaser of how much additional work he wishes to buy. Fortunately, some of the smaller firms continue in business and the gun industry of Liège shows a remarkable resilience, although sadly reduced in size.

In Italy, production is dominated by Beretta and Breda with a very large number of smaller firms still flourishing. The industry in the province of Brescia shows not only resilience but also versatility and guns continue to be made to suit all pockets and all tastes. Manufacture in France is centred in St Etienne where the truly remarkable firm of Manufrance make a range of side-by-side, over-and-under and automatic guns, one of which, the 'Ideal' side-by-side double employs a quite unusual mechanism which has stood the test of time. The French firm of Darne make a shotgun in which the barrels are fixed and the breech slides backwards and forwards, not unusual for a gas-operated autoloader but unusual for a side-by-side double!

In recent years Spain has gone to considerable trouble to improve the image of her firearms industry. Today she makes a range of sporting shotguns which are traditionally British in style and decoration. Germany still produces fine firearms. Guns are still made in Suhl and the names of Sauer, Merkel, Krieghoff can still be found on the top ribs and lock-plates of shotguns offered in Germany. The dominance of the home product is challenged not from Belgium, as it used to be, but from Italy, Czechoslovakia, Hungary, Finland and Russia. Czechoslovakia has had a gun industry for many years and firearms have been made in Russia and Hungary also. New however, is the name Miroku and one of the post-war phenomena has been the rise of the sporting gun industry in Japan. Certainly the man now in the market for a shotgun cannot overlook the products of the Japanese firearms industry, particularly if he favours the over-and-under barrel configuration.

CHOOSING A GUN

When all this has been said, the question that still faces the shooting man is what kind of shotgun he should buy.

The first principle is this: if you shoot for pleasure and alone, then your choice of gun is a matter for you alone. If you shoot in company, then the situation is different, for you owe some consideration to the views, attitudes and prejudices of those you shoot with. To take one extreme, you may find pleasure in shooting with a muzzleloader, but your friends may well take exception to the smoke, smell and possible hazard. They could well be very annoyed about the delay as I well know after a day's shooting at clays with my own muzzleloading Greener. At the other end of the scale, exception could be taken to your using an autoloader or even a pump repeater under certain conditions. I used a Winchester Model 12 pump shotgun for wildfowling for a short time and this was known to the other members of the shoot as my 'gangster gun'. The feeling, not expressed but latent, was that this weapon was dangerous and unsporting. Since I never loaded more than two cartridges at a time, the latter assertion was unfounded and in fact two shots could be got off a great deal faster from a double. The safety aspect did have some foundation, since a conventional double shotgun can always be seen to be safe merely by opening it.

30

Even bearing in mind the limitations imposed by finance and whether or not you shoot in the company of others, you are still left with a rather bewildering choice. It will help if you produce a check list. Some of the criteria may not be important: if this is so, cross them out. What are the criteria? For use in the field the first group of qualities are weight, recoil, balance and handling. Then come ease of operation and, of course, safety. Then qualities which could perhaps be the deciding ones where you are left with a difficult choice. These would include: ease of dismantling and ease of cleaning. If it takes you half the day to take your gun down, then cleaning will be neglected. Other factors which you may have to seek advice on would include reliability, durability and whether or not repairs can be made if anything does go wrong. Allied to the reliability and durability factors is the question of retention of value or depreciation. Will the gun you buy today hold its value or even increase in the years to come or are you buying merely a tool which will serve the immediate purpose and can then be discarded?

If you buy with the intention of retaining the gun in the years to come, then you must also consider another aspect of a gun, beauty. Here we are talking about functional beauty, not just applied decoration. As mentioned earlier this is something which takes one time and effort to acquire, but an awareness of beauty is important and it could well be the deciding factor in your choice of gun. A consideration of the elements of decision as outlined should help you to decide whether or not you buy a new gun or a secondhand one. Do you retain the one you have been given or sell it and buy another? Do you buy British, German, Italian, Spanish, French or American? Do you buy from an established retailer or take the splendid offer of the chap you met in the pub? Certainly, you may get a bargain in the pub, providing your judgment is not clouded, but in any case you must insist that the gun is checked by a responsible person before the bargain is made.

It is important to ensure that the gun bears the correct proof marks and that it is within proof. The provisions of the Proof Acts apply to all small arms except for most of the weapons made for the use of HM Forces, and airguns, not being firearms, are, of course, excluded. The Proof Acts lay down that 'no small arm may be sold, exchanged or exported or exposed for sale or

31

A selection of proof marks old and new.
If in any doubt about the meaning or
interpretation of proof marks, readers should
seek expert advice or consult the booklet
Notes on the proof of Shotguns & Other Small Arms,
available from the London and Birmingham Proof Houses.

exchange or pawned unless and until it has been fully proved and duly marked'. The alteration or forging of proof marks is also an offence. Any offence in dealing in unproved arms is committed by the seller, not by the buyer. Any small arms which are imported and which do not bear acceptable foreign proof marks must be notified to the Proof Master and should be delivered to the Proof House in London or Birmingham within twenty-eight days of arrival.

Shotguns can be submitted for proof or reproof direct to either of the Proof Houses but it is better to submit the guns for proof or reproof through a reputable gunmaker. It should be noted that guns will not be accepted for reproof unless in a fit condition, and since the Proof Houses will not accept responsibility for damage to stocks it is better for the stocks to be removed. If a gun is rejected or fails to stand proof, then the existing proof marks on the gun will be defaced and the weapon should be rendered unserviceable.

Although not yet a legal requirement, it is very advisable to take out an insurance policy against accident and loss or theft.

The greatest single factor in obtaining the maximum benefit from your chosen sport is confidence. You, the user, must be satisfied with the man/gun/cartridge combination and this satisfaction and confidence can only be gained as a result of practical experience.

Today, most reliable gunshops accept that a sale is not enough;

what they need is a customer, and they know that the satisfaction of the customer is largely a matter of confidence in the man/gun/ cartridge combination. For this reason, a visit to the shooting grounds is of paramount importance so that the performance of the gun can be demonstrated. The cost, in time and money, is well spent.

Confidence in the gun can only be gained and retained when both the potentialities and the limitations are known.

Shotguns are essentially short-range weapons and any attempt to extend the range carries with it penalties. For most shooting in the UK the standard $2\frac{1}{2}''$ 12-bore firing $1\frac{1}{8}$ or $1\frac{1}{16}$ oz of shot from moderately choked barrels will give satisfactory results. Avoid excess, the penalties outweigh the advantages.

It is well worth spending time on choosing your gun. It may well represent the greatest capital outlay but, in the long term, it provides best value for your money.

How to Shoot

Tony Jackson

THE WEAPON

Every time the man behind a shotgun attempts to shoot a flying bird he must, as a mathematical fact, squeeze the trigger when the barrels are pointing at a determined spot ahead of the target. The reason for this is obvious: the bird is moving at a certain speed – it may be ten miles an hour, it may be forty – while shot leaves the muzzle at a nominal velocity of 1,070 feet per second and maintains this speed over a fairly short distance. The mental processes involved in the decision to fire, and the actual carrying out of the order by the muscles, add an additional split second to the calculation. It is clear that if the gun was fired directly at a moving target, a miss behind would result. The shotgunner has to place his charge on the moving target. To do so he must fire the gun when the muzzle is ahead of the bird. All this can be proved mathematically. Various books have, in the past, published tables showing just how much forward allowance must be made to ensure a kill. As far as the practical shooting man is concerned, ballistic theory is all very fine but it has no bearing on the realities of shooting in the field.

As a matter of academic interest, the forward allowance for a bird crossing at forty mph, using a standard velocity cartridge, i.e. 1,070 feet per second, is as follows:

Range in yards	30	35	40	45	50
Forward allowance	5 ft 6 in	6 ft 8 in	8 ft	9 ft 6 in	11 ft 1 in

It is hardly necessary to point out the absurdity of these figures as far as field work is concerned. Nevertheless, while I firmly believe that successful shooting is simple shooting, it is as well to appreciate just what is involved ballistically and to understand something of the several schools of thought on the subject.

Before becoming enmeshed in practice and theory, let's take a look at the shotgun and its capabilities.

It is a fairly sobering thought that the modern shotgun, seen to supreme advantage in that thoroughbred of the shooting world – the 'best' side-by-side sidelock ejector, has gained virtually nothing, in terms of range and killing power, over its ancestor of a hundred years ago. Indeed, one can whisk back to the long-barrelled, muzzleloading flintlocks of the late eighteenth century and discover that these delightful weapons could hold their own, in terms of killing range, with any modern London-made 12-bore.

Of course, today's side-by-side is streamlined, light, well-balanced and eminently safe. Its firepower is considerable and it is doubtful if it can be further improved. Yet it still remains a short-range weapon of no great accuracy. Compared with a rifle, a precision instrument, the shotgun is a bludgeon.

In theory the range of a 12-bore shotgun may be considered as being up to sixty yards. In practice, unless the gun and its load have been specifically designed for greater distances, forty to forty-five yards is the maximum killing range for the game shot. Up to this distance the shot pattern should still be holding together sufficiently well to ensure a kill. At ranges above this distance, the pattern starts to disperse and lose velocity. While it is still possible for a bird to be killed by a stray pellet at say seventy or even eighty yards, it will only be by a fluke. It is far more likely that, if the bird is hit at all, it will be 'pricked' or wounded, something which no sportsman would wish.

RANGE

I have already explained that an estimate of range and the speed of the target must be made if the shot is to be successful. As far as the beginner is concerned it is probably the former which causes him the greatest headache. The speed of the bird is incorporated in what I term the 'natural method' of shooting and will be dealt with later. An instant assessment as to whether a bird is in, or just out of, range can really only come with experience. A useful exercise is to set up a dead bird, such as a pigeon or pheasant, at varying distances, so that a mental image can be cultivated. It is a fact that in inland shooting, and particularly where game is concerned, the majority of shots are taken within twenty-five to thirty yards; so-called high birds are often well within killing range and it is indeed rare for a pheasant to be above forty-five yards. As an example of this I recall seeing feral pigeon passing level with the top of the 120 foot tower at the West London Shooting Grounds and appearing completely out of range, yet they were no more than forty yards up.

On the other hand, on the foreshore or where he lacks some physical object such as a tree or bush to give him a sense of distance, the gunner lacking experience will often find himself shooting at birds well out of range. Mallard at sixty yards may resemble teal at forty, while geese are probably the most deceptive of all, for their size tends to deceive the tyro into supposing that they are much closer than they really are.

In order fully to grasp the limitations of a shotgun, it is necessary to have at least a working knowledge of shot charges and patterns. After all, it's not guns that kill, but the contents of cartridges − a fact too often overlooked. For consistent killing, even, well-distributed patterns are essential. Such patterns are not obtained through the use of magnum or high velocity loads, nor are they common to guns with excessive choke. It is vital that the shotgun shooter carries in his ballistical subconscious, burnt in fire, the message that patterns fail before velocity. In other words, although a heavy load backed by a man-size charge may, on paper, add yards to the potential range of a gun suited to accept it, the pattern will have deteriorated long before the striking energy of individual pellets has failed. The result is likely to be misses or pricked and injured birds.

FOUR METHODS

Ask the average good shot just how he achieves his high kill-to-cartridge ratio and he will probably pause, scratch his head and mutter something about just firing at 'em or swinging through them! All of which is singularly unhelpful.

There are, in fact, four recognised methods of hitting moving targets with a shotgun. Two totally impractical; and two workable: the Churchill method, and that of Percy Stanbury or what I call the 'natural method'. Neither, of course, invented their particular systems of shooting, but each analysed and made clear what had hitherto been a dark jungle of leads and forward allowances. The late, great, Percy Stanbury was, in my view, possibly one of the finest and certainly most elegant shots of this century and it is worth noting that he won numerous clay competitions, from local to national level, not with an over-and-under, but with his battered old Webley side-by-side.

The first two, impractical, methods are the intercept and the forward allowance methods. In the first, the gun is held still, pointed at a distance ahead of the target and fired when the shooter judges, by some obscure mental computer, that the bird will literally fly into the shot charge. It is obvious that such a method is totally impracticable and we will brush it aside.

In the forward allowance method, the gun is swung at a pre-determined distance ahead of the bird, the amount varying according to the dictates of the table on page 34. The only problem is judging what, say, six foot eight inches of lead looks like at thirty-five yards!

Robert Churchill's idea, and one which he practised with considerable success, was to teach the shooter to mount the gun on the target, swing with it consciously for a brief period, keeping both eyes open, then overtake 'subconsciously' and fire when the subconscious dictated. There can be no question that, with a well-fitted gun and correct teaching, this method can prove deadly. Nevertheless, it is not so versatile or reliable, in my opinion, as the Stanbury method, the one which, I suspect, the majority of successful shooters use, whether or not they are aware of it.

Here the gun is mounted behind the target, swung smoothly through and fired when the gun points at the target or, in the case of a large bird such as a goose, at its head. Rather I should say that the shooter *decides* to fire when he reaches this point for, owing to the reaction delay which I have already described, an appreciable delay occurs before the shot charge is sent on its way. During this reaction pause the gun has still been swinging smoothly. If the speed of the swing has been estimated correctly, the charge should strike the target.

This method is best exemplified when shooting at a bird which calls for an energetic reaction − a bird such as a snipe twisting out of a wet patch or a duck glimpsed for a brief instant when flighting. In each case the shooter, if he is successful, will only be conscious of having 'snapped' at the bird. Obviously, through the ballistical laws which we have already considered, we know that he swung the gun ahead of the bird but was not aware of having done so.

I have never believed that successful shooting, a sport which demands a close and critical cooperation between eye, brain, nerve and muscle, can be taught entirely successfully through books. Methods can be described, but in the final analysis it is in the field, under 'battle' conditions, that a shooter will have to go through the correct procedures and he will not have a book open beside him.

SHOOTING SCHOOLS

This is where the shooting school comes in. I have often pondered on the extraordinary outlook of some game shots. They are prepared to fork out hefty sums for their shoot subscription, guns and equipment, but go through season after season, shooting consistently badly, occasionally having a brilliant spell, but not really in control of the situation or aware why they are hitting or missing. Suggest lessons at a school and they shy at the idea like frightened teal. 'Too costly, by half − I'm no clay pigeon fanatic − Ruins your style, clays are slowing down and birds speeding up.' The lame excuses are trotted out, the disastrous shooting continues.

But surely, if one is going to invest a sum of money − large or small − in the sport, it is only reasonable to make every effort to acquire at least a passable skill. In the hunting field, only a fool would ride to hounds lacking all but a rudimentary knowledge of horsemanship. In the shooting field the beginner should make it his business to put himself in the hands of a qualified instructor at a shooting school. The expense involved is a drop in the ocean compared with the costs of years of missing.

If we assume that the beginner has acquired a gun, that it fits him and that he has digested the four methods of hitting a moving target and, I hope, conceded that the 'natural method' is the one for him, all that remains is for him to put theory into practice. This, of course, is where the inevitable crunch comes. Yet shooting need not be difficult. If you will consider the case of the twelve-year-old who is given a 20-bore, some basic instruction and told to get on with it, you'll perhaps see why. The boy has a mind unsullied with theory, leads, stance, swing and all the rest of it. What does he do? Why, simply picks up the gun, loads, fires *at* the clay and smashes it. Not once, but again and again. I've seen it happen and any clay instructor will cap the story a dozen times.

To the lad it has all seemed so easy. All he's done is point the gun at the swinging target and fired ... and that's the whole secret. We both know that although he *thought* he fired when the gun pointed at the target, in fact he overswung and the shot charge hit the clay.

Let's suppose you're ready for your first clays. We'll make it easy—a nice, slow going-away bird that gives you plenty of time to get yourself organised. The gun is loaded, the butt just under your armpit, your right index finger lies alongside the trigger guard and your thumb is on the safety catch ready to move it forward when the gun starts swinging; your left hand is in such a position that the gun feels balanced. Personally, I prefer a *fairly* straight left arm because with this you are going to point at the target and must also point the gun. The left thumb should lie beside the barrel. Be careful that the fingers do not curl over the side of the barrel and so partially obscure the target. Don't grip the gun tightly, merely hold it firmly and try to relax so that tension is kept to a minimum.

Keep your feet fairly close together with the weight on the forward leg. You're ready for the shot. Bear in mind that you have all the time in the world. Call for the bird and as it whirrs up, start to slide the butt in to your shoulder, bedding it firmly, push the safety catch forward and at the same time swing those barrels smoothly to catch up the clay ... when the barrels point *at it*, pull the trigger and watch it powder. If you miss, speed up your swing just a fraction next time and keep going until you get it right.

Half the battle is knowing your gun so that when you pick it up, it automatically slides into the balanced, safe position and feels like an extension of your body. Every day, practise stance, swing and general feel; try dry shooting, using snap-caps, at starlings or swallows. Remember that all the time you are swinging the gun, you have *both* eyes open and fixed on the target so that you are barely conscious of the barrels. Shooting, like cricket or tennis, is a test of coordination; the batsman, striking a ball which is a mere blur, is totally unaware of his bat, but he is supremely confident that his highly tuned and linked eyesight, nerves and muscles will do the job for him. It is the same for the shooter who must know, understand and have that same confidence in his gun.

Of course, you're not going to get simple shots all the time at the clay school and as soon as your instructor feels that you have grasped the essentials of the thing, he will move you on to something harder . . . a crossing bird, for instance, or one thrown at you to imitate a driven partridge or pheasant. Don't let yourself be distracted by the fact that you're in a simulated butt awaiting a 'driven grouse'; it is simply a clay slung towards you and whether it is ten yards up or forty it can be smashed by sticking to the same routine. Just swing up through the bird and fire as you overtake it. If a pair are thrown then you will have to take the first well in front, in order to give yourself time to switch to the other so that you can kill it just above you. It is surprising just how much time you do, in fact, have. Watch the real expert and see just how easy he makes the whole thing look. There are no unnecessary movements so that he can concentrate on powdering that first clay almost before it leaves the trap.

SHOTS HARD AND EASY

The transition from clay ground to live shooting in the field will throw up a whole new range of problems. At the shooting school the ground was level, ordered calm ruled the day and you knew precisely where and how the clays were going to come. A far cry from a draughty wood on a wild March evening with woodpigeon whipping over like stones from a boy's catapult, unheralded and unexpected; or a muddy gutter on the foreshore where stance is unheard of and fleeting shadows call for the reactions of a hawk. Of course, it's not always like this and there are numerous occasions, by the covert side, in a well-built pigeon hide or when shooting driven grouse, when the ideals of the clay school can be practised.

Part of the fascination of live shooting lies in the variety of shots; this is particularly so in the case of the rough shooter who may, in the course of an afternoon's stroll, deal with a twisting snipe, a crafty old pheasant streaking from the wrong side of a hedge, a pigeon batting over as high as they come, a rabbit bolting like a furred cannonball and a teal, a black blur of bottle-shaped speed, ripping past his ear at dusk. The variations are endless, the excitement calculated to keep you coming back again and again for more.

It would be fruitless to discuss every contingency in the shooting book, so let's just take a look at some of the more obvious shots, the sort which, if you pull them off, give you a glow that'll last for the rest of the day.

We've mentioned snipe and these feathered bolts are indeed worthy opponents, yet they are not, in my opinion, as difficult as their reputation would have one believe. One school of thought would have you fire the moment they·rise, catching them on the first zig; another suggests that you let them get well out when they have both zigged and zagged and finally straightened their flight-path. Personally I opt for the latter method, for one's pattern is considerably larger and the margin of error is reduced, moreover, the bird is unlikely to be smashed as it may well be if shot at close range. I have shot scores of snipe on my marsh, invariably with No. 6 shot as I find this covers every sporting contingency I'm likely to encounter. Use No. 8 or 9 if you wish, but a gun throwing an even pattern of sixes through the cylinder or improved choke barrel will do the work equally well; it only takes one pellet to knock down a snipe, for it is a fragile little bird.

What of that *bête noir* of the beginner, the driven grouse? Much has been written of grouse, most of it well deserved, but I still have a sneaking feeling that, fast though it is, low though it flies, creeping over the contours like a bomber under a radar screen, the grey partridge has it beaten for sheer explosive velocity. Much of the mystery of driven grouse lies in the aura that surrounds them ... the purple moors, the line of turf butts, the magnificent scenery and perhaps also the sense of occasion which they invoke. Yet are they difficult? Well, I answer, hesitatingly, yes and no. Much depends on the wind, for, make no mistake, grouse with the wind in their tails can be almost untouchable − but then so can some of those downland back-end pheasants which give the best guns palpitations when they slide down the wind at extreme range.

Grouse shooting is largely what I call 'reaction shooting'. In other words you will probably, as a beginner, do best if the birds are upon you almost without warning; their sudden presence stimulates you into stabbing at them without any thoughts of lead. It is the covey seen half a mile away which may cause the bother. Too much concentration can lead to pokey, stiff shooting and inevitable misses.

Those high pheasants I just mentioned, what of them? Well, I doubt if I shall ever get the hang of them, probably because I shoot at only a handful or so each season. These are, indeed, specialised shots which call for experience and although the expert will tell you to deal with them exactly as you would with a lower bird, just swinging that little bit faster, I find that with those I kill I am conscious of having pulled the gun way, way ahead of them. They are among the few birds which spoil the natural method of shooting, at least they do for me.

Experience is the real mentor in the field and this can come only with constant practice and by keeping your eyes open. I am quite convinced that many shooting men have a goodly portion of their sport ruined through their apparent inability to remain on the alert and to take every chance as it is offered. It is always the unexpected which catches the unwary shooter on the hop. He may think he knows his ground but time and again a pheasant or duck will appear from cover where least anticipated.

Loading Your Own Cartridges

David Garrard

Shooters contemplating home-loading naturally think first in terms of saving money. In fact the opportunities to do so on the general run of 12-bore loads are minimal but savings of the order of 20–30% can be made on the heavier 12-bore and magnum loads as well as on small bore cartridges.

'Big Bore' loaders can make savings of at least 50% soon enabling the cost of equipment to be recovered. Hand-loading offers much more than cost-saving, including the facility to produce loads not available commercially such as heavy, low-velocity loads for wildfowling, special loads for lightweight game guns as well as practice loads for clay busting etc. The ability to turn out small quantities of ammunition of a type not available at discounted prices – for example, cartridges for predator control – confers another very real advantage on the man who loads his own.

To all these material benefits may be added one, not so simple to define, but possibly the most convincing of all, the interest in an absorbing hobby that adds another dimension to the shooter's sport. To watch a bird fold up to a cartridge of his own loading gives the shooter very much the same feeling of achievement that comes to the fisherman who lands a trout on a fly tied with his own fingers.

Cartridge loading demands no profound ballistic knowledge or unusual skill. Given an intelligent approach and a moderate degree of handiness on the part of the loader, the required techniques can soon be mastered.

Most shooters have some idea of what is involved in hand-loading used cases. The sequence can be summarised as follows:

1. Resize the metal cartridge head to the original dimensions.
2. Remove the fired primer – often combined with Stage 1.

3. Seat the new primer at the correct level.

4. Meter the correct powder charge into the case.

5. Seat the wad onto the powder.

6. Meter the correct shot charge into the case.

7. Close the case by re-forming the crimp closure in 2 or 3 stages.

The loading machines now available perform all these functions efficiently if operated in accordance with the maker's instructions. They are available in all gauges from .410 to 10-bore. The machines you can now buy in Britain are, save one, of American manufacture and designed primarily to load plastic cases. The British 'Rapid' by Bowman is the exception. Although it is now out of production, spares can be obtained from the makers.

Loading machines can be divided into two types.

First, single-stage machines load one cartridge at a time and can turn out 150−200 loaded cases per hour. Such machines meet the needs of the great majority of shooters and are ideal for relatively small scale, diverse loading.

Second, progressive or multi-stage machines perform all the loading operations at every stroke of the operating handle and can produce 400−600 loaded cartridges per hour. This can be quite hard work. They are of more complex construction than the single-stage jobs and correspondingly more expensive, and are for those who need large quantities of uniform ammunition such as the committed pigeon shooter.

Among the machines listed below, the novice loader should have no difficulty in finding one ideally suited to his requirements.

SINGLE STAGE MACHINES

Lee Loadall (£45). Cheap and cheerful incorporating much plastic. A good first buy.

MEC 600Jr Mk 5 (£130). In all gauges. Simple and durable. I have used the 600Jr with every satisfaction.

MEC Sizemaster (£190). Collet resizing. Auto primer feed. One of the best of its type. Recommended.

Ponsness Warren 375(c) Du-o-Matic (£290). The Rolls Royce of its type. In all gauges including 10-gauge. Virtually everlasting and a real long-term investment. Strongly recommended to committed handloaders. Used by the author for over twenty years without replacements.

MULTI-STAGE MACHINES

Lee Loadfast (£120). Not yet fully assessed. Like the Loadall, could be a good first buy.

MEC 650 (£250). Not fully automated. A practical compromise between the single stage machine and the more expensive fully automatic models. Makes an excellent job.

MEC 9000G (£535). 12- and 20-gauge. Very reliable and highly recommended. 500−600 cartridges per hour capacity.

MEC 9000H (£900). A powered version of the 9000G which eliminates all the hard hand work. Ideal for club or group use.

Ponsness Warren Size-o-matic Elite (£760). In all gauges. Practically indestructible and a lifetime buy. Very reliable. The top of the multi-stage range. The Elite can be fitted with the hydromatic powered modification (£1100) which not only cuts out the muscular effort but raises potential output to around 1000 loaded cartridges per hour. The ultimate choice for group or club use.

The Pacific (Hornady) Model 366 Auto (£450). The only machine of this make still in production. Makes a good job but for maximum reliability production should be focussed on compression-formed cases.

Auxiliary equipment includes universal charge bars for all MEC machines. They are fully adjustable for powder (12−55 grains) and for shot ($\frac{1}{2}$−$2\frac{1}{4}$ ozs). They have proved practical and accurate and a sound investment in the long run. MEC can also supply adaptor plates for the 600Jr and Sizemaster models that enable them to cope with $67\frac{1}{2}$ mm cases. The only other essential piece of equipment that every loader should possess is a powder scale or balance. With this he can make the very necessary checks on powder charges and be confident that they are precise. There is a wide choice from RCBS, Hornady and Lyman.

Having purchased the machine of his choice the next apparent problem facing the loader is the choice of loading components from the bewildering array now available. In fact this problem is nothing like as difficult as it may appear and can be safely solved by using only those components stipulated in the tables of recommended loads. Simplicity is thus combined with safety. Here is a brief review of the components likely to be required by the novice loader.

CASES

The heart of the cartridge. Normally, fired cases will be utilised at no cost to the loader, this being the principal source of cost saving. There are three types:

Parallel plastic tubed cases: The very familiar case found in 90% of all shotgun ammunition. A parallel plastic tube is set in a metal head with a plastic base-wad. Available in all gauges and lengths. Paper-tubed versions of this type are not recommended for reloading.

Compression-formed cases: as marketed by Winchester/ Remington, e.g. Trap 100/200, Blue magic etc. Very durable, comprising a single plastic unit with a metal head. Ideal for reloading and strongly recommended for this purpose. In all gauges, $2\frac{3}{4}''/3''$.

The Activ case: A newcomer that combines the durability of the compression-formed case with the high capacity of the plastic-tubed component. In 12/20 gauge. No metal head. Eight-fold crimp. Perfect for reloading but supplies appear to be dwindling.

Acquiring an adequate supply of cases is rarely a problem as only a very small proportion of the 200 million cartridges fired annually in the UK end up on the loader's bench. The home-loader will naturally husband all fired factory loaded cases and induce friends to do likewise. A walk round the stands after a driven shoot can be productive and often reveals that those with the most money to spend buy the cheapest cartridges. By far the best source of cases are the clay shooting grounds that are proliferating everywhere. A request to garner the empties is rarely refused and several plastic sacksful can be harvested at the end of the day. Small bore shoots and those sponsored by cartridge manufacturers can supply special wants.

PRIMERS

Loaders are advised to restrict their choice to those that appear in the concluding table of loads (pp. 54−55). These include:
Group 1. CCI 109/209, WW 209, and Cheddite. All are of medium strength − the technical term for this is *brissance* − and suited to virtually all the powders listed below.
Group 2. Fiocchi 615, Eley battery-cup primer. These two develop less *brissance* than the others and are ideally matched with the NG 80 series or the Neodisc powders.

POWDERS

Choice of the correct type of powder is of vital importance for successful, *safe* cartridge loading. Here the loader should again be guided by the recommendations given in the loading tables both as regards type of powder and charge weight. *Never* depart from 'the book'. Powders can be conveniently arranged in order of burning rate as given below. Note that the 'medium' burners have the widest range of application.

Fastest burners for the lightest 12-bore loads ($\frac{7}{8}$−1 oz): Bullseye, Red Dot, NG 78, N 310.

Powders of medium burning rate for standard 12-bore loads ($1-1\frac{1}{16}-1\frac{1}{8}$ozs): AS, PSB 5, Green Dot, Unique, Clays, GM 3(BD), S4, N320, NG 80.

Slower burners for heavy 12-bore charges and standard small bore loads: A.1., Unique, HS 6, GM 3(Sp), N 340, NG 82.

Very slow burners for magnum charges in all gauges: A0, Blue Dot, HS 7, N 330.

Powders for .410 loading: BA5, SP 3, H 110. Hercules 2400 also has application here.

WADS

The wad may be the cheapest component in any cartridge but do not underestimate its importance. Any gas leaks past the wad reduce the efficiency of the cartridge and can have a disastrous effect on pattern quality. Always use high quality wadding of proven performance. Cost cutting can prove a false economy.

The traditional wadding was of waxed wool/hair/vegetable felt which still does an excellent job and is available for those who prefer it for game shooting. On many clay grounds its use is mandatory since plastic wads are non-degradable and produce a litter situation. The Diana brand is probably the best of its kind and is recommended. It comes in 15 mm, 17 mm, 19 mm and 20 mm lengths.

One-piece plastic wads supplanted the traditional material some thirty years ago. They provide a more reliable gas seal, protect the shot from erosion on the barrel walls and give a much better velocity/pressure ratio. They have everything going for them except the fact that they can litter the ground after firing. They are usually the hand-loader's first choice. The principal brands are: 'G' wads of the Gualandi range; SNIA GT range. These are both proven performers and are available in all gauges and in lengths to suit all purposes.

Other plastic wads include the versatile *Uniwad*, Winchester WAA 12 and 20 for compression-formed cases, *Remington SP 10* − the only wad of this type for 10-bores. The Gamebore 8-gauge wad is essential in all loading in that giant gauge while the WAA 41 and Remington SP410 are containers ideal for .410 loading in the compression-formed case.

SHOT

The final component over which the loader can exercise choice is the *shot*. As well as being as uniform as possible in shape and size, the constituent pellets should be hardened with antimony. Low antimony shot ($\frac{1}{2}$%), e.g. Eley, is on the soft side although it gives acceptable results in normal game-shooting. The best shot is undoubtedly that from Shotwell, a Gamebore C.C. subsidiary. It is excellent, hard 3% antimony shot in all sizes including Nos. $6\frac{1}{2}$ and $7\frac{1}{2}$ and is unhesitatingly recommended.

MAKING A START

It is unrealistic for the novice loader to expect perfect results from his first efforts but intelligent persistence guided by the maker's instructions will soon eliminate early faults. The following notes are based on extensive experience of hand-loading and are offered as a guide to those making a start.

PRECAUTIONS

The highly inflammable powders and primers should always be stored in their original containers both for safety and certainty of identification. Loose powders are an obvious hazard as are primers liable to spill underfoot. No one in his senses would smoke at the loading bench. Any heating should avoid naked flames or radiant units. Common sense and caution should always prevail.

The first stage of the loading operation is a careful examination of the cases to be used. These must be graded for type and length etc. and checked for faults. Check for bulging or distortion of the metal head. Look, too, for signs of the tube separating from the head or of splits in the tube − particularly at the crimp area. An internal examination should check that no foreign matter is present and that the base-wad is in good order with no part missing. Be rigorous in this examination and take no chances as a sound case is fundamental to a good cartridge.

LOADING WITH THE SINGLE STAGE MACHINE

The machine should be firmly bolted to a substantial table or bench. A permanent, rigid bench is not only convenient but will minimise erratic vibration of the machine and thus contribute to the throwing of consistent powder charges, an important aspect of good loading.

STAGE 1: RE-SIZING

This is sometimes combined with de-primering. Feed the case into the die and force the head home in the die thus restoring it and the case rim to their original dimensions. On all MEC machines except the 600Jr a patent collet mechanism effects the re-sizing and may need an initial adjustment. Reject any case which refuses to enter the die as, if forced, the metal head will be damaged. Other problems are rare. Ejecting the fired primer is trouble-free.

STAGE 2: RE-PRIMERING

Place a primer in the recess provided. If an automatic primer feed is fitted, check that a primer is correctly positioned. A pull on the handle will cause the ramming tube to enter the case thereby forcing the primer into the pocket and simultaneously reseating the base-wad. Slight resistance can indicate an enlarged primer pocket and a loose primer which must be rejected, as must be a case with a dished head, caused by the necessity of using extra heavy pressure. Such heads can be a fruitful source of misfires especially in under-and-over guns.

When first setting up the machine, the seating of the primer should be checked. It should be level with the head of the case or .002″ − .003″ below it. Make any adjustment to ensure that this is so and *never* proceed with the loading of a case in which the primer is proud of the case head.

STAGE 3: LOADING THE CASE

(a) **Metering the powder charge** Slide the charge bar across gently, thus feeding the powder into the case via the ramming tube. Avoid slamming the bar across as this can lead to inconsistent powder charges.

(b) **Inserting the wad or wadding** One-piece plastic wads should be placed in the wad funnel and the ramming tube lowered into the shot-cup. Steady pressure will then seat the wad onto the powder using a pressure not exceeding 30 lb. This will eliminate all air space between wad and powder charge. If the wad can be felt to foul the case mouth do not persist in ramming as the obturating cup of the wad will be damaged which will result in poor ignition. Withdraw the wad and start again, if necessary opening up the case mouth with a tapered wooden plug.

After dropping the shot, the column height should be correct for a good crimp. If necessary, slight compression of the wad is permissible to shorten the column which can be lengthened by inserting a card wad in the shot-cup before dropping the shot. If fibre/card wadding is in use, the over-powder card should be inserted first and seated absolutely 'square' on the powder. Thereafter the remainder of the wadding can be inserted and rammed to a level at which, after the shot is dropped, there is the correct 'free tube' for a good crimp closure. Once this ramming pressure is established, usually about 50 lb, the adjustable stop fitted to some machines can be set accordingly.

(c) **Dropping the shot charge** Slide the charge-bar back and leave in position. The shot charge will enter the case via the ramming tube. At this stage there should be the correct length of 'free tube' above the shot to enable a good, tight crimp finish to be made. This should be around $\frac{7}{16}$ for a 12-bore plastic case. If this measurement differs significantly from this figure, an appropriate adjustment must be made. See under (b) above. If the trouble persists it may indicate something wrong with the loading sequence. Check, therefore, that:

> the correct powder/shot charges have been dropped and that the hoppers are not empty.
> the correct wad is in use.
> a case of the incorrect length has not been selected.

A rare source of trouble here is a rogue case with a 'double' base-wad. Whatever the cause, it is essential never to complete the loading of a case in which any abnormality of loading is suspected.

(d) **Pre-crimping** This is an essential preliminary to a good final closure. Check that the pre-crimping head matches the folds in the case mouth, i.e. 6 fold or 8 fold. Lower the head to make contact with the case. On some machines an external mark enables the folds in the case to be lined up accurately with the head. On others, external fingers fitted to the head locate the folds and line up the head automatically. Do not hurry this stage. Keep an eye on the fingers and give them a chance to locate properly. Once satisfied that the head is properly lined up, lower the head until the crimp folds form an angle of about 45° with the tube.

Some cases perversely fail to align with the head resulting in a damaged pre-crimp which must be thrown out. A split at the crimp folds is another aggravating fault. The resultant imperfect crimp is an offence to the eye though it functions well enough. Another reject for the perfectionist! This splitting of the crimp folds occurs frequently on cases made brittle by low temperatures. It can be minimised by bringing cold cases into a warm room for a few hours before loading starts.

(e) **Crimping** It is very important that the final crimp be properly and tightly formed as the ballistics developed by the cartridge largely depend on this strong crimp. Aim at a uniform crimp with a pronounced taper equal to the factory finish. Some machines incorporate the tapering device in the crimping head. Others use a separate tapering head. It is difficult to put too much taper on a plastic-tubed case but compression-formed cases should not be excessively tapered − beyond the factory level − as this can lead to excessive breech pressures. The formation of a perfect crimp is worth going to a lot of trouble to achieve. It is far more than a cosmetic feature.

LOADING WITH PROGRESSIVE MACHINES

It is well worth spending some time 'fine tuning' these high output machines thus avoiding frustating, time-wasting breakdowns or hold-ups. As the throughput may approach eight hundred cartridges per hour it is advisable to have a well organised supply of all components to hand. Do not hurry. As the operating routine becomes familiar, speed of loading will build up to a level that can be sustained. In addition to the advice offered under 'Single Stage Machines' pay close attention to:

Jams or hold-ups in the primer feed.

Wad feed. Watch out for 'tipping'.

Incorrect pre-crimping.

Check indexing between handle movements. Manual assistance may be needed. Avoid the use of sub-standard cases as the machine may fail to handle these properly with consequent trouble and delays.

An assistant to feed in wads and dispose of loaded cartridges can prove invaluable when a really high output is aimed at. There remains the very important job of:

CHECKING POWDER AND SHOT CHARGES

This must be carried out at an early stage of every loading session. A proper powder scale or balance is a huge help for this essential job, otherwise a chemist's or laboratory balance must be used. It is important when making this check that the machine has been completely cycled as the unavoidable vibration associated with all the loading stages affects the weight of the powder 'thrown'. The easiest method of making an accurate check is, having loaded a case or two, to catch the powder charge at the dropping stage direct into the pan of the powder scale and to weigh it. This procedure should be repeated three to four times to strike an average. Individual charges should not vary more than .2 grains each side of the nominal weight; variations of half this value are quite feasible. Parallel checks of the shot charge are occasionally worthwhile. They should lie within 6−8 grains of the nominal weight, remembering that a single pellet of No. 6 shot weighs nearly 2 grains.

FIELD TESTING

Although extensive ballistic and patterning tests have confirmed that hand-loaded cartridges can easily hold their own with the factory product, success in the field alone will convince the loader that his cartridges are first-class. Out onto the shoot therefore with a bag of reloads. The first clean kill will engender an elation and self-confidence that will ensure a total commitment to his new hobby.

SOURCES OF SUPPLY FOR MACHINES AND COMPONENTS

Your local gunsmith should be the first contact, particularly for powders and primers as these cannot be sent by post. In the absence of local service the best first contact is: Claygame Imports, Meer Booth Road, Anton's Gowt, Boston, Lincs. This firm's catalogue contains a very extensive set of loading tables.

Other suppliers are: A Myers, Vicarage Farm, New House

Lane, Winmarleigh, Lancs. (Big bore specialist.) David Adams, 12, Queensberry Terrace, Cummertrees, Annan, Dumfriesshire. (Reloading equipment and materials.) The Gamebore Cartridge Co. aim to supply all loading components. An approach through their agents can often prove fruitful.

LOADING TABLES

Having acquired a machine, components and the know how, the hand-loader's next requirement is reliable data on effective, safe loads. It is clearly not feasible within the confines of this chapter to print a fully comprehensive set of loading tables. Those that follow are confined to the popular 12-gauge loads and should meet the needs of 90% of shooters, particularly the novice loader.

All loads are in 12-bore. *Primers* Group 1 CCI 109, WW 209, Cheddite. Group 2. Fiocchi 615, Eley.

Magnum 12-bore loads

Chamber length	Case	Primer	Powder charge (grains)	Wadding	Shot charge (ozs)
$2\frac{1}{2}''$	$67\frac{1}{2}$mm P.T.	Group 1	21.0 PSB 3	GT 43/23 22 mm 'G' wad	1
$2\frac{1}{2}''$	$67\frac{1}{2}$mm P.T.	Group 1	21.5 AS	22 mm 'G' wad	1
$2\frac{1}{2}''$	$67\frac{1}{2}$mm P.T.	Group 1	20.0 N 310	22 m 'G' wad + card*	1
$2\frac{1}{2}''$	$67\frac{1}{2}$mm P.T.	Group 1	23.5 GM 3(BD)	GT 43/23	1
$2\frac{1}{2}''$	$67\frac{1}{2}$mm P.T.	Group 1	21.0 Green Dot	GT 43/23 22 mm 'G' wad	1
$2\frac{1}{2}''$	$67\frac{1}{2}$mm P.T.	Group 2	23.0 NG 80	GT 41/21	1
$2\frac{1}{2}''$	$67\frac{1}{2}$mm P.T.	Group 2	25.0 NG 80	$\frac{1}{8}''$ card $\frac{3}{4}''$ fibre $\frac{1}{11}''$ card	1
$2\frac{1}{2}''$	70 mm C.F.	Group 2	19.5 NG 80	WAA 12 + card. Uniwad	1
$2\frac{1}{2}''$	70 mm C.F.	Group 1	19.0 PSB 3	WAA 12 + card. Uniwad	1
$2\frac{1}{2}''$	$67\frac{1}{2}$mm P.T.	Group 1	21.5 PSB 3	Uniwad	$1\frac{1}{16}$
$2\frac{1}{2}''$	$67\frac{1}{2}$mm P.T.	Group 1	22.0 AS	22 m 'G' wad. Uniwad	$1\frac{1}{16}$
$2\frac{1}{2}''$	$67\frac{1}{2}$mm P.T.	Group 1	25.0 N320	GT 38/18	$1\frac{1}{16}$
$2\frac{1}{2}''$	$67\frac{1}{2}$mm P.T.	Group 1	21.5 Green Dot	22 m 'G' wad Uniwad	$1\frac{1}{16}$
$2\frac{1}{2}''$	$67\frac{1}{2}$mm P.T.	Group 1	23.5 GM 3(BD)	GT 43/23	$1\frac{1}{16}$
$2\frac{1}{2}''$	$67\frac{1}{2}$mm P.T.	Group 2	24.5 NG 80	$\frac{1}{8}''$ card. $\frac{3}{4}''$ fibre	$1\frac{1}{16}$
$2\frac{1}{2}''$	70 mm C.F.	Group 1	24.0 A.1.	WAA 12 Uniwad	$1\frac{1}{16}$
$2\frac{1}{2}''$	70 mm C.F.	Group 1	21.0 N 320	WAA 12 Uniwad	$1\frac{1}{16}$

Chamber length	Case	Primer	Powder charge (grains)	Wadding	Shot charge (ozs)
$2\frac{1}{2}''$	$67\frac{1}{2}$ mm P.T.	Group 2	27.0 NG 82	GT 38/18 19 mm 'G' wad	$1\frac{1}{8}$
$2\frac{1}{2}''$	$67\frac{1}{2}$ mm P.T.	Group 1	26.0 A.1.	GT 38/18 19 mm 'G' wad	$1\frac{1}{8}$
$2\frac{1}{2}''$	$67\frac{1}{2}$ mm P.T.	Group 1	25.0 N 320	GT 38/18 19 mm 'G' wad	$1\frac{1}{8}$
$2\frac{1}{2}''$	$67\frac{1}{2}$ mm P.T.	Group 1	21.0 Green Dot	GT 38/18 19 mm 'G' wad	$1\frac{1}{8}$
$2\frac{1}{2}''$	$67\frac{1}{2}$ mm P.T.	Group 1	26.5 A.1.	$\frac{1}{8}''$ card. $\frac{3}{4}''$ fibre	$1\frac{1}{8}$
$2\frac{1}{2}''$	70 mm C.F.	Group 1	23.0 A1.	WAA 12	$1\frac{1}{8}$
$2\frac{1}{2}''$	70 mm C.F.	Group 1	24.0 N 340	WAA 12	$1\frac{1}{8}$
$2\frac{3}{4}''$	70 mm P.T.	Group 1	26.0 A. 1.	GT 38/18 19 mm 'G' wad	$1\frac{1}{4}$
$2\frac{3}{4}''$	70 mm P.T.	Group 1	30.0 N 340	GT 38/18 19 mm 'G' wad	$1\frac{1}{4}$
$2\frac{3}{4}''$	70 mm P.T.	Group 1	28.0 Herco	GT 38/18 19 mm 'G' wad	$1\frac{1}{4}$
$2\frac{3}{4}''$	70 mm P.T.	Group 2	27.0 NG 82	GT 38/18 19 mm 'G' wad	$1\frac{1}{4}$
$2\frac{3}{4}''$	70 mm C.F.	Group 1	27.0 N 340	Uniwad WWAAF 114	$1\frac{1}{4}$
$2\frac{3}{4}''$	70 mm C.F.	Group 1	26.0 Herco	Uniwad WWAAF 114	$1\frac{1}{4}$
$2\frac{3}{4}''$	70 mm P.T.	Group 1	23.0 A.1.	GT 36/16 14 mm 'G' wad + card*	$1\frac{1}{2}$ (L.V.)
$2\frac{3}{4}''$	70 mm P.T.	Group 1	32.0 A0	14 mm 'G' wad.WAA 12 Red.	$1\frac{1}{2}$**
$2\frac{3}{4}''$	70 mm P.T.	Group 1	34.0 Blue Dot	14 mm 'G' wad.WAA 12 Red	$1\frac{1}{2}$**
$3''$	76 mm P.T.	Group 1	36.0 Blue Dot	17 mm 'G' wad. Uniwad	$1\frac{5}{8}$**
$3''$	76 mm P.T.	Group 1	36.0 A0	14 mm 'G' wad + card*	$1\frac{5}{8}$**

* Place 20-bore card in shot-cup before dropping the shot.

** For use in 'magnum' proved guns only.

700 mm = $2\frac{3}{4}''$

76 mm	= 3"	$1\frac{1}{8}$ oz	= 32 grams
1 oz	= 28 grams	$1\frac{1}{4}$ ozs	= 36 grams
$1\frac{1}{16}$ oz	= 30 grams	$1\frac{5}{8}$ ozs	= 46 grams

OTHER SOURCES OF INFORMATION

The sporting press regularly publish information on handloading.

A booklet on the Vectan range of powders is obtainable from the Gamebore Cartridge Co., Great Union Street, Hull.

Mountain & Sowden, Town Ings Mills, Stainland, Halifax, can supply a booklet on the Vitavouri powders.

II
GAME
SHOOTING

II
Game Shooting

There are two sorts of game shooters; both are catered for in this book. The driven shooter expects a lot of birds and pays highly for the privilege. He rightly despises low, slow birds and he pays his keeper or his subscription to be shown plenty of high, fast ones. He is a fairly stationary piece of artillery. If he has a dog, it sits, we hope, obediently beside him. It is there to pick up, not to hunt, except to find an occasional runner. It is likely to be a retriever. The covert shooter is often a first-class shot at driven birds. He will be asked to put little of himself beyond markmanship and good sportsmanship into the day.

The other sort, the rough shooter, is more likely to own a spaniel, or possibly a labrador. These days, hunter-pointer-retrievers such as German short-haired pointers (GSPs) are very popular. With his dog he will do much of the hunting himself and, indeed, this may be his major joy. He will probably hope for a proportion of driven birds during the day but will be equally happy to try to put them over his companions. In shooting, more than most sports, you take your choice and you certainly pay your money. I, long ago, made my choice, just as you must make yours. The main thing is that neither type of sportsman should look down upon the other.

According to the wording on the Game Licence which the Law (see page 337) requires you to buy to shoot game, the term 'game' includes pheasant, partridge, grouse, hare, woodcock, deer and, very strangely to my mind, snipe. Yet I suppose for most shooters 'game' really means pheasants and, to an increasing extent these days, partridges. The grouse family is unfortunately usually only at home to a well-heeled few. The same can hardly be said of the great British standby *Phasianus colchicus*. Thanks to the ease and comparative cheapness of modern rearing methods (see page 126), pheasants can be shot by almost anyone with legal sporting access to a hundred or two acres of suitable habitat.

The pheasant possesses in large quantities the prime natural qualities for survival. It is an adaptable customer. How else could a bird as gaudy as a cock pheasant tuck himself unobtrusively into an English winter furrow? The family of birds to which the pheasant belongs is an enormous one. It ranges from the peacock at one end to the jungle fowl at the other, from the flatlands of the fens to above 12,000 feet in the Himalayas. There can be very few 'pure-bred' pheasants at large in the British countryside. The bird who rises up in squawking wrath at the rough shooter's feet in the reed bed, likewise the sky-rocket who soars no bigger than a starling over the covert shooter's head, is a product of six main introduced strains of gamebird. The first pheasant was possibly brought here by the Romans. The Romans caught its forbears in the marshes of the Euphrates. But the first established evidence of pheasant presence comes from the debris found in kitchen middens of the twelfth century. These bones are thought to be those of the Southern Caucasus pheasant, often called 'the old English' or 'blackneck'. Chinese ringnecks arrived around 1768, followed by the Japanese southern green, imported by Lord Derby about 1840. Lord Rothschild brought in the Mongolian about the turn of the century and Colonel M. Sutherland added the silvery Prince of Wales pheasant in 1902. A dark mutant, the melanistic, suddenly appeared in the 1920s and, to most people's surprise, bred true. The natural fertility and adaptability of the bird has done the rest.

Like all chicken-related birds − the pheasant belongs to the order *Galliformes* − it would rather run than fly. This is the explanation of its white breast meat. Birds that rely largely on flight to get them about their business have well-developed chests full of small blood vessels, in other words red meat, like ducks and pigeons. Once on the wing, however, the pheasant is second to none, at least over a short distance. It reaches maximum revs very quickly. When at full throttle, it very sensibly decides to glide since it can't drive itself through the air any faster. At that moment it is probably doing fifty miles per hour in still air. It is also quite possibly 'curling' as it steers itself back towards its home covert. Add a tail wind to this situation and you have the reason why the greatest game shots of the Edwardian shooting heyday − and many guns since − voted the high, curling pheasant, gliding with wings set, the most difficult shot in the book.

Pheasants can also be ridiculously easy, usually when they are badly 'shown' (see page 63) and often when they are walked up, though the whirr and clatter of a cock rising at one's feet is still enough to cause experienced guns to footle.

The natural history of the pheasant is simple. The birds are very nearly omnivorous, though they prefer grain. They have even been known to eat small lizards. Insects, seeds, buds, berries: practically nothing that is nourishing comes amiss. The cocks are highly territorial in springtime, crowing and scrapping with rivals to establish an area of personal sexual dominance. It is nowadays thought that it is the cocks who attract the hens and not vice versa and that a dominant cock needs up to five acres to himself. So you shouldn't end the season with too many cock birds left on your ground.

Hens start to lay in April and sometimes carry on until the end of August, though these late broods will be little use until later in the season, if then. The pheasant's rudimentary ground nest contains anything up to fifteen eggs but more usually around a dozen. Pheasants are nidifugous birds, that is to say they desert the nest once the chicks are out. The hen usually leads the brood away into long grass or corn. Pheasants have the reputation of being slatternly and careless mothers. I am not sure if this is entirely deserved but they certainly aren't as maternally conscientious as partridges. The young cocks start to colour up around the eighth week and the birds should be strong fliers by three or four months. Thereafter they become solitaries, drawn together simply by the necessities of life, notably food and shelter. They won't linger long where both are lacking, an obvious lesson to the shooter in applied natural history. Pheasants roost, or jug, both in trees and on the ground, a fact well known to both foxes and poachers.

There is really only one other basic fact the shooter needs to know about them and that concerns a dead bird. Its taste improves a great deal if it is hung up by the neck for anything from one week to three, according to the weather.

Between the wars, the native English or grey partridge gave the game gun some of his finest sport, the coveys bursting like little grouse over the tall hedges towards the guns lined out on the September stubbles. After World War Two, the partridge, both the grey and the introduced French partridge or redleg, went through a very bad time. Changes in the farming pattern, early grass cutting, use of chemical sprays to kill weeds and the insects on which the young partridges depended were mainly responsible.

The grey partridge still did well in some areas like East Anglia but now, happily, there are signs of a return in many other shooting counties. Rearing methods have improved. Farming changes, including the preservation of headlands and compulsory EC 'set-aside' − 15% of land annually taken out of production − can act in the little bird's favour. Keepers have learned more about rearing and holding birds on their ground so that many shoots can now enjoy a couple of partridge days in September and early October before pheasant shooting begins. Pheasants are not generally ready until they are strong on the wing and the leaf is off the trees in November.

The game gun new to partridges will have to learn to take birds well out in front, turn and take them behind as well. Because partridges tend to fly low he will have to be especially aware of safety angles.

About grouse shooting I am not really qualified to write. On the few fortunate occasions I have shot these aces among game birds I have been staggered at their speed of approach and ditto of departure, often, in my case, saluted but unscathed. Driven grouse are the cream of game shooting, those who can afford it on a regular basis tell me, and I see no reason to doubt them. All well-managed game shooting is exciting, however. Its finer points are dealt with in the chapters that follow.

C.W.

Driven Pheasants

Tony Jackson

Until the first half of the last century, game was almost invariably shot by the sportsman hunting his birds – pheasants, partridges or grouse – using setters, pointers or those large, rather clumsy-looking spaniels so often depicted in early prints. It was a leisurely, pleasant manner of sport which suited slower days and long-barrelled flintlocks. On the continent, however, during the eighteenth century organised shoots, sometimes on an incredible scale, had captured the imagination of those who were in a position both to pay for and require 'instant' sport. From these shoots, when literally hundreds of animals, big game and small, might be driven to the guns, was born the *battue*, as it was first known when imported to this country.

It met with a mixed reception; the older generation, bred on flintlocks and slowly converted to the percussion system, would have little to do with it. 'Stonehenge' writing in his *British Rural Sports* remarks scathingly: '. . . as well might "mobbing" a fox be called foxhunting, as a *battue* be considered genuine pheasant shooting'.

However, a new up-and-coming generation of shooting men, armed with the new breechloaders and long purses, saw merit in the system. The day of the covert shoot had arrived.

The organised driving of pheasants over the line of guns has, through the years, inevitably borne its share of criticism – sometimes justified. For while driven pheasants, if shown correctly, can prove incredibly difficult, by the same token they can also offer pathetic sport, lumbering low from a covert, just clearing the guns' heads. Such birds are simply not worth raising the gun to.

The principle of covert shooting is obvious: a team of beaters, ranging from perhaps ten to twenty in number, by adroit ma-noeuvring, pushes the birds towards and over the waiting line of guns who, we hope, deal with them skilfully. Put simply thus, the novice may suppose that there is no great art involved. He would be very wrong; for a successful day's covert shooting involves a degree of tactical organisation and diplomacy on the part of the keeper which might be the envy of any embattled general.

The problems are considerable: the keeper must be certain of his birds and have a practical knowledge of the numbers to be found in each covert, field of kale or game strip. Pheasants cannot just be driven into a void. They must be sent to another covert or perhaps, having been 'walked' and dogged into a game strip, driven back to the home covert. It is essential, of course, to make sure they are not driven over the boundaries. Experience will have told the keeper that the birds will have set flight patterns and that reversing the order of procedure may spell disaster, yet at the same time he must take account of the wind and be prepared to put emergency plans into operation should they be required. A wise keeper will try to make use of any available high ground, as his aim is to 'show' the birds as fast and as high as possible. The keeper in hilly ground is fortunate, for with little difficulty and some intelligent disposition of game crops he may be able to send over real screamers. I know one shoot in Devon where, though the bag may not be large, every bird is an absolute corker and if you can hit one in three you need fear no man. Few shoots are as fortunate, many have to cope with flat ground.

Yet even here, provided that there is some reasonably tall timber, that sewelling is used (this is a cord which stretches across the covert with coloured rags attached at regular intervals – the plastic variety used for sealing off road repairs does excellently), and the birds are forced to fly long before they reach the end of the covert, good sport can be shown. Under these conditions the guns should be set well back so that the pheasants are at their maximum ceiling. Perfectly reasonable birds can be shown from kale by standing the guns perhaps a field back; I can see little sport or sense in knocking down pheasants lumbering over at zero. Not only are the birds likely to be smashed, but under these circumstances gun safety can often be neglected as shots are taken at low birds.

Basically the pheasant dislikes flying; it is a bird of the marshes which would sooner run than become airborne. Fortunately, although no long-distance flier, once in the air it can move with surprising speed. Few birds, for instance, have the edge on a hen pheasant curling downwind and piling on the coal.

TWO SHOOTS

Perhaps the best way to explain pheasant shooting is to consider two shoots, one small, the other large, and a day's shooting on each. The first shoot, one which I knew well (see map pp. 68–69), is a typical driven or walked-up shoot of some four hundred acres. The farm is divided by a minor public road and the farmhouse and buildings are set in the middle of the shoot on the north side of the road. The guns, eight in number, consist of four who pay a small subscription of perhaps £100 to help with the cost of rearing about a hundred birds, and the farmer's friends and guests. The farmer chips in with free tail-corn from his own granary and one of his two employees helps out with part-time keepering. Both the workers help to beat on shooting days, while two or three local folk with moderate-to-good dogs bring them along to assist with the pick-up. There are always one or two friends who are only too pleased to beat or generally assist.

It is, as you can see, a cheap shoot, subsidised to some extent by the farmer who, because he has an interest, is willing to provide the facilities for rearing, modest keepering and feeding.

There is a reasonable stock of wild pheasants and a constant exchange of birds between a neighbouring shoot which borders almost one half of the ground. On the other side of the coin three public footpaths run directly across the shoot, over half the boundary adjoins unkeepered land from which there is a constants traffic in vermin, and forestry on the south boundary presents several problems, not the least of which is that the timber, in various stages of growth, extends over the boundary for some fifty acres and is a source of continual trouble. Birds wander and stray into the forbidden area. There is no possibility of reaching an agreement with the owner and relations are strained. However, by the judicial use of game mixture, pheasants are held as far as possible on the north side of the shoot. The forestry is extremely difficult to drive as the undergrowth is, in some places, almost impenetrable.

The shooting plan follows a set pattern. While the guns and beaters are still fresh and the dogs are raring to go, the forestry is attacked first. To get to it the spinney along the south-west boundary is walked. A gun is placed forward by the edge of the forestry to deal with birds flying forwards, as do the majority, while one gun walks behind to catch any trying to break back; those that go over the boundary are lost. There are seldom more than a dozen birds in here though it is a favoured port of call for woodcock.

Experience has shown that it is useless attempting to drive the forestry towards the centre of the shoot; any birds that do come out, and they are few, immediately swing right or left and dive back into cover. The only way to deal with it is for the guns and beaters to line up at the west end to work their way down the long sausage-shaped strip until they come to the bend. Two guns are left on the outside, one behind and the other in front of the line, to deal with any birds breaking out. Once the bend is reached a halt is called and the two outside guns hurry forward to the edge of the Round Copse (see p. 68) to await any birds that may come out and curl towards this obvious refuge.

The forestry operation usually takes at least an hour, for the line is constantly being held up while guns, dogs and beaters search for birds down. Under these circumstances orderly springers are a blessing and guns are warned not to shoot at birds which might fall into cover which is too dense. Self-discipline is called for as rabbits abound and the odd woodcock may flit up. It is vital that the line be kept as straight as possible.

Once the guns have surmounted this obstacle, the Round Copse is attended to. The Copse is, in fact, an overgrown quarry with a pool at the bottom. Guns surround it and beaters and dogs are sent in to give the place a thorough rousting. Usually a couple of crafty old cocks or a hen will clatter up, often when the Copse has been pronounced empty and the guns are ready to move on. The cover is so thick that the dogs have the utmost difficulty pushing them out.

By now, it is usually pressing on towards lunchtime and as sandwiches and soup are taken at the farm, a move is made in this direction via the two hedges running north/south, for both are wide and thick and often hold a bird or two. The bag for the morning may be something in the region of ten to fifteen pheasants and half a dozen various.

After lunch the kale beside the farm is walked towards Finch Wood, two guns walking in the line to deal with any birds breaking back, and the remainder of the guns surrounding the kale in a semi-circle on the plough; they stand well back to give the birds a decent chance to gain altitude.

The plan for the remainder of the afternoon is now fairly obvious; the Long Wood is driven from the road with a walking gun on either side and the remaining guns in a semi-circle at the far end. Birds normally fly towards Dog Leg Wood, though in a strong west wind they may veer more towards Finch Wood. Dog Leg Wood is driven next from the broad northern end, pushing the birds towards Finch Wood. There is a narrow valley between these two woods which enables the guns to have some reasonably fast, high birds. Finally the kale adjoining the fallow is walked, half the guns lining the edge of the tract and the remainder going with the beaters.

It will be obvious that throughout the day care has been taken to try and ensure that the birds are kept on the gound. Every drive has been planned so that the pheasants are pushed to another piece of cover within the shoot. Obviously, variations on the theme are called for each season as kale is planted in different areas. The average day's bag will be in the region of twenty-five to forty pheasants, though this will naturally tail off towards the end of the season. From January 1 no hens are shot and there is often a penalty of five pounds for anyone who makes a mistake.

A shoot of this character, small though it may be, can provide consistent sport for several not too ambitious guns. For those who enjoy 'doing it themselves' this sort of set-up is ideal. Rearing on a small scale, amateur keepering, feeding and all the rest of it will usually attract one or two keen men only too willing to undertake the work.

For those who prefer their sport on a larger scale and simply do not have the time to engage in active assistance, the formal covert shoot provides the obvious answer. The cost will, of course, be considerably more but then you pay for what you get. Subscriptions for the average driven shoot, employing a keeper and perhaps one assistant, range around the £2,000 to £3,000 mark. Something in the region of fifteen hundred to two thousand pheasants may be reared and the annual bag, supplemented by a wild stock, could be in the region of a thousand or so. There will probably be about eight full-scale formal shoots in the season with one or two early skirmishes round the boundaries and a cocks-only day at the end of January.

Once again we will take a look at such a shoot and have an imaginary day there. It will be the first time through, the second

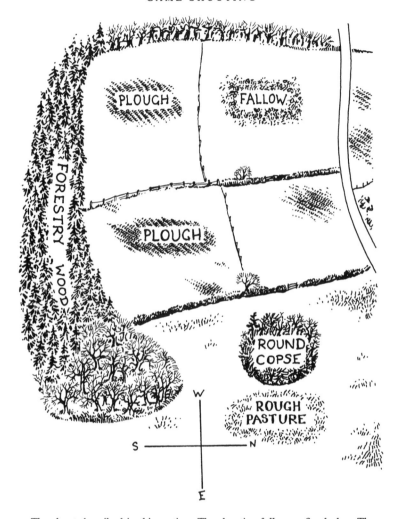

The shoot described in this section. The shooting follows a fixed plan. The forestry on the southern boundary is tackled first, being beaten from west to east, after the south-west boundary has been walked in. This is followed by the Round Copse. After lunch, the kale is driven northwards towards Finch Wood beyond

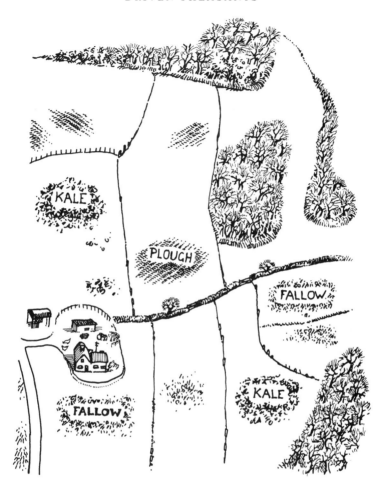

the plough; then Long Wood, on the north-western boundary is taken northwards. Then the long, narrow Dog Leg Wood on the northern edge is taken from the east with most of the birds crossing the valley to neighbouring Finch Wood. Finally the kale in the north-eastern corner is beaten out to finish up the day.

week in October, although a preliminary walk-round on the outside hedges with half-a-dozen guns might have shown a modest bag of twenty-five pheasants and a few various.

The shoot covers some eight hundred acres in East Anglia and, owing to the flatness of the ground and the desire on the part of the owner to show some really decent birds, considerable care has been taken over a period of years to plant shelter belts and strips of cover to try and force the birds to fly as high as possible. There are four main coverts, totalling some fifty acres. These consist largely of old indigenous wood, such as oaks and ash, but planting round the edges to provide shelter has been undertaken, while rides have been cleared and widened in the bigger coverts of fifteen and twenty acres. Some light has also been let into the denser parts of the woodland by clearing small patches and planting them with snowberry and lonicera.

It would be tiresome for the reader if we detailed the day drive by drive. Instead, let's follow our beginner on this his first formal shoot and see what tips we can offer.

In the first place our gun should remember that driven game shooting does demand a certain degree of formality. His behaviour, clothing and gun should correspond. It is not essential to wear a plus-two or tweed knickerbocker suit, though this is undoubtedly ideal, but provided one's garments are practical, loosely fitting and reasonably tidy there should be no cause for complaint. In other words don't appear at the covert side wearing camouflaged jackets or apparently equipped ready for the marsh or foreshore! While the side-by-side has always been the traditional game gun, over-and-unders are now just as acceptable by the covertside. Automatics and pump guns are quite out of place, both on the grounds that they are aesthetically unpleasant and also because they imply that the user is possibly prepared to expend more ammunition than is considered reasonable. Logically it is dificult to oppose the use of a two-shot automatic, but tradition says that it is wrong − and I stand by tradition!

Don't, whatever you do, be late. You will have been told to meet at such-and-such a place at a stipulated time. Be ten minutes early by all means, but not a minute late. Nothing is more infuriating for a host than to have his guests trickling in at their leisure, while his beaters and keepers are tapping their fingers instead of their sticks.

It is customary to draw for stands and you will probably be offered a wallet of ivory slips, each of which is numbered, the figures downwards. Numbering is normally from right to left, though a few shoots reverse this. At each drive one moves up *two* places, thus if you have drawn number three on the first drive, you will be five on the second and so on. Simple enough but guaranteed to create havoc among the more obtuse guns or those incapable of solving such a mathematical problem.

Guns are usually taken to the drives by Land-Rover, or perhaps a trailer. Whatever the conveyance, watch out for your gun barrels. Knocks and dents are easily come by. It is best to carry your gun in a padded slip between drives. Many a good weapon has received a near mortal blow in a jolting Land-Rover.

While you have been preparing yourself for the big day, the keeper and his assistants have been out, long before breakfast, dogging and tapping in the outlying hedgerows, laying out rolls of sewelling and generally making sure that all is well.

The beaters – sixteen assorted farmworkers, two lads and even a girl, renowned for her courage and skill in the most outrageous cover – have assembled shortly before the guns. As the first drive involves a complicated manoeuvre, they are already setting off in a farm trailer. Two 'stops' have been in position for half an hour, tapping steadily and not too loudly at the junctions of two hedges with the main covert to prevent any birds sneaking down there when the action begins. Sewelling – a long cord decorated with coloured strips of cloth or plastic – is being adjusted across the middle of the wood; the purpose of this is to stop birds running forward – pheasants distrust strange objects – and to encourage them to rise and so offer high shots when they come over the guns.

The first covert is roughly L-shaped and a field of kale must first be blanked in by the beaters to send any birds into the short leg of the L. This is then quietly tapped through, the line swings and the main wood is driven forward over the guns who surround it in a semi-circle at the far end. There is a walking gun on each side of the line of beaters outside the wood to deal with any birds breaking sideways and back.

The line is now in position. Glance round carefully and mark your neighbour's positions and those of stops and the pickers-up behind the line. Make a mental picture of your field of fire and

71

determine to fire no low shots in front, no matter how far away the beaters may be, nor down the line on either side. Try to relax, stamp out a firm foothold by your peg and arrange your cartridge bag, having given it a good shake. This tends to leave most cartridge bases pointing upwards. The lead in the other end sees to that. Personally, I always use a cartridge belt as well as carrying a supply in a bag. I like to raise a dozen cartridges in the belt so that they can be flicked out of the loops with no fuss.

The start of the drive is usually signalled by the host, either by a whistle or horn. The beaters are now moving slowly through the wood. If they know their job, they will be walking quietly, tapping gently at trees and bushes. One or two well-trained spaniels are worth their weight in gold here, but they *must* be steady and proof against rabbits. A noisy, straggling line is a sure sign that the keeper in charge does not know his job. The art of driving pheasants is to send them over the guns at evenly spaced intervals. A gigantic flush of birds at the end of a drive may impress the innocent onlooker but it is of no value to the guns who will be unable to deal with more than a tithe of the birds seen.

The first sign that something is afoot comes from the squawking blackbirds and the crafty jays looping through the tree-tops, alerted by the beaters entering the covert. Most hosts will require vermin such as crows, jays and squirrels to be shot but it is wise to ask the form beforehand. As for foxes, I would ask you to turn a blind eye, no matter what instructions you have received!

A few pheasants are now coming forward. Watch how the gun on your right deals with high hen – see how he slowly straightens from his shooting seat as it appears over the trees and, with apparently all the time in the world, kills it neatly in front of him. No hurried, nervous poking and slashing, just a smooth machine-like action and a minimum of fuss.

One of the 'sins' of driven shooting is to 'poach' another man's bird. Every pheasant coming forward will be dealt with by one gun and it is appalling bad manners to attempt to shoot a bird which was obviously going to provide your neighbouring gun with a shot. Greedy shooting has no place in the sport.

As the drive proceeds, mark those birds you have down and keep an eye on any pheasant which you think might be a runner. With experience you will come to know at once if a bird is hit, even though it may evince no signs of damage. Careful observation, however, will reveal a slight jerk as you fired and the pheasant is likely to glide for some considerable distance. Doubtless the picker-up behind the line will have marked it, but it is as well to be able to give him precise instructions.

The end of the drive will be signalled by a whistle and the keeper shouting 'all out'. Once the pick-up is under way and the guns have seen to it that all the birds down have been attended to, you will move on to the next stand. Walk quietly and remember that pheasants have very sharp ears. I never cease to be amazed by guns who gossip at the tops of their voices, alerting the entire area to the fact that danger is afoot.

If you are modest, keep your eyes peeled and show that you have every respect for gun safety, you should survive the day unscathed and qualify for a further invitation. At the end of the shoot it is customary to tip the keeper. This is always a tricky one but if you work on the basis of £10−£15 per hundred birds in the bag you won't be far wrong. If in doubt, ask your host. He will

appreciate the gesture and put you on the right lines. Be sure to thank the keeper and his assistants, while a word of thanks to the beaters, without whom there could have been no sport, will not come amiss.

Shooting Partridges

C. L. Coles

NATURAL HISTORY

The common or grey partridge (*Perdix perdix*) is a native of the British Isles: it is found as far south as Iran and as far north as Russia. As an introduced bird it survives the winter snows of Canada. It prefers light soil, arable or mixed farming, though a rugged strain sometimes called the 'hill partridge' has adapted to the bleaker grassy environment.

Young partridges can be distinguished from old birds quite easily. In September and early October the familiar dark beak, yellowish legs and relatively soft bones of the young birds will readily differentiate them from the grey-beaked, grey-legged and hard-boned adults, but later in the season the simple flight feather test is to be recommended − the pointed primaries (two outer feathers) indicating a young bird. In September a few partridges in their second year may not have moulted these sharply pointed primaries of the juvenile plumage, but these feathers will be faded and abraded to such an extent that the bird will be easily recognised as old. The 'bursa test' on shot birds is infallible. Probe the anal passage with a matchstick. The presence of a bursa (a blind-ended duct) means a young bird; absence of one denotes age.

As to differentiating cock and hen, the presence of shoulder feathers which have only a light 'backbone' stripe indicates a cock, whereas the hen has additional transverse bars across the central stripe. The dark brown horseshoe pattern on the breast is not always a reliable sign of a cock.

Perdix is a very territorial bird and particularly jealous of any close neighbours in the mating season. The highest density recorded was about a pair to three acres, a rare enough stocking these days! Pairing − or covey break-up − usually starts during the first protracted spell of mild weather in the New Year. This is often accompanied by trial pairings and sometimes fighting. By

75

The dark horseshoe mark on the breast of the cock is not always a reliable means of distinguishing the sexes. But the cock always has shoulder feathers with a light 'backbone' stripe and the hen has additional barring on the shoulder.

mid-February things have usually settled down. Though we have recorded a few cases of pairs changing their mates, cock and hen normally mate for life − assuming that both survive the shooting season. If the ground is not shot over they rarely live to a third breeding season.

Partridges do *not* mate within a covey; so the old-fashioned 'change of blood', or swopping Yorkshire eggs for Hampshire clutches was certainly a waste of time. Old birds − to dispose of an old wives' tale − are every bit as good parents as young ones, and old hens lay just as many eggs, with the same hatchability as young ones. As to nesting statistics, the hatch is about 92% from an average clutch of fifteen eggs. The first 'scrape' with an egg in it is usually found towards the end of April in the southern half of England, the eggs being laid at the rate of ten in fourteen days. When the hen is off feeding − unlike the redleg − she covers her eggs over. The incubation period is about twenty-four days.

The average new brood consists of ten chicks, if we include the unsuccessful parents that lose their nests − and nest losses are high. Thereafter, the survival of chicks — particularly in the last twenty years or so — can be very poor indeed. The crucial period concerns the week on either side of June 15. At this time the baby chicks need a supply of easily available insects, without which they cannot survive — and reasonable weather. Insecticides and herbicides (often killing the 'scaffolds' or plants upon which the insects live), and other agricultural practices such as mono-culture and hedgerow removal have diminished the vital supply of food insects. Selective spraying is essential. In this respect, recent research into conservation headlands, which can fulfil the functions of breeding areas for both valuable food insects for partridge chicks, and insect predators able to control aphids, has greatly contributed to a revival in wild partridge populations. 'Set-aside' crops — provided they can be sited with game require-ments in mind — can also feed and shelter increased numbers of partridges and pheasants. But at the time of writing the agricul-tural planners have not quite settled on the best compromises for all-round purposes. Fortunately our game scientists are now in a better position to know which are the most insect-rich crops, and in which way the farmer can provide a survival diet at little trouble to himself. Lucerne and clover are certainly insect-providers; undersowing is always a helpful practice; winter cereals are better than spring cereals; even a grassy, barbed wire fence produces insect communities some way out into the field. Hedgerows are naturally still more bountiful. And the development of 'beetle banks' as field divisions is a new and beneficial feature both for farmer and game manager. Incidentally, the attractiveness of a hedgerow as partridge nesting cover depends on the amount of dead grass at its base in early spring.

After the age of three weeks, the young partridges turn rapidly to plant food, and their winter diet consists mainly of greenstuff, though whether from choice or necessity we are not quite sure. Certainly grain and weed seeds provided in hoppers are avidly taken, and have about four times the calorific value of green food.

Though not strictly natural history — perhaps more a matter of management — it must be said that there can be competition between the pheasant and the partridge, if it is a question of *reared* pheasants being put down in large numbers. Pheasants lay eggs in the partridge nests. They sometimes compete for actual nesting cover and food supplies, and they certainly compete for the keeper's time. Lastly, reared pheasants in heavy densities can put gapes — a disease caused by a worm in the windpipe — into the soil, to be picked up by the partridge. The larger pheasant does not normally succumb to the disease, but the partridge can certainly do so.

REDLEGGED PARTRIDGE

This species, *Alectoris rufa*, which is a different genus, was introduced into this country from France (and is often called the French partridge) in the latter half of the seventeenth century, but the attempt failed. In about 1770 some eggs were imported — again from France — and the resulting young birds were turned down in Suffolk. Gradually the stock prospered and spread out across East Anglia. Now in some areas Frenchmen outnumber the native grey partridge in the bag.

When partridges were commonly shot over pointers and setters, the redlegs became unpopular, as they would not flush readily but crept away stealthily, leaving behind a puzzled dog and a frustrated sportsman. The other difference is that, when driven, they tend not to come over the guns as a covey, but in ones and

twos, which can greatly assist a shoot owner when a beat is rather thin! The birds also fly straighter than greys. These two factors mean that the redleg is shot out of proportion to its true numbers.

At the present time redlegs are deservedly most welcome. Oddly enough for a southern bird they sometimes survive our winters better than the grey. They are occasionally dual-nesters – the hen making two nests, one of which the cock incubates. Lastly, as reared birds, they survive better after release and stray less. They can be treated much like pheasants. In captivity trios can be penned, as the birds become more or less polygamous.

There is no proof that the larger redleg is aggressive to the grey and will drive it away. If anything, the reverse is the case. The two species lived happily side by side on a large Game Conservancy study area. If, as an experiment, all the redlegs were shot out, it is not thought that the grey partridge would fill the empty spaces. Both suffer from the modern agricultural pressures, except that redleg chicks feed *on the move* and can therefore take in more ground. This helps when insects are in short supply. The daily range of a redleg covey is many times greater than the area occupied by greys. Its diet also allows a wide choice, and it can make use of a wider range of habitats. Further, the chicks can exist on vegetable protein and do not need the animal protein (i.e. insects) essential to the survival of the greys. They also have a different digestive system which allows them to grind up and assimilate hard unripe weed seeds: if these were eaten by the grey chicks they would pass straight through. The hatching bracket of the redleg is also less restricted, which can be an advantage if the weather is inclement during the normal peak of *perdix's* hatch: the early and late chicks may escape the killing period.

Its normal range, outside England, embraces France to the south of the Loire, Portugal, Spain, northern Italy and Corsica. There are various other related species, such as *graeca* (sometimes called the rock partridge), *A. barbara* (the barbary partridge of North Africa) and *A. chukhar*, which ranges from the Greek islands to the Far East. The latter species becomes very domesticated on a game farm and lays three or four times as many eggs as the pure redleg. As a result some breeders imported it into the UK and crossed it with *A. rufa*. The cross-breeds were extensively released mostly for 'put-and-take' shooting. The survivors rarely bred and in time a notable deterioration occurred in the stock on the ground. It is now illegal to release either the pure *chukhar* or the hybrid.

The redlegged bird lays a slightly smaller clutch than *perdix*, i.e. eleven to twelve eggs, not forgetting the habit of dual-nesting. The incubation period is the same, twenty-four or twenty-five days. As stated earlier, the eggs are left uncovered when the hen leaves the nest. In Spain and Portugal, on numerous estates visited by the author, the percentage of deserted nests was found to be extremely high – possibly because of the eggs not being concealed and the greater number of uncontrolled predators. During incubation the hen tends to be more nervous than the grey bird, and a keeper has to be more careful when 'dummying' or visiting nests.

With regard to distinguishing cock from hen, no plumage difference is apparent, but the adult cock is usually 3–4 oz heavier than the hen, and stands and postures in a more masculine fashion! In old birds a knobbly spur will be seen on the cock's leg: these are sometimes present on the legs of hens, but are invariably much smaller with only a single protrusion. As to age differentiation – apart from the rather technical bursa test – the young bird has its two outermost flight feathers tipped with cream, whereas in an old bird these feathers show no such variation. These primaries are also more pointed – as in the young grey.

SHOOTING PARTRIDGES

Partridge driving (walking-up is dealt with under Rough Shooting) came into being in the middle of the last century, as a result of the breechloading gun taking over from the muzzleloader. Oddly enough this new form of shooting increased, rather than decreased, the stocks of birds on the famous East Anglian manors, though not because driving tended to kill old birds out of proportion to young. The reasons were complex, and are now only history.

Most sportsmen, when asked to choose their favourite type of shooting, would put partridge driving first – and would also probably list the grey partridge as the best eating!

Although the season opens legally on September 1st, birds are rarely worth driving until three or four weeks later. In the 1880s and 1890s, when holding crops were abundant, November was the peak partridge shooting month.

Any shooting day – large or small – should always be most carefully planned, though I personally always try to ensure *that no one is aware of it*! Organising must be unobtrusive. Shooting is a form of relaxation and guests do not like to be pushed about in order to squeeze in a last drive before lunch, or alternatively to hang about in the cold while the host and his keeper decide what to do.

Food, transport, picking-up, the positions of guns, stops and flankers, should be carefully thought out beforehand – with alternative arrangements made ready in case the unexpected turns up: i.e. a change of wind overnight. Partridges will not face a really strong head wind. Should there be a cross wind, extra gun pegs can be sited at either end of the line, so that the guns can move to the left or right. At the same time the flankers should be told to move sideways, in order to counteract the effects of the wind on the birds.

Plans must always be flexible.

The first thing for an owner to decide is how many days' partridge shooting the ground will stand, without killing the next year's breeding stock – remembering that the natural winter wastage will be of the order of 30%. It may be that two partridge drives, as part of an early pheasant day, will be more than enough!

If a full day's shooting is intended, the owner must plan the sequence of drives to be fitted in to the day, perhaps five in the morning and three or four in the afternoon. The number will entirely depend on the stock, the holding crops, and the beaters available. It is important not to be greedy, and to stop shooting in plenty of time so that the coveys can re-group and have their evening feed before they jug for the night.

TACTICS

The general tactics of partridge driving are normally to start where the stock is plentiful and drive towards a good piece of cover. One can then have a return drive or a drive at right angles, so that birds from the two lots of cover can be shown. By the second drive the coveys will tend to have been broken up, and provide more even shooting. Having said this, it must also be accepted that successive *long* drives will tire the birds. At all times remember the effect of strong winds and the natural flight lines of the birds themselves.

It is sometimes possible to plan the whole day so that the birds are mostly moved towards the centre of the shoot. The last drive of the day should then provide a lot of birds, bearing in mind what has been said about tired birds. Wild partridges will not, however, stay for too long outside their own particular territory, so timing is important.

Where a lot of blanking-in is necessary, the ideal procedure is to undertake this at the start of the day, and later, in preparation for the first drive after lunch when the beaters can get on ahead of the guns. When partridge driving the beaters should be silent rather than vociferous. Yelling and whistling will not encourage the partridges to fly any better! Selected beaters should carry coloured flags which they can raise above their heads at appropriate moments − if hidden by a hedge or rising ground − to show the guns that they are approaching.

Signalling the approach of coveys, when the guns are screened from view, is an accepted practice on most shoots; a short whistle for one or two birds, a longer one for a covey or coveys. The start and finish of a drive should be indicated clearly by horn or whistle: the guns will then know when they may take their first shot − perhaps at a passing pigeon − without upsetting anything else that may be going on. And the signal at the end will tell them that picking-up can start. This will, incidentally, be a lot easier if the guns are not placed in the middle of a thick crop.

Another small point, always tell the guns clearly what they may and may not shoot. It may, for example, be unwelcome to shoot hares early in the season during the warmer weather.

Little need be said about placing the guns, other than that safety is obviously all-important. Where the pegs are *not* in a straight line, the guests must be warned.

After safety comes sporting quality − and as to whether the guns are placed right on the hedgerow or stood well back, depends on the nature of the ground. The only thing to avoid is putting the guests just far enough back from a tall hedge so that they cannot get off a shot in front. There is nothing more irritating!

SHOOTING CROPS

Planning some of the farm crops, so that they are conveniently sited in relation to sloping ground, belts, high hedges and so on can make all the difference to the quality of the birds. If the land is farmed by the shooter this will not usually be too difficult. Similarly, in places stubbles should be left as cover until the end of the partridge season, and where the land would otherwise be bare, crops such as post-harvest mustard can be put in. A fairly thin crop is all that is required, with a seeding rate of 8 lb per acre or less. If a warm, wet spell sets in after sowing, the mustard will be ready for the partridge days, and the later pheasants. But in cold, dry seasons germination and growth can be poor. However, any cover is better than no cover on the bleak, open landscapes of today.

On the actual shooting day the crops involved should not be unnecessarily disturbed, which is not always so easy if you are only a shooting tenant. It is embarrassing to the host if a flock of sheep are driven across the partridge ground, or tractor and trailer arrive to cut kale or lift beet just as a drive is due to begin.

A word with the farmer beforehand, and a brace of birds at the end of the day will usually get results.

Other crops that are satisfactory for holding partridges are beans, buckwheat, canary seed, carrots when not too wet, clovers, fodder radish (also not favoured when wet), kale − if a thin crop − and preferably varied with drills of turnips, swedes etc. Or a mixture made up as follows: $1\frac{1}{2}$ lb rape, $1\frac{1}{2}$ lb giant rape, $\frac{1}{2}$ lb marrowstem, $\frac{1}{2}$ lb thousand-headed, $\frac{1}{2}$ lb swedes and $\frac{1}{2}$ lb turnips.

Linseed and its stubbles are also quite good, though rarely grown these days. Lucerne can be useful as an all round crop and, if also required for pheasant cover, its winter life can be prolonged by additionally sowing 14 lb of barley and 4 lb of canary seed, *before* the lucerne is drilled (which goes in at a shallower depth). Oil poppy is attractive where grown, and potatoes always a great favourite. The birds should be driven *across* the ridges, or the coveys will simply run down between the rows and flush at the end of the field.

Rape usually makes good holding cover, though if thick it can hold the wet a long time. Savoy cabbages, like sugar beet, will act as a good collecting crop; the latter particularly when it is the only cover around after harvest. But beet is generally unattractive after rain and will often serve only as a blanking-in crop, to contain birds for a limited time. A great many new game crops have now been developed for different soils and climates by the Game Conservancy who can be contacted for advice.

DRIVING REDLEGS

Redlegged partridges, as has been said in the natural history section, behave differently from grey partridges when driven – tending to flush in ones and twos.

This can be disastrous on a warm day in flat country, as a covey can be shot out, one at a time, while providing less sport than a posse of hedge-hopping blackbirds. However, when shown in hilly country on a windy day they can provide wonderful sport. Englishmen returning from shooting the redlegs in Spain rarely criticise the way the birds fly! I have been lucky enough to shoot them driven across rocky gullies in Portugal and found them very exciting, presenting a great variety of difficult shots.

More and more estates are now rearing redlegs to provide October shooting – treating them in much the same way as pheasants, except that they should be liberated after seven to eight days in release pens in small groups of about twenty. One or two 'callers' can be left in the pens for a few additional days, and their familiar feeders, water pots , etc., and some friendly straw bales positioned nearby as a 'meeting point'. Forty per cent of the released birds are often put in the bag – sometimes more – a far greater percentage than from reared grey patridges. It is therefore worthwhile to show them properly, and not to waste their qualities. Incidentally they have one advantage in these days of large fields, often devoid of stubbles or any other cover after the harvest, in that they can be shown quite satisfactorily from bare ground, and do not necessarily require to be put into a holding crop. Even in the open, if carefully driven, they will flush at intervals and not in a cloud at the end of the beat.

Because redlegs will hold to belts and scrubland, all hedgerows and bushes should be well beaten through. Reared grey partridges will often hold quite well to their release ground – depending on the crop patterns, freedom from disturbance and so on, but they do tend to be less easy to anchor.

CONCLUSION

At long last there are signs of a resurgence of interest in partridge conservation and shooting − after the swing to the obliging pheasant for the last thirty years or so.

Landowners have on the whole again become conservation-minded. A hedge is not now pulled up *automatically* because it is there, and groups of shrubs that provide nothing to sell are actually being planted on some estates! There are also signs that in many places the bleak landscape of monoculture is giving way to something nearer to the old four-course system, and that our spraying is becoming more selective. Is it really ecologically sound to kill the good insects as well as the bad ones?

Such an approach to farming and land use will provide a more attractive countryside, with its natural crop of wildlife species like partridges. For the grey patridge this is the only hope, for *perdix* will never qualify as 'instant game', a fact that some of us do not in the least regret.

Rough Shooting

Tony Jackson

The rough shoot – a misnomer if ever there was – can provide some of the most versatile and exciting shooting to be found in this country. Size is no criterion. Some of the smallest acreages have the essentials of a rough shoot. I recall a friend who, from a mere fifteen acres adjacent to a reservoir, had some splendid shooting with duck and even the odd partridge, snipe or pheasant thrown in as a bonus.

Who would deny that a low-ground Scottish shoot is in the five-star category! Grouse, pheasants, partridges, blackgame, even capercaillie, may all figure in the bag in the course of a season, not to mention hares, rabbits, snipe, duck and woodcock. A shoot of this nature, walked-up with two or three well-tried friends and some good dogs, is a pearl beyond price. The rough shoot can be any size, it can be shot by one gun or half a dozen and the bag will, we hope, always be varied. It does not aim for the formality of the covert shoot and, apart from the impromptu snipe or golden plover drive, organised driving with beaters does not enter the picture. Opportunities must be seized as they arise and there is far more scope for dogwork. Indeed, most successful rough shoots are to a great extent dependent on one or two spaniels and/or retrievers who really know their job. As far as I'm concerned, one breed for the job is the English springer spaniel. A good worker can literally treble the bag, bustling with drive and thrust through hedgerows and thickets, turfing out wily cock pheasants and dashing rabbits.

Exceptions apart, to provide regular and varied sport one must think in terms of one hundred and fifty acres and upwards. Much, of course, depends on the siting of the shoot. If it is surrounded by covert shoots where pheasants are reared, then there will almost certainly be a steady supply of birds, certainly enough to keep one or two guns satisfied without recourse to taking advantage of the situation by feeding in the boundaries. It is the easiest thing in the world to arouse ill-will by blatantly attempting to draw off another shoot's pheasants, but in the long run you are likely only to lose your own sport, for no landlord is going to tolerate a vendetta with his neighbours caused by the greed of a shooting tenant.

Curb any such greedy propensities and doubtless all will be well. Fair enough to site a few feed hoppers in the middle of the shoot, for no one can complain about that. You will earn good marks if you rear and release a few birds yourself.

However, your shoot may, perhaps, be a block of forestry with a small adjoining acreage of arable, surrounded by a wilderness of unkeepered ground. Your few acres will probably act like a magnet to birds, but if you want to see any return for your money and efforts, you will have to wage an unceasing and relentless war against vermin. The odds will be weighted heavily against you, both by four- and two-legged predators, but you will learn

One of the joys of a rough shoot is the
variety of game which it can offer.

an enormous amount about keepering and the art of producing and shooting game.

Two examples give some idea of the contrasts: one is a Forestry Commission shoot in north Lincs, let on tender. The rent is £400 and the acreage is one hundred and fifty − the sport superb. The surrounding land is heavily keepered, but no attempt is made by the rough shooters to feed in, nor is there any need to. They have a natural oasis for pheasants and other game. I recall our best day with ten guns was eighty pheasants and fourteen woodcock.

At the other end of the scale is a so-called shoot in Sussex of about twice the size of the above shoot. It *looked* all right but despite the distribution, via a release pen, of fifty pheasants to supplement what we were assured was a healthy wild stock, nothing ever came of it − the birds seemed to vanish into thin air. It transpired, however, that most of them were leaving the shoot in the game bags of the local lads who were pleased to take advantage of an absentee rentee situation and a farmer who turned a blind eye.

RENT TO PAY

What rent can you expect to pay? No easy question to answer this, for the situation is complicated by several factors, the two obvious ones being the size of the shoot, the sport it allegedly offers and its situation. The days are gone when a shoot of two or three hundred acres cost the tenant a brace of birds and a bottle of whisky at Christmas. Cheap shoots *can* still be found, be sure of that, but they will usually be in remote, outlying districts. The closer a shoot to a large town, the greater the rent and the smaller the bag − thus reads Jackson's law of sporting rents. The inverse is also true. It is a fact that a few acres close to London, holding perhaps a handful of harassed pheasants and some indifferent pigeon shooting, may command as much as £4 or more an acre. Each season it will be shot out, and the unfortunate tenants, some of whom may go to the trouble and expense of rearing and releasing a few pheasants, will learn their lessons the hard way. There are exceptions no doubt, but be wary, devilish wary, before engaging to take on what at first sight may appear to be a lucky snip. You may even find that you are not the only tenant and that while you shoot at weekends, someone else has the privilege of following you round during the week. Unscrupulous landlords have been known!

If you are prepared to pay *from* £2 an acre then you will, I think, not go far wrong and may even find yourself agreeably surprised. You will almost certainly allay the cost by forming a tiny syndicate of friends and possibly raise the ante slightly to cover a modest rearing programme and the price of traps and tail-corn. If the shooting is worth renting it is probably worth retaining, so be sure and have a legal form of contract between yourself and the landlord. Try to obtain an agreement for at least five or six years and make sure there is a let-out clause with, say, six months' notice on either side.

Perhaps one of the most exciting aspects of rough shooting is the construction of a genuine sporting shoot from what was once derelict, sterile ground. I am firmly of the opinion that the majority of rough shooters fail to realise the full potential of their shoots. So many shooters are content just to potter round the shoot, pleased if they bring back a rabbit or pigeon, delighted and surprised if a pheasant graces the bag. Others have, they will tell you, tried to rear and release a few birds which subsequently 'disappeared' without trace. Close questioning will reveal that no attempt was made to construct a release pen, the pheasants being literally turned out of the crates at the mercy of foxes, the weather and two-legged predators. Little wonder they never featured in the game book!

TO STOCK OR NOT TO STOCK

Before taking any decisions on stocking the shoot, the rough shooter must sit down and make some honest assesments: what number of pheasants will his acreage support? Does he, in fact, need to supplement the wild stock? Is he prepared to sustain a vigorous campaign against the vermin, particularly rats and crows? If he decides to rear is there a steady supply of tail-corn? Above all, is he in a position to ensure that a watchful eye is kept on the shoot? Indeed, if a trap-line is being run, in the spring for instance, then the traps *must* be visited daily.

To be practical, it is seldom possible to obtain a shoot virtually on one's own doorstep. Quite often one must face the fact that if one wants a good shoot, then one has to travel. Nevertheless, it is usually possible to find a genuine, keen local chap who, in return for a gun in the shoot, will undertake to feed regularly and keep a daily watching brief.

If the rough shooter, having weighed the facts, decides to stock the shoot with pheasants, it is vital that he has the cooperation of the farmer. The latter is probably in a position to provide tail-corn, assist in putting in one or more game strips, lend tractors and/or Land-Rovers and generally ensure that the operation runs smoothly. Get on the wrong side of him, perhaps by leaving gates open or trampling on young corn, and you might as well forget the whole idea.

If your ground is bordered by organised shoots then it is obviously a tactical move to make an approach to the various keepers. They will appreciate the gesture and, if you frankly explain that you hope to rear a few birds but have no intention of trying to feed their pheasants in, some sort of cooperation should be possible.

Good shoot relations are immensely important if a sporting atmosphere is to prevail. Not least among those whom you should approach is the local MFH. He may, perhaps, have not the slightest desire to draw your ground, but on the other hand if he knows that you will cooperate then, should the necessity arise, he will contact you to ensure that there is no clash of shooting and hunting interests. Remember that you are both engaged in a field sport and there is no reason why you should not rub along together.

As far as the actual production of pheasants is concerned I still believe that, for the rough shooter dealing in a moderate number of birds, the broody is best. Despite assertions to the contrary, broodies *can* still be obtained. A far more reliable mother than any artificial hen, her hatching success will be in the region of 80%, she is very little trouble if treated correctly, and I have a suspicion that her adopted offspring acquire the preservative instincts of the wild far more readily than their cousins reared by a tin box.

The problems associated with the release of pheasants on both a small and large scale will be dealt with elsewhere (see page 134), but I beg you to make every effort to ensure their safety and to see that their basic requirements of food, water and shelter are readily available. Pheasants will wander a considerable distance in search of their daily intake so that, if it is wanting on your ground, they are darned well going to find it elsewhere. Feed hoppers, which at their simplest and most effective are simply metal drums with slits in the bottom through which corn can trickle, set on bricks or pegs, should be placed at strategic points round the shoot. Feeding points must also be established in the vicinity of the rearing pen with a view to holding the young birds as they release themselves. These points can consist simply of a sheet of galvanised iron on four wooden 'legs' to provide shelter; straw is scattered underneath and corn mixed into it. This will keep pheasants scratching happily for hours as they search for the grain. Your object is to keep the birds working for their food so that boredom does not set in, leading to straying, yet a full crop should not be obtained too readily. If the tin 'roof' is set at an angle, rainwater will run off into a basin or half-tyre, ensuring a steady supply.

MARSH SHOOT RAMBLE

Probably the easiest, and at the same time most interesting method of examining the problems and explaining the practices of a rough shoot is to describe a ramble round my own Sussex marsh shoot. The month is December and there will be just you and me and our two dogs, both springer spaniels. Set in a shallow river valley, the shoot is by no means large − a mere two hundred acres − but it has the advantage of marshy water-meadows, prone to flood, a tidal river bounding its eastern flank and a disused railway line on the other side. The higher ground to the west is criss-crossed by thick, overgrown hedges and, because it is relatively undisturbed, it provides a natural haven for pheasants and wildfowl.

The duck shooting − mallard, teal and a few wigeon − really only comes into its own from the end of November when the heavy autumn rains have filled the gutters to the brim and, in particular, one corner of a water-meadow with a few inches of water covering sweet cattle-grazed grass. This spot is beloved of teal and mallard, but their numbers are dictated by the amount of rain and resultant floods − if there is too much water in the area the duck will be dispersed, but if we are fortunate enough to have a premium on water then the shooting can be exceptional.

In the early part of the season, September and October, the duck, mainly mallard, will be found tucked away in odd corners of the shoot wherever there is some water. One soon comes to recognise that there are certain gutters (or rifes as we call them in Sussex) where there is always a chance of a duck. Before the floods come, tail-corn is sprinkled along the edges and in the shallows at such spots. However, duck are inconsistent, so one must always be alert for them in even the most seemingly unlikely places. Mallard, early on, are often reluctant to rise, preferring to skulk in cover until pushed out by a questing canine nose.

The secret of success on most rough shoots is to be thorough; every piece of cover must be examined and one must always be ready for a shot. Your chances may be few and far between so they must be fully exploited. Never be caught napping, for duck and game have a knack of rising from the most unlikely spots, usually when you least expect it! Bearing this in mind, from the moment we climb over the boundary gate we must be ready, literally, for anything. The first likely draw is a high, tangled hedge, a maze of brambles and thorn with a shallow ditch which rarely floods. Today, although there has been sufficient rain in the past few weeks to provide half an acre of water in the duck splash, this part of the shoot is fairly dry. Such hedges as this, where there is a chance of a pheasant, must be covered on both sides. The technique is to stand back about fifteen yards from the hedge, put in the dogs and keep level with them as they work it down. Both springers are alert and, at the command, dash for the hedge. Slowly and quietly we move, ready for a shot. Suddenly one springer pops out of the hedge, nose to the ground, 'hoovering' on a strong scent. Back into cover it dashes and almost simultaneously there is a clatter, a whirr of wings and a hen pheasant bursts from the hedge on your side − she comes out almost beside you, so don't hurry the shot. There is plenty of time as she skims low for the far hedge. These shots are by no means as easy as they appear, for there is a tendency to shoot underneath the bird. Swing hard at her and as the barrels cover her fire and keep swinging. There! She crumples and a spaniel is already racing to the fall.

On we walk, carefully climbing over a barbed wire fence, both guns broken and unloaded; down now beside an over-grown rife, the dogs working like fiends till we come to a muddy gateway, heavily poached by cattle. With a startling 'scaaap' a snipe, no two, flicker up, flashing brown and white. Wait a second till they are twenty or so yards away and have cut out the aerobatics, then shoot as though you really mean it. One snipe bounces on the ground, the other keeps flying.

At the shots a dozen teal lift from the corners of an L-shaped rife where it broadens and is overhung with alders. Keep still and hiss the dogs to 'hup'; the tiny duck swing backwards and forwards like a pendulum, rising and lowering, uncertain where the danger lies. Keep your head lowered and just watch them from beneath the rim of your cap. Now they head straight at us, perhaps thirty-five yards up. Up with the guns but don't make the mistake of firing into the 'brown'; pick a bird and, if you hit, quickly swing to another. Four shots and the teal flare at full boost, apparently untouched. Watch them, though, as they head for the river – see, one is peeling off, flying lower and lower until, a field away, it collapses. Mark the fall and walk straight to it; keeping your eyes fixed firmly on the spot.

Always make a point, when you have apparently missed, of keeping an eye on the bird until it is obvious that it is untouched. With experience you will come to recognise the slight jerk given by a hit bird even though it keeps on flying.

Although it might seem unlikely that any duck would remain in the pool from which the teal rose, it is well worth making sure. The dogs hunt out the bank, hard on a strong scent, but it is a moorhen which flutters up weakly and is quickly shot. These birds are an absolute pest on the shoot for they will-consume vast quantities of corn intended for the duck.

On we ramble across a narrow, tussocky field, guns held ready for the chance of a partridge or hare. Sure enough, half way across, a jack hare bounds up almost at your feet. There is ample time, so let him get away before firing. Swing the barrels over his ears and see how he cartwheels, killed cleanly in the head. For my part I seldom shoot more than two or three hares in the season, for I like to see them about and to know that there is one there when the beagles draw the ground.

The pattern for the next hour is much the same. Every corner is diligently worked. Two more snipe are added to the bag and a duck mallard which rose from a puddle in the middle of a field.

Each hedge in the high ground is drawn, with a gun on either side. Feeding hoppers have been placed in these hedges and, judging by the feathers and droppings, are being well patronised. A cock pheasant is caught napping but a hen sideslips and is missed cleanly.

There are two resident coveys of partridges on the ground – usually with eight or ten in each. In the early part of the season there is a chance of walking them up and perhaps killing a brace as they erupt from the ground in a whirr of wings, but they swiftly become educated, rising at a hundred yards or more. By October they are as wild as hawks and rarely make a mistake.

If you are lucky enough to have several coveys on your shoot and a root crop more or less in the centre of the ground, adroit driving may enable you to push them into the roots where they can be walked up or a small drive attempted.

Take your time with walked-up partridges rising close to you. There is a natural tendency to fire both barrels too soon. But, if the birds have jumped within fifteen yards, there is all the time in the world. It is useless and unsporting to fire into the 'brown' in vague expectation of killing several birds, for more often than not you will simply not touch a feather or, if you do connect, perhaps send one or two birds away wounded. Pick a bird on the outside of the covey and, if you miss, don't switch to another but try to kill it with the second barrel.

Even if you think you have missed, watch the covey with care until out of sight or it drops. Occasionally a bird will suddenly break away and fly straight up until, head back, it collapses, stone-dead. This phenomenon is known as 'towering'; what happens is that the bird is hit in the lungs which gradually fill with blood, causing it to throw its head back for air and so fly vertically. Such birds are invariably picked up dead, lying on their backs and with their beaks filled with blood.

Back now to our shoot. Time is drawing on and the sun is sinking towards the distant hills. There is still time to investigate a long bank, the side of the disused railway line. Choked with brambles and coarse grass, it is a likely spot for a pheasant or rabbit. This is where a bold, thrusting spaniel proves its value as, bursting the undergrowth asunder, it seeks the tantalising scent of game.

A bank such as this should be covered from both sides, but don't stand too close or your field of fire will be restricted and a pheasant, if one gets up, may be badly damaged if hit at all. Far better to keep level with the dogs, but well back from the bank. Whenever two guns are working opposite sides of a hedge or bank, gun-safety must be stricter than normal. Don't risk low shots, unless away from the hedge and remember that a bolting rabbit may have a spaniel hot behind it. A friend of mine killed his dog under such circumstances and has never forgotten the distress it caused him. With luck we may turf out a pheasant or, perhaps, a rabbit or two, but remember that the afternoon is drawing on and the pheasants should not be chivied too long but given a chance to draw up to their roosting areas.

Dusk is coming on apace, a barn owl flits like a ghost moth across the flooded splash where, a week before, a hundred-weight of tail-corn was tipped. There is no need to prepare hides, for the thick tussocks of reed grass provide ample cover. There is a slight breeze from the east which is ideal. The duck, if any, will come in to land against the wind. By facing the afterglow of the sunset we will see the birds silhouetted long after it is black-dark behind us. There is also a thin cloud layer which will help us to spot birds. Against a cloudless sky they become virtually invisible.

Half-a-dozen decoys, the rubber collapsible sort, are dropped into the foot of water in the centre of the splash and then, dogs under control, we settle down. There were no duck on the water when we arrived but had there been we would have nobly refrained from shooting. There is a sound theory that, if shot at under these circumstances, they are unlikely to return at dusk bringing back friends with them.

The first sound to shatter the calm is a sudden tearing rasp and a slight plop. Again and again the pattern is repeated as snipe, like feathered darts, dive hard for the pool, braking at the last moment and landing lightly. They are virtually unshootable but herald the duck which are to follow.

Abruptly, with no warning, two black blurs race across the water and land with a splash before there is a chance of a shot. They are only yards away and, perhaps sensing danger, erupt like miniature rockets. No hesitation now! Snap at the nearest teal and as it falls, swing up its partner's smoke-trail as it wildly races for the stars. Bad luck! You were a foot or so behind. These tiny duck fly with verve and call for fast reaction shooting.

Gather your bird at once, unless further duck are coming in. It is sometimes difficult to know what to do under these circumstances, though if you have a reliable dog the pick-up can be left till the flight is over. Personally I usually compromise by picking any duck which have fallen close, choosing a moment when there seems to be a lull, and leaving the outliers for the spaniel to work on when we pack up.

Back to our pond where a lone mallard is circling the water, high up and suspicious. Each circuit brings it lower, but don't fire until it is well within range, preferably when it comes in for the final touch-down with paddles lowered and wings cupped.

This type of shooting can be tremendously exciting. To obtain the best from it, cool nerves and good eyesight are essential. Always recall the position of your companion and never risk low shots unless you are absolutely confident there is no danger. Once in position, don't change it without warning your partner and make sure that he understands this as well.

Personally, I would never shoot an evening flight unless I had a dog and one which does not run in. If it cannot be trusted, then peg it down or tie it to a clump of rushes. You should always carry a torch. This can be vital in assisting the pick-up and hunting for dropped cartridges or pieces of equipment. But don't be greedy and delay your pick-up too long. Allow the remaining duck time to come in.

I have drawn a sketchy and possibly ideal picture of my own shoot but, of course, the great joy of rough shoots lies in their infinite variety. On some there may be virtually no water and apparently little chance of a duck in the bag, yet even there, if the farmer is cooperative, there may exist the possibility of dredging or blasting a flight pond. The results that can be achieved with duck are positively astonishing. Small, stale ponds, stuffed with old bicycle frames can, when cleared, enlarged, planted and fed in, show remarkable sport. One must not be greedy and once a flight pattern has been established one should not normally shoot more than once a fortnight. A great deal depends on local conditions and the weather; the occasion may arise when a sudden fall of continental duck offer an opportunity not to be neglected,

even though the water may have been shot the week before. Common sense is the guiding factor. If you overshoot you will merely ruin your own sport in the long run. Rough nights are the ones to pick for they do least damage by way of disturbance.

On some shoots, where there is one or possibly more well-established flight ponds, permanent hides can be constructed, taking into account the prevailing wind. The best I have seen consist of growing alders trained into a circle with a narrow entrance. A word of warning. Beware of placing hides where they can be readily spotted by the public or you may find yourself acting as unwitting host to the local lads with an eye for sport and an absent tenant.

I have been a wildfowler, I have shot driven game, and although I would rate driven grouse an experience to be seized at every opportunity, for sheer *sustained* enjoyment rough shooting, in my book, tops them all. It is the joy of the unexpected, of never being quite certain or knowing for sure the outcome of the day. Large bags mean little to me and I would sooner hunt my birds with a good dog, killing only a few perhaps, but recalling each shot. This really *is* sport.

Grouse Shooting

John Phillips and Willy Newlands

Fifteen species of grouse are found around the northern hemisphere, but for the British sportsman there is only one grouse – the prince of upland gamebirds. The red grouse of the heather moorlands of the British Isles is known to science as *Lagopus lagopus scoticus* and until recent years it was usually described as the only bird species which was uniquely British.

However, unsporting systematists have now taken away this honour and lumped it in with the circumpolar willow grouse as a humble sub-species. The red grouse is quite distinct from its close relatives because it does not turn white in winter or display white wings in summer. And its change of scientific status has not reduced its value as one of the world's most justly famed sporting birds.

The excitement of shooting driven grouse has attracted thousands of sportsmen to the hills of Scotland, England and, to a lesser degree, Wales, for more than a century. Wealthy businessmen, crowned heads and celebrities have joined hill farmers and moorland syndicates in this challenging sport of late summer, which has done much to maintain the typical appearance of the hill country of northern Britain, most of which would revert to forest if unburned and ungrazed.

The authors will never forget the look of glazed ecstasy on the face of one American game biologist (a very keen and widely travelled shot) after a pack of grouse had hurtled over his butt. He lay back on the heather, gasping: 'Oh, boy! This makes pheasant shooting look like a coconut shy.'

Red grouse are the typical birds of treeless moorland from sea level up to about 600–700 m and are very visible in autumn when the cocks make display flights over their newly-claimed territories, challenging rivals with far-carrying *go-back*, *ka-wow*, *grrrrr* calls which are highly evocative for anyone brought up in the hills.

The number of these speedy birds bagged and the quality of the shooting is ultimately dependent on the lie of the land and the productivity of the moorland soil, but there are many shoots which can confidently predict bags of a hundred brace early in the season in most years. On the very best grouse ground, the density of birds in August may be as high as one to two grouse per acre (two to five per hectare). This high figure indicates just how well the species is adapted to life on what, to human eyes, appears to be rather barren and monotonous uplands.

The record books make clear just how abundant grouse can be. At Littledale and Abbeystead moors, Lancashire, on August 12, 1915, eight guns killed 2,929 grouse; on August 30, 1888, Lord Walsingham, shooting alone, killed 1,070 grouse.

The north of England is the stronghold of red grouse in the British Isles, mainly thanks to a continuing tradition of careful management of the stocks and their heather moorland habitat. In Wales, the species has all but disappeared, although one or two shoots have shown that birds can be produced where effort is put into keepering, and grouse are now much less common than they once were on the moors of south-west England and throughout Ireland.

Grouse find it difficult to compete where land has been reclaimed for agriculture, or where moorland has been fragmented by afforestation and the numbers of crows and foxes have increased. The predators are encouraged by the suitable cover, plentiful carrion (where slipshod farming is subsidised by EC payments) and the availability of invertebrate food in the improved grasslands.

If you ask the average shooting man what constitutes good moor management, he will probably suggest, in descending order of importance: vermin control, supply of grit, drainage, shooting sensible numbers of grouse, and burning heather.

In fact that afterthought, heather burning, forms 50% of successful management. Get it right and grouse will thrive, if given the secondary support of fox and crow control.

This is demonstrated when an energetic young keeper takes on a neglected moor with many acres of even-aged heather, much of it woody and old. He starts by burning numerous small fires, 25–40 m wide, through long heather, and he kills the crows and foxes. In the first years of his new job, grouse numbers increase rapidly because their breeding success is higher. The rate of improvement slows after a few seasons, but, by the end of a decade, a moor which was carrying a breeding pair of grouse to thirty acres may have been transformed into one carrying a pair to five acres — a sixfold increase.

By diversifying the age classes of heather through the use of fire, the keeper creates more 'grouse houses' or territories. The birds find the varied heather habitat they need for feeding and shelter. The population responds to the fires, depending on the speed of heather regrowth, within three to five years. Thanks to this quick reaction, the improvement of grouse shootings may actually be faster than the creation of a pheasant shoot, where new woodlands will probably take ten years to reach a size which can hold appreciable numbers of birds.

As a result of two decades of scientific work through the Seventies and Eighties, Dr Adam Watson and his team of moorland researchers at Banchory, Kincardineshire, showed that heather quality is the basis upon which grouse shooting is built: good heather produces good grouse. *Calluna vulgaris* is not just the pretty plant of romantic songs — the bonnie bloomin' heather is the source of prosperity in our hills.

Heather forms almost unbroken stands over much of the uplands of eastern Scotland, the Pennines and eastern Ireland. Cock grouse take up their territories on these moorlands in autumn and they defend them against all other males throughout the winter and spring, although they may join other birds of both sexes to form packs during blizzards and to roost at night.

Where the heather is well managed by the setting of small and widespread fires and the heather is nutritious, growing on base-rich soils, territories will be small and the overall population of the moor will be high. With poorer heather on low-grade soils, no amount of management effort will achieve the same high levels of population.

Heather can be damaged when the moor is grazed by too many deer and sheep, particularly in winter. Competition results in the best food being lost to the grouse and cover is reduced, exposing them to predators. Red deer numbers have more than doubled in thirty years although the range available to them has been greatly reduced by afforestation and land reclamation for agriculture.

Sheep numbers have also increased in response to generous subsidies under the Common Agricultural Policy (CAP) of the European Community. The national flock in England has grown by 30% in the ten years to 1992, resulting in hill sheep levels which are unsustainable without serious loss of heather cover and severe environmental damage and erosion.

Red deer are also important hosts of the sheep tick (*Ixodes ricinus*) which is the vector of a virus disease, louping ill, a serious sheep ailment which is a lethal disease to grouse. The long-term decline of grouse in much of north and west Scotland is likely to be linked to these increases in deer and sheep numbers.

In the face of this competition, food quality is particularly important to the hen grouse in spring. She is confined on her mate's territory throughout winter, leaving only in the severest of weather. The assessment of the dietary value of the heather was made by the cock in staking out his patch in October and she has to live on the rations he is able to guard for her.

Provided the young shoots of heather have not been eaten by deer, sheep or hares, or damaged by dehydration during frosts, the hen's body condition reflects the quality of her winter diet. As the days lengthen, her internal clock starts to speed up and the number of eggs she will lay is determined.

However, the female grouse exists on a biological knife-edge every spring. The winter diet will not have been rich enough to provide all the nutrients needed by the developing eggs. She needs an early burst of spring growth to give her the nutritious shoots of blaeberry, heather, cotton grass and flowering plants on which production of a successful clutch depends. A week or two of warm weather at the critical time leads to high-quality eggs and large broods of thriving youngsters.

Breeding success is connected to the hen's own behaviour, which is again dependent on her diet. If she is well-nourished she mothers her chicks with gusto, spends much time brooding them, is highly aggressive when enemies such as crows or hen harriers approach and is likely to rear a large proportion of her chicks, even if the weather turns bad during the rearing period.

In years when the onset of spring growth is very late, or heather is dehydrated and 'frosted', the hens will not rear many chicks. In extreme seasons, the parent birds themselves will die in April, May or even June. Such deadly years are noted by owners and keepers as those when 'the disease' killed grouse stocks.

Of all the predators, crows and foxes are by far the most serious. The moor manager must keep their numbers down.

The hawks, owls and falcons – totally protected by the law – are insignificant in their effect on a well managed moor. The grouse bag is more certainly and easily increased by greater attention to burning than by the illegal persecution of birds of prey.

Weather is not a serious hazard. The red/willow grouse is a bird of Arctic places and can even find a cosy living on the mountains of northern Norway, where it does not see daylight for a quarter of the year and has to feed on the high tundra by moonlight in temperatures which fall to minus 40°C. It shares with its close relative the ptarmigan the title of the hardiest of all bird species.

By comparison with the high Arctic, the British moorlands have a comparatively gentle climate. The red grouse is not attracted for long by sheltered hedgerows and rich stubbles, and it has to be remembered that in Britain the species is at the southern edge of its range, while the grey partridge (naturally) and the pheasant (by introduction) are reaching towards the northern limit of theirs.

Record grouse bags can follow torrential rain in late May and June, in just the same way that an 'ideal' mix of warmth and showers may be followed by disastrously poor shooting days. The key lies in the food available several months earlier.

There are freakish variations which can affect this general

picture. Late snowstorms with falls of several inches can cause hens to desert their nests and can kill chicks, but these circumstances are very unusual. Rain, even if it is cold, will not by itself kill young broods. Falls of up to three inches in one day have been recorded on moors where chicks were, on average, a week old – and a splendid season has followed.

Sleet and frost at night during the egg-laying period may destroy eggs and waterlog nests, but well-fed hens will lay again, even if this happens during the early stages of incubation. If it occurs after a fortnight of sitting, however, the hen will not usually re-nest.

Grouse need grit to grind up their tough, fibrous food and release the nutrients it contains. Only on moors overlying soft rocks or on extensive areas of deep peat is there any possibility that grit will be in short supply, but even there, the birds seem to find enough for their needs and do not take extra territory just because it contains supplies of grit.

Heather is typically a plant of dry ground. If the soil is water-logged, the heather will not grow strongly and it will not compete very well with lower-grade grasses and sedges. Drainage may improve the growth of heather, but may also destroy the wet flushes which are important sites for the insects on which young grouse feed for the first two weeks of life.

Poor drainage can occur on thin peat on steep slopes in north-east Scotland and the remedy is to pull a heavy tine through the ground to break up the sub-soil's hard pan.

Access and recreation are words which arouse strong emotions among the owners of hill land. Moor proprietors who have roads over their hills are often concerned at the numbers of picnic-toting ramblers who stop their cars and wander over the heather looking for a place to eat their sandwiches. However, research has shown that grouse take territories of equal size and rear just as many young on areas of intensive human use as they do in places which few people reach.

Day-trip tourists do not wander over the moors in any numbers until after hatching. By the time disturbance does become obvious, the birds are no longer confined to a small area and can move away from people without coming to any harm. Humans are also natural herd animals and can be encouraged to use certain picnic spots and pathways.

Scattering young chicks in cold, wet weather can be serious, but few day-trippers brave the hills at such times.

What is much more deadly than walkers and picnickers is the ill-trained townee dog. Sheep farmers and game managers unite in condemning the family pet which is running wild and 'having a marvellous time'.

The matter of public access to moorland does affect grouse and it is a complex one, which will take patience and goodwill to resolve, particularly in England. Some landowners and sportsmen see the conservation of moorland for grouse and other wildlife threatened by this invasion, but they will undoubtedly have to put themselves on the same side as the hundreds of thousands of members of such powerful bodies as the Royal Society for the Protection of Birds (RSPB) and the Ramblers Association. If it came to a trial of strength, there would be no contest: the shooters, their sport and their management expertise would be blown away.

The future welfare of the uplands and all the species that live there lies with the conservation and management bodies which, if they pooled their resources, could boast a membership of more than a million people. A policy is needed which accommodates everyone's interests.

Unless this compromise is found, the future for grouse and upland wildlife − and the heather moors themselves − is bleak.

Over-grazing by subsidised sheep, over-burning of heather in large fires by shepherds, and the increase in fox and crow numbers have already been responsible for a massive decline in grouse over most of the west of Scotland and north-west England.

Heavy grazing and trampling by cattle, particularly on small areas of heather hill in winter, can be just as harmful. In general, however, moderate grazing by cattle and sheep in summer improves the productivity of heather, by keeping it short and nutritious.

The present economics of sheep farming, with reliance on the hill ewe subsidy, has resulted in a progressive degradation of hill land, with serious effects on wildlife and on what is rightly called 'the Prince of Upland Gamebirds'.

SHOOTING GROUSE

Grouse shooting is actually three different sports: shooting over dogs, walking up, and driving.

The typical method of cropping a thin population on extensive moors, typical of Caithness, Sutherland, Ross-shire and parts of Inverness, is shooting over dogs. About 150 years ago, nearly all game shooting in Britain was done over bird dogs and there is a revival of interest today in the traditional sport, which is still the favoured method of harvesting upland game in North America and parts of Europe.

Where bags are below around twenty-five brace a day, dogging becomes a worthwhile alternative. Its devotees describe it as 'an aesthetic experience' with one or two guns, three or four dogs running in relays, a dog handler and assistant to carry game and lead the resting dogs.

The dogs commonly used are pointers and setters. A warm, humid day with a steady breeze is ideal. Under such conditions in late summer the grouse will lie well and their scent carries for some distance.

As far as possible, the ground is covered across the wind or upwind and a brace of dogs will work it at a fast gallop, ranging out a hundred yards or more on each side, crossing and recrossing in front of the guns, who can talk quietly, admire the dogs and the view, and enjoy one of the most pleasant sights in field sport.

The climax is sudden, as one of the dogs scents grouse and stops dead, rigidly pointing with aligned head, body and tail in the direction in which the covey is lying. The second dog, which will not usually have the scent, will 'back' the first by stopping and taking up the same point, although some distance away. This is very useful on broken ground, where one or other of the dogs may be out of sight for much of the time.

The guns take up position, one on each side of the pointing dog, while it is encouraged to draw slowly forward towards the hidden grouse. When birds rise – a moment of startling excitement – the dog 'drops' and the guns shoot.

Dead birds may be pointed by the dog, but under British conditions dogs are not usually required to retrieve, although in North America and Scandinavia this is considered to be part of their job. Dogging works best on areas of rank heather where the coveys will lie well.

Shooting over pointers used to be much more widespread than it is today. The decline came about partly because success in managing grouse for driving from the 1870s onwards resulted in moors so crowded with birds that the dogs could not work properly.

It was also thought that the season for grouse was so short — little more than a month — that the year-round effort required to keep and train the dogs was not worthwhile, particularly when partridges declined and very few estates had enough to dog on stubbles in September and October.

Modern enthusiasts hunt snipe, woodcock and wild pheasants with their bird dogs, extending the season into autumn and winter. The dogs can be surprisingly versatile and provide months of varied sport, even returning to grouse in open weather in winter, after the stalking is over, when the wily birds are a considerable challenge for the hunter.

Walking-up can be described as dogging without the artistry. The basic principles of working the ground are the same, but the party of guns may be as many as six or eight, with followers to carry the bag. The only dogs are the guns' normal pheasant-day companions — spaniels and labradors.

The shooting tends to have a certain sameness about it as there is little chance of intentionally varying the angles of the birds, by flushing them from different directions, such as occurs with dogging.

If birds are plentiful, the line never gets going, and stops every fifty yards while a bird is picked up or a wild dog is caught and chastised! Walking in line when birds are scarce is very dull. When they are numerous it is quite tedious, unless the party, can be kept small (which it never is).

DRIVING GROUSE

To most discriminating sportsmen this represents the *crème de la crème* of shooting. This high esteem is reflected in the price put upon it. The endless variety of shots, the country, the time of year, all combine to make the driven grouse invitation one of the most sought-after in any sportsman's calendar. The organisation which has to go into a day is considerable and success is often in the balance until the last minute as speculation about the dawn breeze and the lingering mist results in anxious discussion between keeper and owner. Once decisions are made, the guns assemble, draw numbers and set off for the first line of butts, sometimes on foot, more usually by Land-Rover.

For those fresh from office desk or smoky town, the climb to the butts can be a lung-bursting business. Heat and flies torment the guns as they zigzag higher and higher up the hill.

At last the cartridge bag is opened and put carefully on the edge of the stone and turf butt, the gun is slid from its sleeve and loaded, the dog is parked carefully out of the way and it is possible to brace aching legs on the shooting stick and take stock.

The first consideration is safety. This butt is No. 2, so there are no worries about flankers. What features can be picked out in front to mark the safe arc of fire? To the left, that big grey stone on the burnside with the white lichen, sixty yards away, catches the eye. To the right, the patch of rushes where the sheep drain starts.

The beat can be seen lining out nearly a mile away on the far ridge, so nothing much is likely to happen for a few minutes yet. There is time to take in the glorious panorama which extends below, patchwork valleys and nestling farms, a glimpse of the distant sea. Racing cloud shadows on a far slope. A wonderful place to relax, sit and dream in the hot sun.

A double shot suddenly rings out below, followed by a whistle from the neighbouring butt. Galvanised into life, the dreaming gun sees on the horizon, sixty yards in front, six or eight apparently motionless birds.

The inexperienced think they have ample time. The experts move into action at once: in a split second the gun is on the shoulder, bird covered, shot fired. Any hesitation and the chance is lost.

The great maxim with grouse is to shoot fluidly and fast. The man who has quick reflexes and can allow himself to be uninhibited and shoot by instinct will miss a few but he will kill a lot. The 'old poker', on the other hand, is always caught napping, rarely gets two shots off in front and is always turning round. He is the first to complain of blind butts and is unable to produce even a 3:1 ratio of cartridges to kills.

The flight pattern of grouse differs in many ways from that of lowland game. The pack skims along the contours and is not usually very high off the ground. This low-altitude speed is deceptive, and every bird in the group is actually doing something different.

Grouse rarely fly straight. If they are flapping, they are rising. If they are gliding, they are falling. In each case, they will be swinging to left or right, slicing across the baffling interface between sky and heather at breathtaking speed.

No amount of conscious calculation can accommodate their changes of pace and direction in time to put the shot where it ought to be. Let the subconscious do the work − and get your gun off well in front.

As the ice is broken on the first drive and shooting has started, confidence increases. The next birds to come are a pair over the rushes to the right, swinging up hill and slowing as they brace themselves to land in front, thirty yards out. Both fall, and morale is high, only to be shattered a moment later when a covey comes on the same line but with no intention of stopping. Two shots are yards behind them. A singleton straight in front, followed by a group of three, increases the bag by a couple, and a high swinging bird missed by your left-hand neighbour is killed overhead and falls almost on top of the man below.

A covey streaks in over the big stone. Only time for one in front, dismount the gun, pirouette and fire behind as they tear down the hill. The chosen bird staggers but picks up and is tidily killed by your neighbour. A quick 'thank you' wave, concentrating all the time on the front, and another covey comes hurtling in, straight at the butt.

Too slow, missed in front. Turn, miss behind. While fumbling to reload, another covey and single sneak past, just in time for a sternchaser shot after the last bird — the only effect being to leave the shooter even more rattled.

The beaters are close, three hares potter through the line of butts, followed by a string of sheep. The keeper's horn signals 'No shooting in front' — the drive is over.

Considering it is the first day, not too bad: fifteen shots and seven birds to pick, excluding the cripple killed by the next gun. The retriever, skittish at first, soon settles and the birds are all quickly gathered. A dogless neighbour has a runner down and an offer to help is gratefully accepted, with the dog completing the job.

Two pickers-up appear. Standing three hundred yards back, they have three birds which fell near them. Perhaps that was not a double miss near the end after all... On to the next line of butts on the steep hillside, the next sweating climb, the next drive.

The day is a mixture of relaxation in glorious surroundings and moments of intense, heart-stopping excitement. There are very few guns who don't mean it when they thank (and tip) the keeper for a great day, take their brace of birds, and praise the host's skills and organisation.

PTARMIGAN: THE GAMEBIRD OF THE HIGH TOPS

Climbing up from the heather moor, the hunter reaches the high tops. The plant cover is dwarfed by cold and wind, so that only mosses, blaeberry and tiny alpine plants can survive among the scree and boulders. This is the home, year round, of the ptarmigan.

Slightly smaller than the red grouse, weighing 400–600 g compared with 650–750 g, the ptarmigan (*Lagopus mutus*) is otherwise similar in appearance — with the dramatic distinction that it moults into almost completely white plumage in winter, only the tail remaining black.

The only bird capable of living at all seasons in such inhospitable Arctic places as Spitzbergen, the ptarmigan shelters in the Highland scree and finds a living where any other living thing would perish. The falls of stones are just as vital to its way of life as heather is to the red grouse. Otherwise suitable ground cannot carry

ptarmigan unless there is scree to shelter them from the wind.

Ptarmigan are usually found above two thousand feet, except in the far north-west of Scotland, where exposure is so severe that they are found at lower altitudes, almost down to sea level in Sutherland.

The birds are often absurdly tame, running about making noises usually described as 'croaking', but most accurately imitated by running a comb across the edge of a table. They might seem easy targets for the hunter, but the landscape is on their side. After a three hour walk, climbing two thousand feet, carrying lunch, cartridges and increasingly heavy gun, the birds are met on a 45° slope of unstable scree, the only footholds covered in damp and slippery vegetation.

To load the dice even further in the ptarmigan's favour, they rise as quietly as owls, unlike the rumbling flush of grouse. They may be thirty-five yards away before they are spotted and the gun, poised between mountain top and abyss, and without much contact with either, does well to get off a shot before they are gone around the boulders and into the next corrie.

It is small wonder that ptarmigan numbers are little affected by shooting. A twenty-brace day for four fit guns would almost get into the record books.

Pursuit of this fine bird will produce the most interesting of bye-days in a week's stalking or grouse shooting and takes the sportsman to places he would not otherwise explore. The little grey and white ghost of the misty corries is a worthy gamebird, much respected by those who have hunted it on the high tops.

CAPERCAILLIE AND BLACKGAME

The giant grouse of the Scots pinewoods, the male capercaillie (*Tetrao urogallus*) weighs up to 4.5 kg and is one of Britain's most impressive birds, with his bearded throat and green-glossed dark

plumage. At nearly three feet in length, he is twice the size of the female. The plumage of the capercaillie varies in both sexes and no two birds are exactly alike.

This pine forest bird became extinct (or nearly so) in Scotland and was re-introduced in about 1837 from Scandinavia. Adult birds were brought over and also clutches of eggs, which were put into blackgame nests. The re-introduction was very successful and the species steadily expanded its range from Perthshire, where it was first established on Drummond Hill on Loch Tay side, into most of the eastern and central Highlands.

In Europe, the capercaillie is looked upon as big game, the cocks being stalked individually during their spring display or 'spel', notable for its performance of strange cork-popping and gargling noises.

Still regarded by some foresters as a pest, a family party of caper can make an impressive swathe through a plantation of young pines, eating most of the leading shoots. Loose groups of birds feed on the ground in summer, in the tops of pines in winter, where their diet consists almost entirely of buds and needles.

While still relatively common in places where there are extensive tracts of Scots pine, including Deeside and Speyside, the 'King of Grouse' has suffered a substantial decline in recent years. Causes may include the ever-greater mileage of deer fences, into which birds fly with fatal results, the increase in fox and crow numbers previously mentioned in connection with red grouse predation, and, possibly, a run of unfavourable summers. Although the bird has a northern range, the young need warm, dry days in midsummer if they are to get a successful start in life.

Some estates may have over-exploited their caper populations and there is now a widespread voluntary shooting ban. It is hoped this will be only a temporary measure. Attempts to 'protect' the species by law are so far unwarranted.

The black grouse or blackgame (*Lyrurus tetrix*) is among the most magnificent of our native birds, with the most dramatic communal display, the lek. Males have glossy blue-black plumage with white under the distinctive lyre-shaped tail, and weigh 1–1.4 kg. Females have slightly forked tails but are otherwise readily confused with red grouse.

This is a gamebird of the marginal land between forest and moor. Although it is the least specialised of our grouse, it is the most sensitive to human interference and people pressure, even where there is no shooting. The population graph has shown a steady downward trend for decades because of habitat loss and increased predation. A few districts seem to go against this general trend for reasons which are not yet understood.

Shooting blackgame should always be done by driving. Shooting immature or moulting birds during August grouse days is a travesty of sport when they can provide such marvellous shooting from October onwards. Although they are really birds of the woodland fringes, they are found on open heath early in the season. They like mixtures: largest numbers are found where mixed-age birch and pine are interspersed with patches of heather, bracken, blaeberry and arable crops.

There was a time when estates in south and north-east Scotland used to enjoy annual blackgame days, but nowadays they are nowhere sufficiently numerous. The best that can be hoped for is a black grouse drive on a back-end grouse day, or possibly a few coming forward with 'outside' pheasants in October.

The whole range of upland in Scotland is home to capercaillie, blackcock, red grouse and ptarmigan. The grouse family are the primary game inhabitants of six million acres of agricultural and forestry ground. They are among the most important birds to the sporting economy of Great Britain – and certainly among the most prized.

The Management of Game

C. L. Coles

The golden age of game shooting lasted from about 1880 to the start of the First World War. During this period most farms looked like Constable landscapes. There was no shortage of food or cover for the birds, the use of poisonous sprays and seed dressings was minimal, and farm machinery was horse-drawn and harmless. Wetlands were for the most part left wet, and, in the traditional game counties our woodlands consisted largely of mixed hardwoods such as oak, ash and beech, often with compartments of coppice, and always with a warm forest floor. Many coverts were planted with pheasants and landscaping in mind, rather than the sawmill. The era of dark even-aged spruce forests blanketing the countryside had not yet arrived.

The job of the gamekeeper was comparatively easy. His duties were to police the estate, keeping poachers away, and to protect his game from their enemies. Apart from the weather, 'vermin' constituted the major factor which influenced the fluctuations of his birds — particularly the replacement of young.

There were also rabbits to be dealt with, ride-trimming in the coverts, winter feeding — either on foot or from a pony cart — and rearing where necessary. In those days this was far less widespread. In the wild pheasant counties of East Anglia it was unheard of. But where rearing was carried out it was often on a very large scale indeed.

On the partridge manors, 'hedgerow keepering', which consisted largely of finding the nests, protecting them, 'dummying' them (i.e. the Euston system) if in a dangerous place, was the main job from May onwards. In that epoch, the partridge — not the pheasant — was the common gamebird and the sportsman's everyday quarry.

Nowadays the job of the keeper and the game manager is very different. Farms are often intensively cultivated, frequently disturbed by machines and heavily sprayed. The old chessboard pattern of mixed crops has in many areas given way to large

Modern intensive farming has destroyed
many of the hedgerows that provided
the partridge with its nesting sites.

hedgeless fields and monoculture until a more wildlife-friendly agriculture started to develop a few years ago. Almost everywhere, the gamebirds' habitat has deteriorated. Additionally, there are just more people, motorcars, electric wires and cables — 'birdcage Britain' an ecologist has called it — in our shrinking countryside.

In spite of this, and perhaps surprisingly, shooting is on the whole in a healthy state. Since the early thirties, game conservation has become a science in its own right. Game is regarded as a supplementary 'crop' or by-product of the land, which, if carefully husbanded, can be harvested just like cereals or potatoes. To get the best results, the game crop must be planned as part of the agricultural or forestry enterprise and not just as an afterthought. Put like this it may sound too prosaic and businesslike, but the fun aspect of it is still very much present. Game management and keeping, either as a spare- or full-time occupation, is absorbingly interesting. The challenge is just a little greater than it was thirty or forty years ago. Nevertheless, the pendulum has swung and many land users are once again concerned with improving the habitat. And whatever we do for the partridge benefits other forms of wildlife equally.

116

HABITAT

The key to the high survival of game is the maintenance of a suitable habitat. A great part of the Game Conservancy's time consists of advising on and improving the environment. Game is valuable: a good shoot increases the capital value of the land. Softwood timber crops are to some extent less economic than they were. People talk more of leisure and amenity. Farmers and landowners are therefore more willing to put in a few game spinneys – the modern version of which can be shot during the first year, the rows of young trees being intercropped with artichokes, kale, canary grass, Texel greens and other suitable nurse crops. Other small areas of game cover should, where possible, be planted on banks or in unproductive corners which cannot be cultivated economically. And often landowners – requiring good shooting and wanting a more attractive landscape than the normal intensive cereals or milk 'factory' can produce – will devote three of four per cent of their land to amenity woods, belts, special game crops or perhaps wildfowl pools. It is not much use just increasing and improving the cover. It must be sited where it will be of greatest value. A good interspersion is needed – not too much of one thing in one place and too little in another.

There are several dual-purpose crops like kale, which are planted mainly for the farm, but which can be used by game. Obviously, three separate ten-acre fields of kale are a better proposition than one thirty-acre block. The way it is fed off, the resulting shape, the direction of the drills and so on will all have a bearing on its usefulness during the shooting season. Seed kale is particularly valuable. Mustard is another excellent dual-purpose crop, and is often valuable when disced in or put in with a spinner after harvest on what would otherwise be bare ground. It is best sown in mid-July and not later than mid-August. Artichokes are also a favourite, being often sited beside a small insignificant woodland of a couple of acres to make something of a worthwhile size for the shooting season, but they must be managed and not left to run riot and deteriorate. Kale can be similarly used. There are also a number of special game crops, which can either be planted as pure stands or as mixtures. Maize is an excellent game crop and is the basis of all food patches in North America.

The various game mixtures should be chosen according to soil, elevation and climate. In addition to kale and maize, other plants commonly included are buckwheat, canary seed, white millet, tic beans, sunflowers and cereals. Simple cocktails are sometimes the best, for instance maize and millet: The Game Conservancy can advise on a local basis.

With regard to more permanent cover in the form of woodlands, the landowner should try to aim for mixed species and mixed ages. As to the design of a covert, the golden rule is to let the sun in and keep the wind out – with an outer hedge and/or a perimeter windbreak of conifers. The pheasant indulges in most of his daytime activities as a pedestrian, and hates draughts. The provision of carefully planned collecting and flushing areas is vital: the accent being on high, fast birds of quality, not quantity.

Lastly on the subject of woodlands, we should remember that in addition to the timber and the pheasants, there is a third crop of increasing importance – roe deer, which are valuable as a trophy quarry and as venison. Roe do not interfere with pheasants. They can cause some fraying and browsing damage to certain trees and thereby incur the wrath of the forester, but careful management and a suitable shooting programme will usually reduce this to acceptable proportions. The compensations for having roe on an estate can be very great.

FARMING PROCESSES

I have touched on the problem of farm chemicals and the damaging effect of some machines. The chemicals are here to stay: they are recognised as valuable aids to maximum crop production – though we hope their use on farms will become more sophisticated and selective. Some are toxic to gamebirds, others have harmful indirect effects by destroying insect life or by removing the weeds upon which the insects live. This shortage of insect foods, which – as we have said – are absolutely necessary for grey partridge chicks, is one of the main causes why this species is at present in a state of decline.

To reduce the danger to wildlife, here are some of the precautions that should be taken with farm chemicals.

(a) Always use the least toxic chemical which will do the job efficiently.

(b) If it is necessary to use a dangerous chemical, restrict it to the area (one crop, or part of a crop) where it is needed.

(c) Keep the sprayer away from hedges and banks, especially at nesting time, and do not contaminate any water which birds might drink.

(d) Complete any weed-killing with known poisonous sprays as early in the season as possible, before partridges hatch and before there are many pheasant chicks in the corn.

(e) If poisonous sprays have to be used on brassicas (cabbages, kale, rape, mustard etc.) spray before the cereal harvest so that birds still have safe alternative cover in the standing corn.

(f) Do not leave in the fields any tins or receptacles which have contained poison, any puddles of concentrated spray, or heaps of dressed seed corn.

(g) Where toxic seed-dressed corn is concerned, make sure the seed is properly buried under the surface, and no heaps of corn are left as tempting food.

As to the heavy fast machines that must be used on farms these days, probably the silage cutter is the worst − mowing over partridge nests, maiming young pheasants, as well as roe deer kids which are often dropped in silage crops, or left to rest there while the mothers are away feeding. Obviously, if there is no shortage of *safe* nesting cover, birds will be less inclined to nest in the grass crops. However, some losses will be inevitable and a few safeguards are worth considering. If late cuts for silage and early cuts for hay *can* be avoided, major losses will be averted. The fields are most likely to be full of birds between May 21 and June 21. Early in the season, light rolling − before the grass is six inches high − will often drive the nesting pairs off to safer ground.

As to cutting, after many years of trials, flushing bars have not proved their worth behind the average tractor driver! But there are various methods of cutting that can reduce casualties, such as leaving an uncut grass headland of fifteen to twenty yards wide until last. The centre of the field should be cut in strips in the normal fashion and broods from the centre will tend to filter into the uncut headland, which is cut from the inside towards the hedge. This method gradually drives any broods towards safe cover.

Whatever method is used when grass-cutting, if an area of standing grass is rapidly decreasing at the centre of the headlands, it is always worth walking through alone, or with a dog, to flush any birds concentrated in the remaining cover. If the last little patch to be cut is in the centre of the field, it will materially help young pheasants in the crop if the final cutting can be left until the following morning, thereby enabling the birds to draw out at night.

With regard to protecting baby roe from slaughter, recent trials have shown that flashing road warning lights, placed at strategic points in the field the night before cutting, are effective in emptying the crop of roe. A chemical deterrent which can be sprayed along the sides of the field and act as a barrier against the deer crossing into the crop has been successfully developed. However it is not likely to be available commercially for a year or two. Its barrier properties last for up to two weeks.

There are a number of operations on the average farm that can either destroy wildlife or so reduce the game-carrying capacity of the land that a good shoot cannot be developed. The most important thing is obviously to have the cooperation of the farm staff. On a large estate one answer is to give the farm manager or foreman a 12-bore, and always ask him out − perhaps as a walking gun − on shooting days!

WINTER MANAGEMENT

In addition to doing all that can be done to minimise the damaging effects of some farming operations, there is the problem of winter conditions. The modern farm − often with its lack of hedgerows and rough corners, its early ploughing of stubble and so on − can be a very hungry place for game in hard weather.

Two considerations will help. Firstly, planning the crops so that the resulting mosaic will spread the food, shelter and escape cover as evenly as possible. And secondly, providing supplementary grain food in hoppers.

As regards the cropping, all winter cereals are beneficial, because in addition to providing early cover and early bite, they produce far more insects for the partridge chicks the following June, than spring corn. Undersowing is similarly of great benefit.

Hopper feeding is a well understood practice. The containers can be made from five gallon oil drums, preferably with the feeding slots *underneath*, where they are to be used for pheasants (though not for partridges) and situated at peck-height above the ground. This prevents any sparrow, finch, crow or pigeon from scavenging the gamebirds' rations.

Hand-feeding on strawed rides in coverts is still the ideal method for pheasants, but it is time-consuming. Hoppers can also play a very important role in holding birds on a shoot, and in some cases in actually preventing starvation.

Although not strictly a part of winter management, shoot owners should not forget to provide a network of drinkers for all reared birds at strategic places all over the ground.

PREDATOR CONTROL

If the land can provide enough food and cover, and man-made pressures are kept to the minimum, game will prosper. But so will the predators − this is nature's way of regulating things. However, the game manager's job is to provide a surplus to *shoot*, not to feed every hungry mouth and beak in the district. The enemies of game must therefore be controlled, humanely, selectively, and in most cases only during *selected* periods of the year, when gamebirds and their nests are most vulnerable. This is now a good deal harder to achieve than it was when the keeper was legally allowed an armoury of 'engines' such as open spring traps, ride nets, poisoned baits and so on. Today he has his gun; humane traps such as the excellent Fenn to use safely inside tunnels; snares and certain poisons (such as Warfarin) for rats and little else. Judiciously used, the keeper can still protect his game birds by legal means. In the wider interests of conserving attractive and protected non-game species such as, say, tawny owls or sparrowhawks, he will have to accept losses that occasionally may be very frustrating to him.

Predator control is *not* an outdated conservation technique, as

A feed hopper can easily be made out of a five-gallon drum, the bottom can be replaced with wire netting or a slot-dispenser: small birds cannot steal the grain and snow cannot block the outlets. Larger and more sophisticated hoppers can be bought from game appliance firms.

some naturalists would have us believe. In fact reducing the numbers of rats, corvids, grey squirrels and similar pests helps everyone. Earlier studies on the Game Conservancy's experimental partridge area in Sussex showed us just how important it can be. At the same time these studies highlighted the complexities of the problem. To give but one example, the short-tailed field vole (*Microtus agrestis*) makes a nice easy meal for stoats and weasels. When the vole cycle is low, or perhaps when we interfere with their living conditions, the weasels swiftly turn to any partridge chicks that may be available. Plenty of voles can therefore mean safer rearing conditions for young partridges. By measuring small mammals and weasel numbers on an area, and relating them to the seasonal partridge chick survival, we proved this beyond doubt. Balance is important.

Trapping is as necessary today as ever it was, particularly as we have fewer gamekeepers to undertake this task.

A good keeper in well-hedged country should run fifty to sixty tunnel traps on his beat during the killing months. Hedgerows provide good travel lanes for small, hunting 'vermin' and they will use them – as well as ditches, stone walls, grassy barbed wire fences etc – until the crops grow up. The keeper should therefore trap hard all through the winter months until he gets too busy 'egging' or rearing in the spring. Boundary traps and a few strategic 'indicator' traps should always be kept operational.

The best way to learn how to construct a tunnel, how to place the trap inside, where to site it and so on, is to spend some time with an experienced keeper – preferably a partridge man, for he will know that one can never have a good partridge shoot if all the predators are allowed a free run. And there is, too, a fundamental maxim of keepering that 'if you look after the partridges, the pheasants will look after themselves'.

The tunnel trap will pick up mainly stoats, weasels, rats, young rabbits and hedgehogs – the latter unfortunately being serious nest destroyers. Waterside cage traps will deal with mink, and continental box-traps – with a see-saw inside – are also successful, in the hands of a patient man who is prepared to learn a different technique. They can catch a lot of weasels – taking them alive – particularly when they acquire the smell of the field mice that often go in, to the irritation of the trapper! As far as possible, site all traps and snares away from the eyes of the passing rambler.

If the keeper inspects his nests regularly and, obviously, with extreme care, he will immediately see what losses he is suffering – a vixen or stoat with a litter can give a lot of trouble if not checked in time. The crow family – including magpies – are clever at nest raiding, which may not be too important as regards the early clutches, but they can also kill a lot of chicks. Crow cage traps – constructed on the lobster pot principle and judiciously sited and baited according to the season – can be very effective. The Larsen cage trap – preferably used with a decoy magpie – is a most effective corvid catcher, and any unwanted or protected birds can be released unharmed.

To control foxes – which for reasons of good relations should first be discussed with the local hunt – shooting and snaring are the two most effective methods. It must be admitted that foxes are great killers of nesting hens, and can also cause havoc when presented with the tempting situation of hundreds of reared poults in covert. Snares should *always* be sited where there is the least possibility of catching farm stock, deer or domestic animals. Shooting can take the form of carefully organised fox drives using heavy loads and avoiding long shots: also using marksmen with suitable high velocity rifles, fox 'callers', and powerful spotlights.

Rats are pests with no redeeming qualities whatsoever. They should be controlled by means of Warfarin baits in polythene sachets, placed in dispensers such as small gauge drain-pipes. If the rats become Warfarin-resistant, there are other legal poisons that can be substituted.

A tunnel trap will catch weasels, stoats, rats and other small ground vermin.

Coupled with habitat protection, predator control is undoubtedly the most vital and essential part of a balanced game management programme.

The Game Conservancy's recent experiments on Salisbury Plain produced dramatic results in increasing the stock of wild partridges on an area where the predators were controlled. On the neighbouring unkeepered area the stocks remained at a very low level. When the situations were reversed after some years and the poor area was keepered, the partridges rapidly increased; while on the neighbouring land where the predators were left untouched, the high partridge stocks soon dwindled away to a sparse population.

Rearing Gamebirds

T. H. Blank

Revised by Mike Swan

In lowland situations it has become the norm to release gamebirds into the wild each year to provide a high enough population to sustain shooting.

This is largely because increasingly intensive farming has reduced populations of insects on farmland, thereby removing the main food of gamebird chicks. However, recent studies by the Game Conservancy Trust have shown that it is still possible in some areas to produce healthy populations of entirely wild pheasants and partridge. At the same time there are many areas, especially in the wetter western half of the UK, which are unlikely ever to be able to rely on wild production alone to produce reasonable levels of sport.

Even so, the true sportsman will do all that he can to improve habitat and look after such wild game as he has before he thinks about supplementing this with reared birds. For those in need of guidance, the Game Conservancy provides both an on-shoot advisory service and a series of highly acclaimed 'Green Guides' on all aspects of game management. (See end of chapter.) Details are available from the Game Conservancy's national headquarters at Burgate Manor, Fordingbridge, Hampshire, SP6 1EF. Telephone 0425 652381, Fax 0425 655848.

The notes which follow are necessarily brief, but should act as a useful guide to basic practice for anyone who is contemplating rearing. They are written mainly with pheasants in mind, but apply equally to both redlegs and grey partridges in most areas. Any significant departures are noted at the end of the chapter.

The sportsman who pens his own pheasants may set the eggs under broodies or use either a still-air or cabinet incubator according to the number of eggs produced. The low incidence of broodiness in modern laying strains, combined with the chance of introducing disease with the barnyard hen, has drastically reduced broody hatching. Still-air incubators, taking up to two hundred pheasant eggs, rarely give consistently satisfactory hatches unless correctly sited and given constant and expert attention. Cabinet incubators with a weekly intake of five hundred pheasant eggs (i.e. the weekly production of one hundred to a hundred and twenty hen pheasants from mid-April to the end of May) do give fairly satisfactory hatches (approximately 65% fertile eggs) particularly when used in conjunction with still-air incubators for the final hatching period. Eggs used for incubation should be stored in a cool moist atmosphere and culled for unusual size, colour, shape and texture. If they are stored for less than seven days, daily turning is unnecessary. Hatchability declines with longer storage periods. Scrupulous cleanliness is essential if unnecessary losses are to be avoided. All incubator equipment should be fumigated before use and between hatches by pouring a formaldehyde solution on crystals of potassium permanganate.

The ambient temperature in a cabinet incubator is set at 99.5–100.0° F; but in still-air incubators where there is a sharp vertical temperature gradient, a temperature of 103.5° F is recommended at two inches above the egg tray level. Automatic humidity controls are now fitted to some of the smaller cabinet incubators, but, in still-air incubators, humidity is difficult to measure and only crudely controlled. Eggs should be turned thrice daily – by hand in still-air incubators, but in the larger cabinet incubators fitted with automatic turning devices, a minimum of five turns a day is recommended. If a combination of cabinet and still-air incubators is used for setting and hatching, eggs are usually transferred on the twenty-first day. No further turning should take place and after an initial 'drying down' period of sixteen to twenty-four hours a high humidity should be induced in the still-air incubator which remains closed until the hatch is completed on the twenty-fourth or twenty-fifth day. The dried-off chicks benefit by spending a few hours in chick boxes before they are moved to the brooder houses.

On some shoots, where high importance is attached to wild pheasant production, twice the number of pheasants are caught up and penned for only half the normal laying period so that the hens may be released by mid May to rear broods of their own in the wild.

BROODERS AND BROODIES

Rearing with broodies and coops on an open field is now virtually extinct. But where only small numbers of pheasants are required, the use of movable ten feet by six feet pens, containing a fixed coop, protects the vulnerable chicks from predation. Poults reared by broodies under these conditions (fifteen to eighteen per pen) are usually of the highest quality.

Whether the chicks are home-produced or bought in as day-old chicks decisions have to be made concerning the size and type of rearing unit to be used. Except for a few experienced keepers who rear in large units of five hundred or more, by far the greatest number of pheasants are reared in units of one hundred to two hundred and fifty. The method, once commonly known as the Fordingbridge system, is to use a plywood brooder house approximately eight feet by four. Larger brooder houses (eight feet square) have been designed to accommodate units of five hundred chicks. Circular wooden brooder houses have also been built and while this design prevents the dangerous grouping of chicks in cool corners, this is partially offset by the extra cost of construction.

Heat is supplied by a brooder lamp which may be operated by Calor gas (propane) or electricity. Under normal conditions chicks require artificial heat for a four-week period and running costs vary considerably according to the fuel used. In isolated areas, the freedom of movement given by Calor gas may be of overriding importance. Although the source of heat may affect the quality of the feathering, all systems, properly managed, can produce well-feathered poults. With Calor gas, running costs may be reduced by using a brooder incorporating a thermostat or by rearing in larger units.

Some brooder houses of more modern design may have their own 'built-in' heating systems. The low circular 'Rupert' brooder of metal construction and heated by paraffin has long given satisfactory results, while more recently fibreglass brooders heated by Calor gas or electricity have also become available.

Whatever type of brooder house is used, all rearing systems require some form of penning. This is most conveniently constructed from sections which should be ten feet long and either four or five feet wide. Inch mesh wire netting is nailed to the

Pheasant chicks will, under average conditions, require a brooder lamp for the first four weeks of their lives.

framework made from two-by-one timber − strengthened at ground level by boarding which also provides additional shelter for the poults.

The number of sections used can be increased as the poults grow until eventually the pen is approximately fifty feet long by fifteen feet wide. The sections can either be bolted or simply wired together, supported by diagonal struts and roofed over with an inch mesh nylon net. 'Gated' sections allow easy access to the pen. Some penning systems utilise sections only four feet

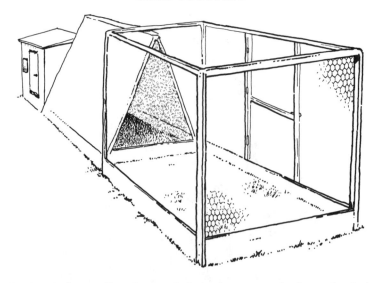

The brooder house will need a pen of wire netting on a wooden frame; the planks at ground level also provide shelter. The ridged section, which is polythene-covered, makes a sun trap for the chicks, and gives shelter at night when they have outgrown the brooder house. Modern pens are far larger than the one illustrated.

wide enclosing a square area with the roof netting centrally supported by additional poles to give adequate headroom.

Sections which have had an additional covering of polythene can be used to form a combined sun parlour for the chicks during the first week or so and a night shelter for the poults at four weeks when the brooder house may be needed for a second batch of chicks. Two such sections, clamped together at the top, provide a ridge-tent structure. This will allow chicks access to grass when only a few days old, without the risk of them becoming wet and chilled. Running of birds between the various parts of the system is facilitated by ensuring that 'pop holes' are sited in the corners of each area.

REARING

Whatever brooder system is used, management is generally similar. Most modern units have a wooden floor with an inch high layer of unheated white wood shavings as bedding. A circular area around the brooder lamp is enclosed with hardboard approximately 50–60 cm high to keep the chicks near the source of the heat for the first few days. For twelve to twenty-four hours before the chicks are introduced, the heating system should be turned on to ensure that everything is warmed up and working smoothly. A temperature of approximately 95°F (34°C) is recommended in the brooding area, but this is often difficult to measure accurately. A comfortable heat on the back of one's hand is a rough guide, but by far the best indication is the behaviour of the chicks themselves. When they have been taken from the chick boxes and placed under the brooder lamp, bunching beneath the lamp's centre will indicate inadequate heat. If the chicks are concentrated on the perimeter against the cardboard surround heat may be too great and the height of the lamp can be adjusted.

For the first night the chicks should remain within the surround and food and water is introduced the following day when the brooding area can be extended. Egg trays are particularly suitable for scattering food (starter crumbs) on for the first few days since the crumbs are agitated by the movement of the chicks. Unless the water fountains provided have very shallow containers, pebbles should be added to reduce the chances of any chicks being accidentally drowned. On the second or third day (if the weather is suitable or if a sun parlour is provided) the chicks can be allowed access to the grass. At first this should be restricted to a small area until they have established the habit of returning to the brooder lamp to warm up.

Feeding ad-lib is commonly adopted but there must be adequate feed space at the utensils provided. Care should be taken not to overfill the trays so that the minimum amount of food (which inevitably becomes 'mouldy') is scattered. The high-protein starter crumb should be gradually changed for a chick pellet at about two weeks while at four weeks growers' pellets are introduced.

At the end of the first week the chicks should have restricted access to the main pen, but will be penned back at night (either in the brooder house or night shelter) until they are taken to the release pen at six or seven weeks.

DISEASES

While brooder rearing with enclosed pens has freed the keeper from the tyranny of the open rearing field, it has brought with it two important disadvantages – the increased risks of disease and feather pecking. Although disease did occur on the open rearing field, the individual units were small. Now with closely penned units of two hundred birds, the chances of disease spreading rapidly are very much greater. Fortunately considerable advances have been made in discovering preventive or curative drugs which are most effective if the diseases are recognised in their early stages. Two of the most commonly encountered diseases are 'gapes' (due to a parasitic worm *Syngamus trachea*) and coccidiosis (caused by one of several different species of parasitic protozoans, *Eimeria spp.*). 'Gapes' is easily recognised by the characteristic 'snicking' – a juicy cough accompanied by the sideways flick of the head – of the young pheasants. This can be cured with several drugs which are administered either in food or water. Coccidiosis probably kills more young pheasants than any other disease. It is most likely to occur in birds of three to five weeks of age and a few listless looking birds standing around with feathers awry, accompanied by a reduction in food consumption, should be taken as a warning of this disease. Curative treatment – there are several effective curative drugs – could be started while veterinary confirmation is being obtained. Although most pheasant foods do contain a coccidiostat at a relatively low level, it may not be effective if the pheasant poults experience a really

As an alternative to beak trimming feather pecking can also be prevented by 'bits', which are, of course, removed before the birds are released.

Beak trimming is best carried out with an electric cauterising debeaker.

heavy challenge. Some disease organisms are quite capable of surviving in the ground for more than a year. While a high standard of hygiene is imperative with brooder rearing, selecting a suitable site for the rearing field is also important. If possible, fresh ground should be used each year since there is no practical and economic way of sterilising infected ground. It is best not to return to the same area of land more often than once in three years.

Feather pecking − a relatively rare occurrence on the open rearing field − can be more dangerous than some diseases. Resulting from a large variety of potential causes − overcrowding, boredom, food content and presentation, lack of escape cover etc. − it reduces the poults' vitality and resistance to disease. It also predisposes them to 'chilling' and may result in cannibalism. Outbreaks of feather pecking may be arrested by beak trimming (in this case the removal of less than $\frac{1}{4}''$ of the upper mandible) at the first sign of trouble. Alternatively, routine trimming may be carried out at three weeks and again at six weeks when the poults are moved to the release pen. In recent years 'bits' (either of soft metal or plastic) have been applied at three weeks and removed when the birds are released. A healthy well-feathered bird undoubtedly stands a much better chance of survival in the wild.

133

RELEASING

With modern rearing equipment, management, foods and medic-
aments, a survival rate of over 90% to six or seven weeks is an
average figure. The real problem now begins – how to ensure
that these birds will not only survive, but also remain in the
area throughout the shooting season! Little is known about the
recovery rate by shooting from broody-and-coop reared birds
which were moved to release sites together with their foster parents
and coops. Probably the average figure was not very different
from the country-wide average obtained today (about 40% of
released birds). This apparently low figure results from lack
of knowledge as well as inability or unwillingness to take the
necessary precautions.

The transition from a completely protected existence to survival
in the wild must be made as gradually as possible. The first stage
is to select a suitable site on which to construct a release pen.
There are several important factors to be considered and inevitably
compromises have to be made. The site should be as central as
possible, sheltered and facing south. Permanent cover, shrubs
and trees to encourage roosting, is necessary, but open sunny
rides are also important. Well-drained ground is always an advantage too since the incidence of 'gapes' is usually lower. The
release pen consists essentially of a six-feet high, two-inch mesh
wire netting fence to keep the pheasants in and potential predators
out. Burying the base of the turned-out netting about six inches
under the surface ensures that the larger predators will not dig
underneath the fence, while the addition of a floppy eighteen-
inch overhanging fringe at the top of the fence will prevent them
climbing over. Alternatively, the same objects may be achieved
with less labour by pegging down the bottom of the wire netting.
In either case it is wise to surround the release pen with a double
strand of electrified fencing wire – about fifty centimetres from
the pen and fifteen and thirty centimetres above ground level.
Although other factors are involved, a rough guide to the number
of birds a release pen can accommodate is to allow fifteen square
metres per bird.

Although our weather is largely unpredictable, movement of
the poults to the release pen should be made when there is a

likelihood of a warm dry spell. To ensure that the poults remain in the pen for at least a two-week period, the primary flight feathers of one wing are usually cut. The stubs are moulted and replaced by adult flight feathers and within three weeks most of the poults will easily fly over the fence. To ensure that these poults can return to the protection of the pen at night, entrances fitted with anti-fox grids are placed at intervals around the pen perimeter. Feeding − gradually adding a proportion of grain − is best carried out in the morning and evening; feed rides, strawed down with fresh straw in which the grain can be scattered, help to hold the birds, and an adequate water supply is essential. Under optimum conditions up to 60% of the poults have been shot in the year of release.

PARTRIDGES

Partridges, both grey and redlegged, can be reared almost as easily as pheasants, employing similar methods and equipment. For egg production, partridges are penned in pairs in wire-floored pens to reduce disease risks. These small pens are most conveniently constructed in blocks of five or six pens, each pen about six feet long and two feet wide. Although individual egg-laying performance varies greatly, hens should lay an average of between twenty-five and thirty eggs. At one time, rearing was carried out exclusively under broody bantams in low, movable pens, but brooder units of eighty to one hundred birds are now the rule. For the first two weeks a special partridge starter crumb, containing a readily digestible high-protein content may be an advantage. Grey partridges are most frequently reared to augment a reduced stock of wild birds. In some areas where they have been shot in the year of release, recovery rates have been disappointingly low. Most successful releases have been made with units of approximately twenty birds, well spaced out in movable pens, from which some of the six to eight-week-old birds are released at intervals. Using a similar method with redlegged partridges, and releasing in an area where there is suitable cover (such as sugar beet or a tall stubble), recovery rates have been similar to those of pheasants.

FURTHER READING

Game Conservancy Green Guides
Egg Production and Incubation No. 5 £8.95
Gamebird Rearing No. 8 £7.50
Gamebird Releasing No. 10 £7.50

Your Shoot by Ian McCall (A. & C. Black £12.95)
Pheasant Health and Welfare by D. R. Wise (Piggott Printers Ltd, Cambridge, ISBN 0 952 11020 2)

III
PIGEON
SHOOTING

III
Pigeon Shooting

Colin Willock

I started shooting pigeons seriously in the early fifties. At that time there were comparatively few experienced practitioners. Most guns still regarded pigeons as an occasional quarry that offered a shot when there was nothing better to shoot. It was the day of roost shooting sponsored by the Ministry of Agriculture, when thousands of half-price or free cartridges were banged off in the leafless woods of February and March without much effect on the pigeon population beyond mild disturbance of their night's rest.

From such casual encounters with the wood pigeon, ring-dove, cushat or quist, more scientifically known as *Columba palumbus*, spring a number of notable and remarkably persistent superstitions, in particular that: wood pigeons are hard to kill; call for big shot; carry a lot of shot; aren't worth serious shooting and, possibly worst of all, aren't worth serious eating.

Even in the fifties, a few others knew differently, among them the late Archie Coats of Dummer in Hampshire from whom I learned most of my trade. Archie was then shooting up to sixteen thousand woodies a year and earning his living by doing so. Today there are many first class pigeon shooters, many of whom learned their technique from Archie Coats' writings and lectures at the annual Game Fair. The increased shooting pressure has to some extent altered the wood pigeon's habits. They are more decoy-conscious and harder to deceive. The proliferation of oil-seed rape has changed their feeding preferences. At various stages in their growth pigeons go mad over rape, even on the stubbles, where they seek the tiny seeds left by the combines. As a result, the flocks have a wider choice of feeding places. Whether their current choice is peas, wheat, barley or rape, the expert pigeon shooter has learned to kill woodies where it matters – on the crop that is in danger. Some of the know-how I shall attempt to pass on here.

NATURAL HISTORY

There are five wild pigeons in Britain. Only one, the wood pigeon, seriously concerns the shooter who kills pigeon over crops. The other members of the family are: the blue rock (*Columba livia*) which belongs to the sea cliffs of the northern coasts. At one time the bird was obviously much more widely spread since it is the ancestor of all domestic pigeons, including city birds and racers (when these go wild they are known as feral pigeons).

The small brownish bird with white barred tail, the turtle dove (*Streptopelia turtur*) is a spring and summer migrant and is protected. Not so its close relative, the collared dove (*Streptopelia decaocto*). This light fawn bird with long tail and two black half-collars at the neck is a recent invader from Europe. The species appears to have taken over Britain and spends all the year here in increasing numbers. Like the turtle it probably doesn't do much damage, eating a great many weed seeds. It sometimes comes in to decoys but is too small to warrant shooting.

The stock dove (*Columba oenas*) was on the shooting list until protected by the Wildlife and Countryside Act of 1981. This lacks the white neck and wing markings of the woodie. Instead, it carries two small dark marks on the wing. These are only detectable in the hand. In the air, size, manoeuvrability, and a tendency towards lack of caution, are the surest giveaways. Finally, the main quarry, the wood pigeon needs little description. It is, as may be judged from its estimated ritish population of over eleven million, an immensely successful bird. It produces up to three broods of two to three young a year. It rejoices in the British pattern of farming which provides it with a mixed, protein-rich diet throughout the year, together with extensive forestry strips and shelter belts for nesting and roosting. It has, I suspect, thrived on a fantastic scale in Britain during the last hundred years. Colonel Hawker, who shot anything that flew, barely mentions it in his *Diaries* and would surely have accept-ed its challenge in the early 1800s had the bird been present in any numbers, especially as Longparrish, his home in deepest

The woodpigeon is distinguished from the smaller stock dove by the white
marking on the neck and the prominent white bar on the wing. The stock dove
also has two smaller dark wing bars.

Hampshire, is these days in the heart of prime pigeon country.
As to the continent, even today, the bird is protected in Sweden.
I have travelled the length of France at harvest time and seen
fewer than a dozen wood pigeon. Leave aside the question of
whether we actually do receive foreign winter immigrants from
Europe – let the ornithologists argue that one out – we in
Britain do seem to have got very nearly the lot. Farmers, of
course, cannot be expected to rejoice. Nor possibly should some
of the rest of us. A woodie in a day eats enough malting barley to
produce a pint of beer. To a wood pigeon, one hundred and fifty
peas are barely a cropful and two ounces of nitrogen-rich clover a
mere snack. Nevertheless, the wood pigeon in pestiferous numbers does provide magnificent sport and its shooting a public
service to farming.

Of all the legendary qualities which shooters have ascribed to
the woodie, one is in every respect true. The bird possesses
the most remarkable sense of caution, reinforced by one of the
keenest pairs of eyes in the world of birds. It can spot a man,
or anyway movement on the part of, or by the part of, a man

at ranges of up to a mile. Luckily for the shooter, it has two compensating failings: an insatiable appetite, combined with a desire to dine in company. These prove its undoing at the hands of an experienced and knowledgeable gun.

PROTECTING THE FARMER

Decoy shooting cashes in on both these weaknesses. What is more, decoying kills pigeons precisely where they are causing the damage − on a besieged crop. Scientists of the Ministry of Agriculture, notably Dr R. K. Murton, have argued that shooting, no matter how intense, can make no real difference to total pigeon numbers. Instead, he says, the regulating factor is 'winter kill' which cuts the pigeon population down to a size commensurate with available food. The result of the sum, he says, will be the same whether we shoot or not. The argument, which may be scientifically true, overlooks one important factor. Ask the farmer whose newly planted ten acres of kale is being enjoyed by a flock of five hundred woodies as a nice fresh green salad, whether he minds waiting for old man winter to thin the marauders out or if he would rather have them killed now. He will probably reply that even if you can't hit them, you're bound to scare the so-and-so's away. Either way, his kale is going to get a chance. If the field were left unguarded, slaughter of the crop could cost him hundreds of pounds in seed and labour. True, the flock, put off by your shooting, will have to dine somewhere else, but maybe their alternative target won't be so young and vulnerable; or the hordes will split up so that damage is lessened; or, with luck, if the birds are determined to set upon an equally important crop, there will be another decoy shooter ready for them. All this argues that it is desirable to have a 'fire brigade' of trustworthy and efficient decoy experts available for farmers to call upon.

EQUIPMENT

I do not believe that a special gun is necessary for pigeons. Archie Coats shot all his with a standard 12-bore game gun. I know one expert who keeps a spare pair of fully choked barrels for pulling down long ones when he is short of dead birds to act as decoys, at the start of a shoot, but this is a refinement I would not advise. Over decoys, 95% will be killed within thirty yards, and perhaps 60% within twenty. Pattern, therefore, is what counts. From this it follows that one needs more shot rather than bigger shot. Sixes are fine but then so are Sevens. When on form, I decoy with one ounce Impax Sevens. If you want to give yourself a bit more chance then go to a trapshooting load with an ounce and an eighth. I suppose the answer is, as always, shoot with the cartridges that give you most confidence. Pigeon, I repeat, do not take a lot of killing, nor do they carry a lot of shot. The belief has grown up because a stray pellet or two from the *outside* of the pattern can harmlessly pluck a lot of downy feathers which look spectacular floating through the air. Centre the bird in the pattern and that is that, at any range up to forty yards.

Next, it is essential that the shooter do his best to escape the pigeon's incredible eyesight but don't go to ridiculous lengths about it. You can't shoot anything as aerodynamically agile as a pigeon if you're uncomfortable. Such trimmings as face masks are 'out' for this reason. Sensible drab clothes, green or brown, and, most important, a hat to match, are all you need. Camouflage smocks are first class in winter but, for my money, too hot in summer. In hot weather, I often shoot just wearing a green or fawn shirt. I once had a magnificently camouflaged pyjama jacket! A hat that hides as much of the face as possible is vital. Never forget that human flesh-tones, particularly when moving, are one of the most easily picked out colorations. I rate the right hat as being more important than body clothing. The latter, if you are properly organised is largely concealed by the hide.

Next for the hide itself. The most comfortable and, in many ways, most satisfactory is a bale hide. Its disadvantages are that it is as immobile as a pill-box and calls for the total cooperation of the farmer. At least fourteen (better sixteen) straw bales are needed, including one to sit on. The back of the hide must be taller than the front, to provide background for the shooter's head. It is only worth building a bale hide on a crop that is likely to be menaced over a long period, such as pig clover, under-sown stubble or peas. I have often built one temporarily during harvest, when there are a number of bales lying about on a stubble that pigeon are working. I've also known the farmer's straw lorry come for the very bales amid which I've been happily sitting! Nowadays, the giant circular bale has largely replaced the small and portable rectangular model. The big bale is useless as hide material except when a net can be placed against it. Apart from the draught-free comfort, particularly appreciated on a winter's day, the advantage of a bale hide is that the pigeons totally accept it. On a large field you usually have to persuade the farmer to build two or three to cover changes of wind and approach and even food faddism on the part of the birds. Pigeons often patronise one part of a crop in the first half of the week, another by the weekend. They are great ones for sorting out the best, both in quantity and quality. Because of its permanence, especially after the bales have become wet and heavy, you often have to bring the birds *to* a bale hide. This calls for a lot of decoys with whose deployment I will deal in a moment. With a portable hide you can, and often do, move your pitch two or three times in a day's shooting. In other works, you can move *to* the birds. No serious pigeon shooter can be without portable hide equipment.

A metal stake to support camouflage netting, the 'kicker' on the side is essential – especially on frosty ground.

The first requirement is a set of five, easily portable, metal stakes. Most shooters design their own and get a blacksmith to make them up. You need three stakes of five feet and two of four to four foot six. They must be both strong and light. The best I have used are tubular. A small metal addition is welded to the top in a V-shape to support the camouflage nets. About a foot from the base, a 'kicker' is welded on to enable the shooter to stamp his stakes into the ground. The resistance of dry or frozen earth is considerable, so both welding and the metal must be strong.

Until recently the pigeon shooter relied on Government Surplus camouflage lorry or artillery nets. Today you can buy excellent lightweight nylon nets. I particularly like the 'Leafgreen' series. They are expensive but do not tear easily. Two will garnish any size hide. You need one coloured dark green and brown, and

144

a lighter net for shooting on ripe corn. Net hides should always make use of some natural or at least permanent feature as 'background'. A barbed wire fence is better than nothing. I have made successful use of lone telegraph poles, cattle troughs, abandoned farm implements, the walls of barns or outhouses.

There is one other solution to the portable hide problem which I originally invented for wildfowling but serves equally as a pigeon hide. It consists of around sixteen feet of 'Netlon' plastic garden mesh to which is attached with string a lightweight net of the 'Leafgreen' type. Half a dozen light wooden stakes are stapled to the Netlon for driving into the ground. The net can be lightly garnished with natural material − wheat stalks, leaves, grasses, etc. The great virtue of this hide is that it can be rolled up like a carpet and a move made to a new position within minutes.

Finally, in the height of summer, natural features can often be adapted for use, with or without reinforcement by nets. Elderberry bushes are especially handy when growing in a pit, or hedge, or edge of a wood. A few strokes with a billhook will often fell and shape the branches to give complete cover without doing serious damage to the countryside.

The bale hide is the most comfortable, but also the least mobile. The one illustrated here is far too cramped.

145

Whatever the choice of hide, the shooter's object must always be to see *through* it, not over it, without being seen himself. This calls for careful hide dressing leaving peepholes — an inch or two will serve — facing the priority arcs in which pigeon will approach. Seeing through the hide in turn demands that the shooter sits low enough. Shooting sticks, except in ditches, perch one up too high. A five-gallon drum with sharp edges first beaten flat with a hammer, and a cushion or folded sack placed on top, puts one at the right height. Archie Coats took practically all of his shots sitting and always advised me to do likewise. Some pigeon shooters find it hard to swivel on their bottoms unless they have a swivelling top to their stools. Such seats take a bit of finding.

Finally, two serious safety warnings. Nets have a bad habit of catching on muzzles, top levers and even triggers. Second, *never* be tempted to shoot two from a hide. If you must share, only one person at a time must do the shooting!

THE RECCE

The next item of essential equipment takes me directly into the tactics of shooting. I always keep a pair of binoculars in my vehicle. They are invaluable during the reconnaissance phase of a shoot. The importance of reconnaissance cannot be over-emphasised. Of course, if like many of us you have only a small farm acreage on which you are allowed to shoot pigeons, the recce becomes simple and resolves itself into two basic questions (*a*) are the birds feeding in worthwhile numbers? (*b*) are they determined enough to stay? Even on a hundred acres, binoculars can prove useful, perhaps to pinpoint the most favoured spot in a field of young mustard (pigeons are pernicketty feeders and prefer their greens *au point*). With kale, for example, their gourmet ambitions are best realised when the tender plants reach their second leaf. Not all the crop in a twenty-acre field necessarily reaches this stage of gastronomic succulence at the same moment. Binoculars will also help you to detect the flight-line into the field. Fixing this to within ten or twenty yards can prove crucial to success.

Again, use of glasses will give you a picture of the whole local traffic pattern. Are more birds flighting to a neighbouring

Dead birds (left) are the best decoys of all – when properly set up with their heads propped up on a twig. Artificials must be coloured with matt paint.

farmer's crop than to yours? If so, can you get permission to shoot there if your own set-up fails. Which is the 'reservoir' wood from which they are flighting? Does the flight-line cross your farm and, if so, might a decoy 'picture' somewhere along that flight path pull in birds going to your neighbours as well as to your own field? It is tiring work setting up hides and decoys in the wrong place. A couple of moves before you start shooting doesn't add to accuracy when you're at last in action. The old service adage that 'time spent in reconnaissance is seldom wasted' applies in a big way to pigeon shooting. The bigger the area to be covered the more time should be spent making certain. I have sometimes gone nearly mad with frustration when accompanying Archie Coats on a recce lasting an hour or more – he once looked after farms covering half Hampshire – while pigeons clattered up in hundreds from the various fields we visited. However, at the end of the recce, the maestro had usually settled correctly on the most productive target areas and placed his guns in the spots which would give the best sustained shooting and therefore the best crop protection. Admittedly, he did on occ-asions go straight to one field and set up immediately, but only because recces on previous days had shown this to be one target that really mattered.

No matter how well recce'd, no crop shoot can succeed without decoys. There is nothing to beat dead pigeons. If shooting regularly it pays to keep anything up to a dozen dead birds, though half that number is worthwhile, as a convincing framework to your decoy picture. In warm weather these birds will become distinctly unattractive to the shooter, at least within two or three days, but will still fool their live relatives. There is little to choose between most rubber, plastic or cardboard imitations.

'Flappers', wire frames on which dead birds can be placed and their wings moved at the tug of a string, are a valuable addition to a decoy pattern. The moving white wing bars of a live bird are a flock feeding signal.

THE DECOY PICTURE

The object of setting out decoys is always the same: to attract pigeons on to the killing ground in front of the hide. Since all birds land into the wind, wind is plainly a crucial factor. Pigeons may approach from any direction, but their final touchdown is always made head to wind. When decoying, the objective is to kill birds as efficiently and therefore as easily as possible. Take fancy shots if you must, once your eye is in, but reckon to kill 80% of your bag at the moment of maximum killability. This occurs once only and then only for a split-second in every single pigeon approach. The siting of your decoy pattern should ensure that the moment of maximum kill is channelled in to the waiting gun, in range, in view, and where the shot can be most comfortably taken. Only practice in setting out decoys can teach you how to produce this ideal situation. I would strongly advise reading the chapters in Archie Coats' *Pigeon Shooting* on advance decoying if you wish to appreciate some of the finer points.

For the moment, I will confine myself to some do's and don'ts. Don't be tempted to place your deeks too close to the hide. This is a natural reaction but betrays lack of confidence and may betray you to the pigeon. Stick them at least twenty yards out in a way that will draw the birds past you, slowing for touchdown and well in range. Place them roughly head to wind, but observe a flock of feeding birds. They do not dress by the right, nor do they stand in close order. There is a fair space between each bird and they do not face the wind at precisely the same angle. Some are even across wind. When using dead birds, stick a sharpened twig into the underside of the head so that the head can be pegged up in a natural feeding attitude. Broken pieces of bamboo cane are excellent for the purpose. It is amazing how much difference this can make to the start of a shoot when the birds are acting shy. Keep pegging up until there are at least twenty birds out. After that it probably doesn't matter. I doubt whether it is worth putting out more dead birds after you've reached fifty, but, please, always tidy up. Birds left belly-up with wings open may warn off the cautious while still out of shot. At the fifty plus stage of a big shoot all you have to do is to lay the most recently slain down on their breasts.

If birds start shying off after a period of steady shooting, something is wrong. Has the wind changed? If it's a definite change, then the main axis of the decoy pattern must be altered to conform. Has it been raining? Or has the sun suddenly come out? In either case, rain or sun glistening on artificial decoys may be giving the game away. Take in the artificials, if you can afford to. One vitally important aspect of hide and decoy siting: where is the reservoir wood from which the birds will be coming? Will the wind carry the sound of shooting towards it to keep the birds there stirred up? If not, should you site both hide and decoys so that you will be shooting *towards* that wood and thus causing maximum unsettlement to the birds there? A pigeon unsettled is a pigeon airborne. Once airborne, it can be tempted to go feeding, which is where your decoys come in. With luck, so does he. Incidentally, such wanderers can sometimes be persuaded to make an approach by lobbing out a dead bird from inside the hide among the decoys. The flicker of falling grey, or a white flash of madly twirling wing bars is sometimes sufficient to trigger off the feeding impulse in distant pigeons that are airborne and as yet undecided where to go.

A DECOY SHOOT

It's a summer day, you're in position, decoys out, hide nicely garnished, everything set out to hand. If you're wise your watch will tell you that it's already midday. In high summer, birds often

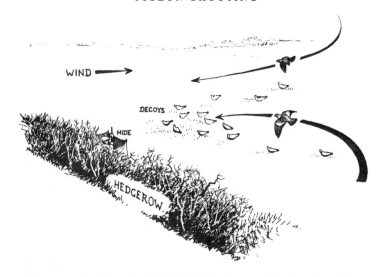

Pigeons all land into the wind (which doesn't mean that they then sit in regimented ranks on the ground). The aim should be to place the decoy 'picture' to funnel them in front of the hide about twenty-five yards out.

have a very early morning meal and then don't feed in real earnest until mid-, or even late, afternoon. Nevertheless, with luck there'll be a trickle to keep you interested and to reveal any faults in your tactics. The first bird comes in confidently almost before you have got your bearings. He lands, but a movement in the hide scares him and he is away and thirty yards distant before you've got your safety catch off. Leave him. There'll be plenty more without starting on a shot that you will probably miss. A lull now for ten minutes. You're begining to regret that missed chance, when two come sailing in, flattening off and air-braking to land among the decoys. You take the front one and kill him in a cloud of feathers. The rear bird jinks wildly and flares away. A difficult shot and you miss him. Your tactics were wrong. You should have let the leader land and then killed the one behind, still in the air. The first shot will put up the grounded pigeon who will become an airborne 'sitter' on take-off.

Never mind, you got one for two. If you keep that up through-out the day you will be at least in the 'Second Eleven'. You rush out to set up the dead bird to add to the decoy pattern. Good idea, bad moment. Sit tight for a minute or so after the shot.

Distant pigeons don't always associate the sound of the gun with your decoy picture. The fall of a killed bird often catches their eye, just as does a dead bird thrown from the hide.

As the afternoon wears on, the pace hots up. Now you can tell directly you see birds leave the distant wood whether they are coming to you or mean to pass wide to another target. Now is the time to make final decisions about your own choice of position or that of other guns you may have placed in different parts of the field, or even elsewhere on the farm.

The traffic pattern is becoming established and will almost certainly continue to build up until the real battle starts which, in hot weather, may be as late as six pm. If one of you is wrongly sited, it's better to make the decision and effort to move now.

As the pace gets hotter, you are bound to have some 'long-droppers', birds that climb away confidently and then suddenly fall dead in mid-flight. Mark these to be picked up at the end of the day. Start walking around now and you may not only miss some productive shooting yourself but will cause birds to sheer away from your companions. Wounded birds you must, of course, dispatch straight away. You will notice that a casualty fluttering on the ground draws in pigeons as does no still-life decoy. Resist the temptation to capitalise on the wounded bird's plight, but ponder instead on what might be done if you had had some string-operated, spring-operated gadget which would persuade a dead pigeon to flutter its wings in the same fashion. One or two of my friends have developed contraptions which work. One, I recall, used the hinged ribs of an umbrella to raise and lower the dead bird's wings when the string was pulled from the hide. Commercial 'flappers' and 'floaters' are now available. 'Floaters' support a dead bird with wings spread as if landing.

If the field is a very large one, you may find, even if there are other guns placed round it, that pigeons start to drop in to an area out of range to all. This can prove serious unless stopped at once, as their movement will draw birds as no static decoy set-up can do. If this diversion of traffic occurs during a lull in the shooting, then the gun nearest to these outliers must put them up by clapping or more often by firing a shot in their direction.

As you hoped, around five pm the birds fairly pour into the target area. It is no longer possible to set out every dead pigeon as a decoy directly after the shot. Now you have to wait for lulls in which to tidy up. There's no longer any need to peg up heads. Just lay the slain down on their bellies. It probably doesn't matter much if you overlook one or two, but do make sure there are no breast-upwards dead on the fringes of the decoy picture. These may cause approaching pigeons to veer off, though even this is unlikely if the shoot has become really set.

You should never show your muzzles above the hide until mounting the gun to shoot.

By now your eye should be well and truly in. You may feel inclined to take some chancey ones but never forget the object is to kill pigeons in the easiest and most efficient way. Even when you've brought off a few corkers, you may be surprised and disgusted because you miss some of the really easy ones. The bird most usually foozled, even by so-called experts, is the one I call the ping-pong ball because it appears to be standing still in the air over decoys, exactly like those celluloid balls balanced on a spout of water in a shooting gallery. All of us miss these at times because, I suspect, we shoot *at* the bird instead of realising that it is travelling, however slowly, forwards and downwards.

Swing in the direction of its flight path, that of a helicopter touching down with slight forward movement, and you will kill every time.

At around seven pm the pigeon traffic begins to tail off. If you are tempted to stay shooting until the last raider returns to roost you may be very late off the field. There's still quite a lot to be done. If you have a dog with you now is the time to use him. But remember there are probably young game birds about, so keep the dog well under control to seek only those birds you have marked, ones that have fallen into ditches, thick patches of cover and even, with restraint, on the edges of standing crops, though you will rightly incur the farmer's wrath and probably lose your right to shoot if you do any damage. Better lose a bird or two than let an unruly dog loose in a field of prize barley. On a hot summer's day there is one rather nasty chore to be performed before you pop your pigeons in the sack. Blowflies delight in laying their clusters of tiny, oblong, yellow eggs on dead pigeons laid out as decoys. Their favourite spots include: round and inside the mouth; under the wings and, of course, in the region of a shot wound. If the eggs aren't removed, maggots will quickly hatch out and can spoil your birds. If you're going to pluck them next morning, it probably doesn't matter too much. However, I always prefer to de-fly my birds on the field of action, plucking away contaminated feathers and where the head is badly affected simply pulling it off. Cleaning the bag in this way is especially important if you're selling the birds to a game dealer. Finally, when you get home, I advise tipping your birds out of the sack to cool as soon as possible. The heat generated by thirty or forty recently killed birds in close proximity is pretty formidable and certainly does nothing to improve the condition of the meat.

WINTER SHOOTING

About winter decoying I have little to say, except that days are shorter both for pigeon and shooter. The pigeons consequently start feeding earlier, often as soon as it is light, and the shooter must be prepared to be on the field to greet them. Feeding habits change once the harvest is over. At first, in October, and sometimes on into November, the birds clean the stubbles. Frequently,

153

about this time, there is a disconcerting departure to the woods, especially if it is a good acorn and beech mast year. Then pigeons can be hard to come to terms with as there is still a lot of leaf on the trees and, anyway, decoys, except for a 'lofter' or two, won't do you much good.

A word or two on 'lofters', a form of decoy I haven't mentioned to date. A 'lofter' is simply a decoy perched up high and clearly visible in a suitable tree. Trees with a lot of leaves on them aren't suitable, for obvious reasons. Dead and bare trees most certainly are, especially if they command a good field of vision. Being cautious creatures, pigeons like to spy out the land before deciding to feed. Archie Coats termed such lookouts 'sitty' trees. If you can perch a 'lofter' high in their branches it will often act like a magnet to passing pigeon traffic. The snag, I have always found, is that it is extremely difficult to get a lofter high enough, securely

154

perched and facing the right direction. Friends of mine have tried shooting up lines with which to loft the decoy with catapults and even bows and arrows. One or two of the more athletic have had more success using climbing-irons. The best answer I have come across to date is a set of lightweight lofting poles. The top one ends in a plastic petrol funnel in which the decoy sits. Once you've found a suitable perch, all you do is withdraw poles and funnel, leaving the decoy behind. Two lofters in a 'sitty' tree are twice as convincing as one. In an acorn or beech mast situation,

A 'lofter' is often a good way of attracting passing pigeon traffic.

when birds are scouring the woods for food, a lofter or two on the edge of the wood, *plus* a normal decoy display on a field immediately outside the wood, will sometimes pay dividends.

After stubbles and acorns, what? High on the winter menu come delicate greens, sprouts, lucerne and, as a staple hard weather diet, clover. Clover is rich in nitrogen and pigeons always seek food which will give them maximum energy. In sharp frost and snow they are almost certain to turn to crops that stand well above the ground and are therefore less prone to freezing. Sprouts come in for a bad caning at this time as do kale, cabbage and even turnip tops. In respect of a pest operation, pigeons are easy to exterminate at such times but their value as food deteriorates rapidly if the frost persists. A diet of greenstuff, kale especially, gives them the stomach ache. They soon become thin and their flesh poor. In snow conditions they are difficult, if not impossibe, to decoy. Pigeons, for all their remarkable eyesight, appear easily dazzled (notice the way they will often fly directly over you when you are in the open with the sun low behind). Likewise, against snow, I doubt whether they can make out your immobile decoys at all clearly for the glare.

ROOSTING

One other aspect of winter shooting remains – roosting. This can give productive and most exciting sport. The first requirement is a good roosting wood. Pigeons have very definite preferences, not only about which hotel they choose for the night but even concerning the room they select to sleep in. They don't much care for badly furnished or draughty establishments. Wide open woods of beech or oak are seldom favoured, but fortunately most woodlands are mixed. These are usually some conifers, hollies or ivy-coated trees. These are the sort of lodgings pigeons appreciate on a cold night. Pigeons like to feel a lot of woodland around them so the ideal situation is usually something around a hundred acres or more made up of mixed hard woods. Forestry plantations of conifers sometimes attract very large pigeon roosts, though my experience is that the birds tend to use the edges rather than the dark and dense centres. Anyway, except in old, well-established conifer woods, with tall, well-spaced trees, birds are hard to see and to shoot.

Roost shooting has a good deal in common with duck flighting: it is something that can be fitted in at the end of the day, takes place almost to a schedule and requires much the same kind of quick, instinctive shooting. The first requirement is to find your wood and then to discover whether it is being currently used by a lot of pigeon. The amount of white-splashed droppings on leaves and ground, plus the numbers of *fresh* loose pigeon feathers, will not only reveal whether the hotel is well patronised but also which rooms or suites of rooms are most in demand. This will enable you to form an initial idea of where to stand in order to intercept the guests. If you're wrong, you can easily change your plan once you see how things are going.

As with duck flighting, rough or windy weather is the best for roosting. In such conditions, the birds will often start coming in early. On a wild December day I have started roost shooting at two-thirty in the afternoon, knowing that it would be dark soon after four. In February and March, when most roosting is done, four or even five pm is sometimes early enough. As with duck flighting, you must study local conditions.

It usually pays to have two or three companions with you. A big wood can then be split up or several small ones individually guarded. Once shot at, especially on calm evenings, pigeons are likely to depart in search of a quieter night's rest, so all likely woods should be marked. Above all, guns must not be tempted to shoot at very high birds.

Cover, at least in the latter stages of a roosting shoot, is not particularly important. Usually, a good background is enough, a large tree trunk or bush against which one stands to break up the telltale human outline. A clear space of sky to the front helps, though obviously not too much or birds coming over the treetops will spot you. Pigeons come in to a chosen tree head to wind, so, just as when decoying, wind direction will, to some extent, dictate your choice of stand. Clear spaces do not come to order in woodlands so you must learn to shoot *through* branches. In essence this consists of pretending that the branches are not there and just swinging through them normally. This is easier said than done. Many otherwise adequate shots fail when roosting for this reason. They unconsciously stop their swing because some twigs interpose between gun and bird at the vital moment. It is amazing how much of the shot charge can be absorbed by a tree and a bird still killed. Many times a shot seems to be followed by the fall of an equal volume of bird and timber!

A dog is a definite asset provided he is steady. Birds should be gathered as they fall. It is surprising how difficult it is, once it has got dark, to find birds, or even gun or cartridge bag, if you have laid them down inside a wood.

The two best roosting shoots I ever remember took place when a blizzard sprang up in late afternoon. The pigeons were mad keen to get in early and confused by the snowstorm once they arrived above the wood to find themselves being shot at. They were in large flocks and they milled around and were still coming in when all real shooting light had gone. On one of these occasions, I became as confused as the pigeon. I had seventy-five to pick all told, and had been laying them down in three or four heaps under different trees throughout the shoot. Now I couldn't even find the snow-covered heaps! Fortunately the spaniel's nose solved the problem but it took even him half an hour to sort it all out.

The kind of roost shoot that I find least promising is on a calm evening when all the birds arrive over the wood at the same instant in a cloud. A couple of shots and they usually vanish to a quieter spot. Roosting, I find, provides two of the most tricky shots in pigeon shooting, though I am sure you will laugh in a superior way at mention of the first of them. This is the 'sitter' who has sneaked into a tree-top twenty yards away. 'Sitters' are certainly 'on', at least as far as I'm concerned. Pigeons are to be killed for the pot and for the farmer's sake, so I have no scruples about shooting them in trees. How many times have I drawn a careful bead and fired, only to watch a shower of twigs come down? The answer is to take a full sight at the feet. Use the choke barrel to make sure.

The second difficult bird is a true 'screamer' and one of the hardest shots in all shooting. It is the pigeon who has decided to drop straight in, usually in windy conditions, from a great height. This bird makes the most of his 'variable geometry', closes his wings until they are little more than the size of vanes on a paper dart and slides down the wind, almost vertically, as fast as a high speed lift. If you can kill him once in three shots you are doing extremely well. I know many good game shots who affect to despise pigeons. Truly, they have no idea what they are missing. Where pigeons are concerned, I've seen them do that, too!

IV
WILDFOWLING

IV
Wildfowling

For me wildfowling is the cream of all shooting sport. If I had to abandon all forms of shooting save one tomorrow, wildfowling would be my surviving choice. Name a second and I would give you pigeons. Partridges would come next. Pheasants, I fear, would finish fourth. This is of course, a highly individual choice but one that I, at least, can explain. There is a common denominator present in both wildfowl and pigeons. They are both truly wild. They both need knowledge and hunting skill, fieldcraft in short, if they are to be outwitted. Pheasants, by any stretch of the imagination, do not. They need organising and marksmanship but those are different things. My friend Tony Jackson, who has contributed the section on 'wildfowling', strongly resents the term 'duck shooting'. 'Duck shooting', he says, 'is something you do on a flooded field, a stubble or a flight pond. Wildfowling only happens beyond the sea wall.' It's a fairly purist point of view and I told him so, though I understand perfectly well what he is getting at. Wildfowling on the saltings is a rare, possibly unmatchable sport. The atmosphere and the iodine-scented air you breathe is to be obtained nowhere else. The fowl are more unpredictable, usually far less plentiful and governed by more imponderables – the combined effect of wind and tide for one – than in inland shooting. I prefer to think of it all as duck-flighting, whether done on saltings or inland. It is the habit of flighting between roost and feed at dawn and dusk that makes wildfowl, wherever found, the most exciting quarry on wings. If a distinction has to be made between one side of the sea wall and the other, I like that of a Norfolk friend of mine, John Buxton. He refers to a foray after duck below the tideline as a 'wild flight'. I think that is a fair description. Duck or geese can never be tame, unless you mean those feeble, stocked mallard put down on a park lake and persuaded into the air by beaters. I give you that, once airborne, they can usually fly like a duck should – if only in circles. But here I side with Tony Jackson. This is, literally, duck *shooting*.

Ducks and geese seize the imagination. This is why I asked the late Jeffery Harrison to cover their natural history so fully. They come to us from such far-off places – Spitzbergen, Iceland, Greenland, Scandinavia, Lake Baikal, even from Kamchatka, on the Pacific coast of Russia. They can find their way unerringly in the dark to the merest flash of attractive water. They are beautiful in flight, in repose, even in death – and they are remarkably good to eat.

There has been some wonderful writing about wildfowl which I have tried to distil in another book (*The Bedside Wildfowler*). From Hawker to Hemingway, men of imagination and talent have written about the lure of wildfowl and wildfowling. No writer that I know of has become so lyrically stirred by the pheasant. And that, I suppose, is a fair indication of the difference.

C.W.

Wildfowling Guns

Geoffrey Boothroyd

There are two sorts of wildfowler, the man who exists for this type of shooting alone and the second type, the man who is a part-time wildfowler. Both share or have shared at one time or another, a deep and often frustrated desire for bigger and better guns throwing heavier and yet heavier charges to greater heights through the tightest of choked barrels.

This disease has affected most of us, in my own case it started with a desire for longer and longer 12-bore cartridges, then on to bigger bores until I ended up with a truly massive 4-bore that was more suited to a radar controlled gun turret than to being fired from the shoulder.

For the man to whom wildfowling is a pastime rather than an obsession and who uses his gun for general sport, the pursuit of duck and geese usually arouses a need to discover what is the most powerful cartridge that he can fire in the gun he already owns, a gun more often than not chambered for the standard $2\frac{1}{2}''$ cartridge. It cannot be too strongly emphasised that a $2\frac{1}{2}''$ cartridge does not measure $2\frac{1}{2}''$ either as you get it out of the box or when you take it out of your gun after it has been fired. Taken from the box a $2\frac{1}{2}''$ cartridge can measure about $2\frac{3}{8}''$ or 2.375", say 59 to 60 mm. A cartridge case marked $2\frac{3}{4}''$ or 70 mm can in fact measure a good $\frac{1}{16}$ of an inch shorter than a nominal $2\frac{1}{2}''$ cartridge. Most 12-bore shotguns likely to be encountered today were originally made for 2", $2\frac{1}{2}''$, $2\frac{3}{4}''$ or 3" cartridges. As we have seen, the term $2\frac{1}{2}''$ cartridge is a misnomer; what is really meant is that here is a cartridge intended for a gun with a $2\frac{1}{2}''$ chamber. One would think, of course, that the cartridge case after being fired would measure $2\frac{1}{2}''$ if intended for a gun with a $2\frac{1}{2}''$ chamber. You would, of course, once again be wrong! If your cartridge has a roll closure, it would be over $2\frac{1}{2}''$ in fact about 2.565 and if it has a crimp closure, then it is likely to be 2.725" *not* repeat *not* 2.5" or $2\frac{1}{2}''$. At this point, I would not blame you if you gave up in despair! However, if you can, please bear with me. The case length, *per se* is not all that important, what is important is the load, the weight of shot. The more shot in the cartridge, the more room required, and unless you increase the diameter of the cartridge, (i.e. decrease the bore number *not* the bore diameter), you have to make it longer.

CHOICE OF LOADS

Let's have a look at a cartridge catalogue. A standard $2\frac{1}{2}''$ 12-bore has $1\frac{1}{16}$oz of shot or, if we go metric, a 65 mm cartridge with 30 grams of shot. Also offered is a similar cartridge with $1\frac{1}{8}$oz shot or 32 grams. Now let's have a look at a $2\frac{3}{4}''$ or 70 mm cartridge.

In British loadings this can be had with either $1\frac{1}{4}$oz of shot or, in the Eley Magnum loading, $1\frac{1}{2}$oz of shot. Gram equivalents 35·5 and 42·5. The $3''$ or 75 mm 12-bore has $1\frac{5}{8}$oz of shot (46 grams) and although in America the $3''$ can have up to $1\frac{7}{8}$oz of shot this load is not produced in the UK. The next size up is the 10-gauge. Today, only two case lengths are loaded, the 65 mm and the 75 mm, the first with $1\frac{5}{16}$oz of shot, the longer case holding $1\frac{7}{16}$oz of shot. The longer 10-gauge cartridges, the $3''$ and the $3\frac{1}{4}''$ are now not available. In the 8-bore size the situation is even worse. There used to be five different case lengths, now there is but one, the $3\frac{1}{4}''$ loaded with 2 oz or 57 grams of shot. The largest case is the 4-bore available in $4''$ lengths only and, as with the 10- and 8-bore, the nominal case lengths are the same as the actual. The 4-bore was loaded with $3\frac{1}{4}$oz of shot and the longest 8-bore with $2\frac{3}{4}$oz. It will be appreciated that if you own a 4-bore and can afford to use it, it is now likely that you will be relying on old cartridges and perhaps you may now have got to the stage where you have to reload to keep in business. The main danger is that you might be offered some 4-bore cartridges reloaded by someone else. It would be prudent to check the load before they are used. The same applies to 10-bore cartridges that might be better in a collection than in the chamber of your pet 10-bore gun. Two 10-gauge cartridges are still available but there is now but one 8-gauge. This is the old standard $3\frac{1}{4}''$/80 mm originally loaded with $2\frac{1}{8}$oz of shot and 6 drs of black powder. The eight gauge cartridges went up from $3\frac{1}{4}''$ through $3\frac{1}{2}''$, $3\frac{3}{4}''$, $4''$ to $4\frac{1}{4}''$. Again, you have to watch the case length since longer cases can be accommodated and in many of the eight gauge shotguns there is no indication on the cartridge case or on the shotgun as to the length of chamber. This situation exists, of course, with the 12-bore. I have an old black powder double hammer gun which was originally intended for a $2\frac{1}{2}''$ case, 3 drs black powder and the old load of $1\frac{1}{8}$oz of shot. This gun can chamber $2\frac{3}{4}''$ magnum cartridges and even $3''$ cartridges taking $1\frac{1}{2}$oz of shot. No indication exists anywhere on the gun as to the case length and it needs an expert eye to decipher the proof marks.

PROOF MARKS

In his search for longer range, the wildfowler is more likely to be at risk than the ordinary game shot who is content with his standard $2\frac{1}{2}''$ case and $1\frac{1}{16}$oz of shot. For the man who wants to have a go at wildfowling with his standard game gun, there is the wish to use more powerful cartridges. First of all, check your gun. Take off the barrels and have a look at the marks under the barrels. If of British manufacture or British proof, you should find the letters NP or BNP or the words NITRO PROOF. If your gun does not bear marks similar to these, then it is not prudent to continue to use it with modern cartridges and it is certainly very hazardous to use heavy loads. The wisest course is to submit the gun to a reputable gunsmith for his comment and advice. Your gun may not bear British nitro marks because it was made and went through proof abroad. Austrian guns bear the mark NPV as an indication of valid nitro proof, those made in Belgium the letters PV and those of French origin PT. German shotguns bear the letter N and Italian guns PSF for *'polvere sensa fumo'*. Spanish guns should bear the letters BP inside a shield if suitable for use with nitro or smokeless powders.

Even supposing that the barrels bear nitro marks, this does not mean that the gun is necessarily safe. Has it been altered since submitted to proof, have the chambers been lengthened, ejectors been fitted or have the barrels become enlarged? In connection with the latter comment, the 1954 Rules of Proof limit the enlargement of the barrels by reason of wear or neglect to $0.010''$ greater than the nominal diameter when measured $9''$ from the breech face. The old method of marking the barrel diameter or bore was for 12-bore guns 12/1, 12, 13/1, 13. The decimal inch equivalents were 0.740″, 0.729″, 0.719″ and 0.710″. Any competent gunmaker has a gauge for measuring bore diameter, and is able to tell whether or not the barrels are within proof.

Let us assume that all is in order. What then is the type of cartridge which can be used in the gun with safety? The Proof Marks under the 1954 rules require that the barrels are marked with the nominal bore in a diamond, i.e. $\diamondsuit$12$\triangleright$ and the chamber length. The nominal bore diameter at 9″ from the breech will also be marked e.g. 0·729 in. The barrels will also bear markings to indicate the maximum mean pressure of the cartridge. This is the important figure and was not used under the earlier rules of proof, where instead, the maximum shot load was marked. Service pressure will be given in tons per square inch, i.e. $2\frac{3}{4}$ TONS or where a special proof has been requested, the weight of powder and shot may be marked. The use of service mean pressure allows for a variation in powder and shot load. It is measurable and can be expressed in terms which are understandable. One minor problem is caused by the variation between British and continental Proof. British Proof produces results in tons per square inch and Continental Proof in kilogrammes per square centimetre. Because of differences in the manner by which these results are obtained, the results are not directly comparable on a mathematical scale. As long as the case length of the cartridge bore some relation to the shot charge and the shot charge to the pressure, then the user had some measure of security since his gun would be marked either NP or BNP or even NITRO PROOF and the shot charge indicated, $1\frac{1}{4}$ oz. Alternatively the chamber length or nominal case length would be marked and this could be checked against the type of cartridge it was intended to use. A more recent indication of the suitability of the cartridge has been the use of the mean service pressure in tons per square inch or kilogrammes per square centimetre.

The Proof Act is under constant revision and the 1986 amendments allowed for the use of either Imperial or Metric measurements for a period of five years. After this five year period, metric measurements are to be used, e.g. kilogrammes per square centimetre.

In all matters concerning proof, it you are at all uncertain do seek advice from a reputable source. The Proof Houses in

Birmingham and London will be found to be most helpful.

At long last the situation appeared to have been regularised and then, in America, magnum loads for shotguns were introduced as a result of the development of progressive burning powders. Such cartridges were loaded with $1\frac{5}{8}$oz of shot in $2\frac{3}{4}''$ cases and $1\frac{7}{8}$oz of shot in $3''$ cases. These cartridges were imported into the UK and, of course, presented a very real hazard if used in guns originally proved for black powder only. Because so many British guns were of such superlative quality, a great many have survived and continue in use.

LONGER RANGE

In August 1967 IMI introduced their magnum cartridges in 12-gauge $3''$ length with $1\frac{5}{8}$oz of shot and in a $2\frac{3}{4}''$ case length with $1\frac{1}{2}$oz of shot. It was agreed by the Proof Authorities in Britain that the new magnum cartridge should only be used in British guns which had undergone special proof. Such guns would be marked SP and the word MAGNUM would follow the $2\frac{3}{4}''$ or $3''$ chamber length marking. The maximum service pressure would be $3\frac{1}{2}$ tons for the $2\frac{3}{4}''$ and 4 tons for the $3''$ chamber.

It was accepted that the $2\frac{3}{4}''$ magnum cartridge could be used in the standard $3''$ gun which would bear either the $1\frac{1}{2}$oz proof mark or $3\frac{1}{4}$ tons. With the tremendous increase in the use of shotguns not of British manufacture, the British Proof Authorities agreed that Eley magnum cartridges could be used in guns which for the $2\frac{3}{4}''$ magnum were proofed at 900 kg and for the $3''$ cartridge at 1000 kg. It should be noted that the original recommendation of the Proof Authorities was that 12-bore foreign shotguns should not be used with Eley magnum cartridges unless they had been proved to a level of 1,200 kgs. This recommendation was modified by a statement issued by the Proof Authorities in 1986 which took into account the difference in the method of measuring pressures.

People in search of greater range will be strongly tempted into using the heavier loads. Larger shot means fewer pellets per ounce so to get back the pattern density in go more pellets and up goes the shot load! All well and good if you are prepared to pay the higher price, withstand the heavier recoil and, of paramount importance, have a gun which will safely handle the magnum cartridges. This aspect of shooting has perhaps been unduly belaboured. 'What has this to do with me?' you might well say. 'I've been using this gun for years with all sorts of cartridges – the gun is a good killer and is as tight as a drum.' But, remember that gun is getting older and older, some with black powder proof only might well be over a century old. Abuse, neglect and even honest wear and tear may have taken their toll so that in addition to ensuring that the cartridges are suitable for your gun, you should also make certain that the gun is in sound condition. Failure of the barrels can result in expensive or even irreparable damage and injury. A pair of barrels can be replaced if necessary – a left hand cannot!

Where weight and recoil need not be prime considerations, the weight can be increased and so reduce recoil and if the gun can be carried slung and the distance carried is not far, then heavier loads can be considered and a suitable gun acquired. Such a gun would not be satisfactory if it has to be carried all day and excess weight has a penalty when mounting and swinging. Without going as far as an 8-bore, the man interested in wildfowling would be advised to buy a gun with $2\frac{3}{4}''$ chambers so that he can use $2\frac{3}{4}''$ Alphamax or Hymax with $1\frac{1}{4}$ oz of shot. At the same time, his gun will handle the standard 12-gauge Grand Prix $2\frac{1}{2}''$ with $1\frac{1}{16}$ oz of shot.

THE BIG GUNS

If the desire to throw larger charges of shot into the air cannot be subdued and you have to have a larger bore gun – 10-, 8- or even 4-bore – caution must be observed regarding the cartridges you use. Although large bore guns are still being made in this country (a double hammerless 4-bore is at present being manufactured) most of the 'big bore' men use guns which were made many years ago, many by makers long since out of business. The traditional gun will be a hammer double or single gun with the Jones rotary double grip under lever. These guns, if they have received reasonable treatment, are virtually everlasting! For this reason, a vintage hammer large bore gun can easily be over a century old and bear old proof marks or even black powder marks and be chambered for a long obsolete cartridge. My 3″ 12-bore Alex Henry was built as a .577 double rifle in the 1880s and then subsequently converted to 3″ 12-bore and this gun has given good service for over forty years now! The proof marks that this gun bears are many and very complex since none ever appear to have been erased so they provide a potted history of its life! My own single barrel hammer 8-bore was made by William Evans of London in 1897 and was built on a Webley action for a Mr W.A. Brown. This gun was bought in 1962 for £17.50 and has never given me any cause for concern. Both guns were submitted for nitro proof and both passed without the need for any attention. Both, for many years, have been used mainly with home-loaded cartridges, and I have been fortunate that my initial stock of 3″ 12-bore cases and 8-bore cases has lasted and since they were never overloaded they have all been re-used several times.

Cartridge costs have risen considerably since the first edition of this book was written eighteen years ago. Then, one hundred 3″ 12-bore cartridges cost £9.86; now one source quotes £24.67! Then, an 8-bore cartridge cost 34p, today an 8-bore cartridge by a specialist supplier will cost about £1.00.

The dedicated wildfowler, undeterred by the ever-rising costs of his cartridges and, at times, even the difficulty of obtaining supplies, continues to find work for his treasured gun despite its weight and size. If you still intend to join this happy band, please do some research before you spend your money and seek advice so that you can avoid the pitfalls that await the unwary.

The Natural History of Wildfowl

Jeffery Harrison

Revised by the British Association for Shooting and Conservation

The geese and duck which are the legal quarry of the wildfowler in the United Kingdom are all part of the family *Anatidae* – swans, geese and ducks. The family has a worldwide distribution. They are all aquatic or semi-aquatic birds, with webs joining the three forward toes, which are complete in all species except the magpie goose of Australia and the *Ne-Ne* or Hawaiian goose. All have long necks and broad, somewhat flattened beaks, to facilitate feeding by grazing on land or water. Many obtain their food by diving.

All wildfowl on the British list moult the flight feathers of the wings simultaneously in midsummer and are flightless for about six weeks until the new feathers have grown. In the case of swans and geese, where both parents care for the young until they can fly, both moult simultaneously and regain their power of flight at the same time as their young can first fly.

Duck behave differently, in that only the female cares for the young and then only until they can fly. The males, traditionally referred to as drakes, as distinct from the female, frequently referred to as duck, separate and start to moult often before the eggs have even hatched and seldom take any part in caring for their young. An exception to this generalisation is the Icelandic population of the eider duck, in which the drakes regularly help in this for the first two or three weeks of their ducklings' lives. This has been recorded exceptionally in mallard, harlequin duck and cape teal.

The females do not moult until their young are flying and can care for themselves. At the start of the shooting season, except in bad nesting years, many adult females are still flightless in moult, lurking in dense cover.

Swans and geese comprise a tribe of their own, still within the family – the latter being further subdivided into grey and black geese. Unlike duck, there are no obvious plumage differences between the sexes. The most certain identification characteristics of the grey geese are the colours of their bills and legs. Young birds are like the adults, but duller, except for the white-fronted goose which has a distinctive adult plumage. The family bonds are strong within the wintering flocks, which on the ground are referred to as gaggles and in the air as skeins, the characteristic V formations and lines in which geese, particularly grey geese, fly.

The sub-family of ducks can generally be distinguished from geese by the fact that, in the northern hemisphere, the males are quite differently marked and much brighter than the females. In the southern hemisphere, the marked sexual difference is lacking. They are divided into a number of tribes, one of which includes the familiar, and protected, shelduck, a species which tends to link the true geese to the ducks. Shelduck sexes are almost identical. The birds feed with an upward kink in the neck, as do geese.

The other groups are represented in Britain by the dabbling duck and the diving duck. In general, young duck of both sexes grow their first plumage similar to the female, but less bright. These youngsters moult into their first winter plumage between October and January, so that at any time while this is happening, every kind of intermediate plumage may be seen. Drakes in full plumage should be easy to recognise, but these also become duck-like when they moult into eclipse plumage and become flightless in midsummer.

Thus in early autumn we find both the parents and their young are all in a similar plumage. The most effective guide to identifying any duck is the wing pattern and the colour of the speculum – the bright band of colour formed by the smaller 'secondary' flight feathers. This speculum in dabbling ducks is bounded by two twin lines of lighter colour, one near the leading edge and the other along the trailing edge of the wing. The colours of the shoulder region, particularly of adult drakes, is also very often characteristic. When the drakes assume their eclipse plumage, their wing colours do not change and so they can still be recognised without difficulty. Thus the body colouring of a drake wigeon

173

appears duck-like, but the bird can be recognised instantly for what it is by the brilliant white shoulders and green speculum, which the female and young do not possess.

This eclipse plumage is protective, tending to conceal the male in cover while it is flightless. Geese retreat to large waters and tend to feed on submergent water plants during this dangerous period and most British shelduck undertake a 'moult migration' to remote sandbanks in the Heligoland Bight.

The most reliable means of identifying the different species of duck is the wing pattern, and especially the colour of the speculum − the band of brightly coloured secondary flight feathers on the inner part of the wing, which in dabbling ducks is bounded by two strips of white.

The British Association for Shooting and Conservation (BASC) (formerly WAGBI) is making practical use of these wing characteristics for its duck recruitment and condition studies by asking wildfowlers to send in one wing from certain species of duck which they shoot. Each one can be identified, sexed, aged and measured, so that the production of young for the previous breeding season can be assessed. These findings can in turn be related to the National Wildfowl Counts and in so doing, we can learn about the causes of population changes, and the effects of environmental factors which are of vital importance for conservation, as well as gaining insights into sex ratios, migratory patterns and body conditions.

Diving duck have larger feet than dabbling duck with lobulated hind toes and the limbs are situated further back to give more effective propulsion when swimming under water. Their body shape is also broader and flatter than a dabbling duck or surface feeder. It is interesting that the Greenland mallard, a resident bird which lives much more on saltwater than our own bird and which tends to dive much more to feed on seaweeds, has also developed a rather broader and flatter body than other mallard.

Diving duck have relatively smaller wings and their wing beats are therefore more rapid than dabbling duck, tending to make more noise in flight — thus the goldeneye is often referred to by the wildfowler as 'rattle-wings'.

GREYLAG GOOSE

This is one of the largest of the grey geese, predominantly grey on the head, neck, breast, upper parts and flanks and with paler underparts, becoming white under the tail. The back and flanks show prominent white transverse barring. In flight, the very pale grey shoulders are characteristic, while a broad white bar across the rump and white margin to the grey tail shows well.

175

Occasionally there is a narrow white margin at the base of the bill and the underparts may have minimal black barring.

The legs and feet are pink and the bill of the most westerly Icelandic—British population is orange, but the plumage gets progressively paler and the bill pinker from Western Europe eastwards until the true Eastern form with a totally pink bill becomes differentiated from the Volga eastwards. The call is very like that of a farmyard goose, a low-pitched *aung-aung*.

The greylag nests in Iceland, Britain and from Scandinavia eastwards into Austria, Yugoslavia and northern Greece. The Eastern race extends eastwards from the Volga to Manchuria. In winter, birds from the Scandinavian—Baltic region migrate to Spain; others from central Russia and Czechoslovakia move to the Black Sea and North Africa. Birds from the Volga move south into Iraq and Iran, while others from further east move down into the Indian sub-continent, Indo-China and Burma. It is curious that it is in the west that the greylag has been domesticated, whereas in the east it is from the swan-goose that the familiar 'Chinese goose' is derived.

Greylags nest in heather, long grass or reeds, often on islands, and colonially. In Czechoslovakia they frequently nest in pollard willows during floods and occasionally in Britain under feral conditions. One pair once nested thirty feet up in a pine tree in Ireland making a base on an old crow's nest. Up to twelve eggs may be laid; only the female incubates and both parents care for their young, during which time they are in full moult and flightless. Growth of their new flight feathers coincides with those of their young. As with all geese, a few can nest in their second year, but the majority not until they are three years old. Feral greylags are now regularly nesting in many parts of Britain.

The Icelandic population has increased to some 90,000, although it appears to have stabilised or even declined over recent years. The majority now concentrate in Scotland, particularly in the east—central area. It has been suggested that the increasing and more aggressive pink-footed goose may have driven greylags from some of the traditional haunts such as the inner Solway, where it used to be the commonest goose.

The food of the greylag is mainly grass, autumn stubbles and, in spring, young cereals. Virtually no damage is done, except under extremely wet conditions. Some new foods, such as swede, turnips, sugar beet tops and even carrots have now been noted in Scotland, but in central Europe, root crops are never taken.

The only native British stock now remaining is in the Outer Hebrides, but in the middle of the nineteenth century they were certainly nesting as far south as Suffolk and probably north Kent.

Feral flocks are well established in Britain, having been dispersed in the 1960s and 1970s particularly by wildfowlers. Unfortunately, some are now causing agricultural problems. The most recent count found 19,000 feral greylags especially in eastern and north-western England and south-west Scotland.

Other feral flocks have been established by the Russians in the northern Volga, the Swedes in central Sweden and by Count Léon Lippens at Zwin in Belgium. Zwin birds have infiltrated the Scandinavian–Spanish flyway and it was hoped to establish a new flyway route between the Western European mainland and south-east England. Birds of eastern origin with completely pink bills have been recorded in Kent occasionally over the past thirty years, so this should be perfectly possible.

Greylags, like other grey geese, are excellent table birds, particularly when feeding on sugar beet tops. Where necessary, control by shooting is obviously the ideal method, but it should be noted that grey geese are highly susceptible to toxic seed dressings which have on occasions killed large numbers.

PINK-FOOTED GOOSE

The combination of a dark brown head and neck, with paler underparts and blue-grey upper parts with pale transverse barring, a short black bill with a pink bar (which is occasionally much more extensive) and pink legs and feet make the pink-footed goose reasonably easy to identify. The call is also a characteristic *wink ... wink* or *ank ... ank*, higher pitched than that of a bean goose, with which it can be confused – indeed the pinkfoot is regarded by many authorities as the westernmost race of the bean goose.

It breeds in two main populations, one in east Greenland and central Iceland, the other in Spitzbergen. The former winters in the British Isles, the latter in Germany and Holland, spending some time in Denmark on both migrations. This goose is a

colonial nester, sometimes on cliff ledges or more usually on islets in tundra rivers. The main colony of the Iceland−Greenland population is in the Thjorsavar Oasis, an area threatened in the 1970s with inundation behind a hydro-electric dam. This was of vital importance to pinkfeet, since most of this population nests in that country.

An intensive scientific study of Thjorsavar was carried out by the Icelandic authorities with international help to which the then WAGBI contributed as a result of an appeal for funds.

There has been a remarkable increase in pinkfeet wintering in Britain from 30,000 in 1950−51 to a record peak of 238,000 in 1991−92 with great numbers concentrating in the north-east and central lowlands of Scotland as well as Lancashire.

Their main food on arrival in autumn (from mid-September) is gleaned from stubbles and old potatoes − at which time the geese are doing good by controlling potato disease. As the fields are ploughed, pinkfeet move on to grass and winter cereals, but unlike greylags they do not usually turn to root crops, for their shorter, more delicate bills are unsuitable for such tough foods. In early spring, they cause trouble to many farmers by moving to the 'early bite' for the high protein quality of the new grass, prior to their departure back to the breeding grounds.

The Spitzbergen population which is much smaller, tends to be more conservative in its food requirements, which consist very largely of grass.

Since the sale of dead wild geese became illegal under the Wildlife and Countryside Act, 1981, pinkfeet have taken to roosting on inland waters far more than they ever did when there was a profit motive for shooting excessive bags. This clause in the Act, instigated by the late Earl of Mansfield when President of BASC, has no doubt been a significant factor in the increase of this species. The other main factor appears to have been the increase in protection and the non-shooting refuges throughout their range.

WHITE-FRONTED GOOSE

This is the smallest and most distinctive of the common grey geese when in adult plumage. Together with the very rare lesser white-fronted goose, these are the only two to have highly distinctive adult plumages compared with first year birds, which in other species are merely rather duller than the adults.

Adult whitefronts are generally grey-brown, darker on the head, neck and upperparts, the latter with pale transverse barring. The forehead and front of the cheeks are white with a blackish

posterior margin, but the white does not extend beyond the level of the eye. The lower breast and belly show a variable number of broad and irregular black transverse bars. The juveniles are generally duller and lack the transverse barring and the white forehead, but the feathers in the area which will become white by the end of the first winter are at this stage much darker than the rest of the head. The voice is a high-pitched *ank ... ank*.

There are two highly distinctive races of whitefront which visit the British Isles. The first, from breeding grounds on the west coast of Greenland (lying approximately between 60°−70° N), is the darkest of all the grey geese, some of the adults having underparts which can be almost entirely black. The white borders on the tail are greatly reduced and the bill is a bright yellowish-orange, very much the same colour as the legs and feet of both races.

The Siberian race, which nests in tundra on the Siberian main-land and Kolguev and Novaya Zembla Islands, is distinguished from the Greenland race by being paler and by having a pink bill. The nail in the adults of both races is white, but is blackish in the juveniles, which often causes confusion in identification between this and young Bean Geese.

Siberian whitefronts winter southwards to the Mediterranean, Austria and the Indian sub-continent. Those which visit Britain originate only from the Kanin Peninsula and Kolguev Island eastwards to Dickson Island. They migrate in late autumn via the White Sea direct to East Germany, moving on into West Germany and Holland in November. Although a few reach the main English haunts in Gloucestershire, Somerset, north Kent, Dorset and Hampshire exceptionally as early as late September (as in 1972), these are not generally in peak use until late December at the earliest. Return migration starts from late February to mid-March and takes these geese to the south of Moscow, where they remain into late April until their Siberian nesting grounds have unfrozen.

Greenland white-fronted geese migrate across the central ice cap in autumn and thence across the Demark Straits, some stopping off in Iceland, but others move direct to Irish or western Scottish winter quarters and until recently into Wales in small numbers. This was the one area in which the winter range of the two forms regularly overlapped, but they did not mix, except accidentally.

Peak numbers of Siberian whitefronts in Britain were recorded in 1967–68, when 12,000 were found. Over recent years the total wintering population in Britain has decreased to around 5,000 birds. In Holland, where the majority using the western European flyway pass the winter, there has been a massive increase to over 360,000. Greenland birds are far more difficult to survey, being more widely distributed in smaller numbers, but are thought to number about 15,000, mainly on Islay in western Scotland. The Siberian race feeds mainly on grass in winter, but will graze winter wheat, as will Greenland birds. The latter also take grass and the roots of cotton grass from the peat bogs which they frequent. Both forms like shallow water 'flashes' on their feeding grounds.

The rare lesser whitefront may be recognised by being smaller, having a yellow ring round the eye and a white forehead which extends over the crown, well beyond the level of the eye. Its call is even more high-pitched. Its presence in Britain is accidental, being widely distributed in Eastern Europe and Western Asia. The whitefront can now only be shot in England and Wales, the season in Scotland having been ended in 1981 in order to give protection to the Greenland race which cannot easily be distinguished in the field.

CANADA GOOSE

The Canada goose belongs to the black geese and is the largest goose in Britain. Although almost all our Canada geese date back to introductions which took place from the mid-seventeenth century and are of the big Atlantic race, there is evidence to suggest that some giant Canada geese may have been brought in, a race thought until comparatively recently to be extinct, but which has now been rediscovered in America. Genuine transatlantic migrants, usually one of the smaller races, have occurred in Ireland.

The Canada goose is easily identified by its black head and neck with an obvious white 'cut-throat' marking. The rest of the

body is brownish, the underparts pale, becoming white under the tail, which is black. The upperparts have pale transverse barring. The rump is black with a prominent white transverse bar which shows in flight. The beak, legs and feet are black.

This is a North American species, known as a 'honker' from its loud resonant call, *aahonk*. Feral flocks are now well established in Scandinavia, from where birds migrate southwards as far as Holland in winter, a habit which started about 1945. It is also a most successful introduced species in New Zealand.

In the British Isles, the Canada goose can be described as a parkland bird, so it is not in competition with other geese except feral greylags in similar surroundings, where the Canadas invariably secure the best nesting sites, usually on islands.

The Canada goose has taken every advantage of new man-made waters, particularly gravel pits and has shown a considerable increase. The first census (in 1953) revealed a total of 3,000–4,000. By 1990, this figure had increased to over 60,000, almost all in England, particularly in the south-east, the Thames valley, west Midlands and Yorkshire. Non-breeding birds from the latter area undertake a moult-migration to the Beauly Firth, a habit which was first established earlier this century.

Canada geese were formerly distributed in this country by catching them up while flightless in the moult and redistributing them, both for sporting purposes and to reduce grazing damage, but this practice has now stopped. Since then they have increased and are causing problems in many areas to grassland, public amenity places and collections of waterfowl. Control is attempted by shooting where appropriate (and, in the close season, by licensed egg-pricking, and other methods). If practised properly by flighting them to and from their feeding grounds, it can be just as sporting as any other goose shooting. On their roosting waters, however, they can be exceedingly tame.

They make exceedingly good eating, particularly the young. In the autumn they feed mainly on stubbles, moving to grass and cereals later in the winter. At such times they do no agricultural damage, even the reverse. In the spring however, they may well come into competition with farm animals for the early bite, but can easily be shifted by bird scaring devices. During the summer they feed a great deal on submergent water plants, such as curled pondweed, which is particularly favoured during the moult. Obviously if cereal crops are being grown alongside moulting waters, the geese will walk out into those crops and cause damage, which can be prevented either by not growing the crop alongside the water or with a low electric fence.

MALLARD

This must be the most familiar of all the British duck, a bird which has adapted itself to man more successfully than any other. It nests in every county, ranging from urban parks to open marshland and salting islands, from dense cover on the ground to holes in trees often thirty to forty feet up, from sea level to altitudes of two thousand feet. It will nest in farm buildings or

in nesting baskets put out over city canals totally devoid of vegetation.

The male is unmistakable with his greenish-yellow bill, glossy green head and neck, white neck ring, greyish-brown upperparts, dark chestnut-brown breast shield and grey under-surface. The tail coverts are black, the upper ones with the characteristic double curl. The tail is brownish-white and is prominent in flight. The wing speculum of both sexes is violet-blue with white borders, the inner border extending further towards the body across the tertials in the female. The legs and feet are orange.

The female is predominantly brown, with paler streaked underparts and a prominent pale stripe above the eye. The feathers of the upperparts are prominently outlined in buff and the pale tail feathers are more mottled with brown than those of the male. The bill is ochreous-yellow with darker mottling and the legs are also ochreous with darker webs. The young are similar, but lack the distinctive complete pale outlining to the feathers of the upperparts. In eclipse, the male resembles a darker female, but keeps the greenish-yellow bill and orange legs and feet.

The mallard is more prone to varieties than any other duck, showing albinism and melanism very frequently. In-breeding in town parks causes increasing symmetrical albinsim of the wings and a broadening of the white neck ring to include the whole breast shield, like a male shoveller. Other very dark, almost black, mallard also show a white breast shield and are probably derived from a black East Indian runner strain, the so-called 'Cayuja mallard'. All such birds are of impure genetic stock and should be ruthlessly culled.

Mallard breed across the whole of the northern hemisphere, from the Arctic Circle south to the Mediterranean in Europe and easwards across Asia to eastern China and northern Japan. In North America it is found west of Hudson Bay and Mississippi. In winter, migrants move south to southern Mexico, North Africa, India, Burma and southern China.

So far as is known, wild-bred British mallard are largely sedentary, small numbers only moving into France, very rarely as far as Spain and Portugal. Immigrants reach us in winter from Scandinavia, the Baltic states and western Russia, some from almost as far east as the western Caspian.

Between 1954 and 1987, BASC members liberated well over 250,000 hand-reared mallard on to unshot waters in order to infiltrate the wild population and thus to increase the total number. All were ringed and results have shown a survival and mortality rate which compares with those of wild-bred mallard. A small number have been found to disperse during their first autumn and winter, the majority of recoveries being from Holland and France, but ranging from Denmark to Italy, a certain indication that we have much more to learn of our home-bred wild birds.

Recoveries of abmigrants, i.e. those which have paired with winter visitors from overseas and returned home with them, have plotted out the north-west European flyway from which we get the bulk of our mallard. These have ranged from Tromso on the Norwegian Arctic coast in the north to the foothills of the Ural mountains in the east. One bird recovered on the Danube in Romania was thought to have moved north-east into Russia and later switched into the Black Sea flyway.

Movements during the Arctic winter of 1962−63 showed a marked tendency for hand-reared mallard to move south-west, which was more strongly developed in adults. This showed that hand-reared mallard were well able to look after themselves under stress of severe weather.

The mallard is omnivorous in its diet, taking a wide variety of plant and animal species. In autumn, corn, particularly barley is favoured, being gleaned from stubbles or flattened unharvested crops. Acorns, in good years, are very popular in November and December as they fall. Various favoured seeds include alder, silver birch, hornbeam, all the sedges, bur-reed, reed-grass and true bulrush, red-leg, knotted persicaria, water pepper and flotegrass. Invertebrates include caddis fly larvae, freshwater shrimps and the mollusc, Jenkins' spire shell. On brackish and saltmarsh habitat, mallard take the seeds of sea club rush, fennel-leaved pond weed, marsh samphire and common seablite.

It is very difficult to estimate the total wintering population in Britain since mallard occupy many waters which are never counted. Furthermore, large numbers are released for shooting purposes. The latest National Waterfowl Count gives figures which indicate over 200,000, but it is believed many more winter in this country.

The mallard makes a most excellent table bird, particularly a young corn-fed bird, but they may be said to be excellent eating throughout the season.

TEAL

The smallest of the wintering dabbling duck in Britain, it can only be confused with the slightly larger garganey, which is a local summer visitor. Confusion is, therefore, only likely in early autumn, when the two species may occur in mixed parties, before the garganey departs southwards.

In full plumage, the drake teal has a chestnut head and neck, darker on the crown, with a broad bright green stripe around and behind the eye, outlined in white. Both stripes meet on the nape. The buff breast shield is usually well marked with black spots and is sometimes separated from the neck (as a rare variety) by a white neck ring, which may be only represented by a white spot anteriorly and which indicates a close relationship to the mallard.

The upper parts and flanks are finely vermiculated in grey and white. The scapulars form a longitudinal black and white line, which is characteristic of the European form, being absent in the American race, in which there is instead a vertical white line on the sides of the breast. The belly is white, the undertail coverts black with a prominent yellow triangle on each side. The wing is grey and both sexes have a black and green speculum outlined with a broad light buff line in front and a narrower white line posteriorly both of which show well in flight.

The female is predominantly brown, with paler underparts and an indistinct pale eyestripe. The flanks and breast are mottled with darker brown, the feathers of the upper parts being outlined in pale brown. The underparts of adults are unspotted and of juveniles spotted. The bill, legs and feet of both sexes are grey-brown. The male in eclipse so very closely resembles the duck that only on close examination can they be told apart, by the more uniform and darker upper parts of the drake.

The call note of the male is a high pitched *prip . . . prip*. The female quacks like a mallard, but is higher-pitched, the first quack being loudest, the others falling away in intensity.

The teal breeds across the whole of Europe and Asia from Iceland and Britain through to north-eastern Siberia, Mongolia, Manchuria and Japan. The American race (which occurs almost regularly as a transatlantic drift migrant in the British Isles, particularly Ireland) breeds from Alaska to the middle west of the United States.

In winter, migrants reach North and East Africa, the Persian Gulf, the Indian sub-continent and southern China. Although the Icelandic teal population reaches Britain in winter, the bulk of our immigrants come from Scandinavia, the Baltic States and north-west Russia, south as far as the western Black Sea.

There appear to be two closely related flyways for teal in western Europe. On one, the birds move rapidly from Russia down to the Camargue area of the south of France, moving east in midwinter to the Adriatic and thence northwards back to their nesting grounds. Another, quite possibly closely connected, brings teal into Britain via the Low Countries, birds moving through to Ireland and southwards to the Iberian peninsular, particularly in hard weather.

The British population gave rise to some concern in the mid-1960s. There had been a very large wintering population in

1959−60 and in 1961−62, which was associated with the period when the new polder of East Flevoland was being dried out, displacing a million and a half duck, mainly mallard and teal by the destruction of prime wildfowl habitat. This undoubtedly made the drop to the very low population of 1965−66 − 1968−69 seem even more marked, but the interesting feature of this low period was that it occurred at a time when the production of young, as shown by BASC's wing analyses, was good. For this reason, it seemed likely that the fall in population was due to a migratory shift rather than to any real numerical decrease. This could have been initiated by the drastic changes occurring on the new polder and certainly no such decrease was recorded at the same time in the massive Camargue population. Now the British population is estimated at a minmun of 164,000, again the numbers being very difficult to determine on account of the teal's small size, secretive habits and liking for small bodies of water.

Teal feed freely on fresh, brackish and saltwater habitats, often congregating in packs many hundred strong. Inland, the seeds of common spike rush and creeping buttercup are particularly favoured, together with insect larvae. In brackish water, the seeds of sea club rush and tassel pondweed predominate and on the saltings, orache and marsh samphire seeds. In a peak seeding year for the latter, in 1969, no less than four thousand teal congregated on twenty acres of flooded marsh samphire in Kent. The small mollusc, Laver spire shell is also taken in large numbers from the uncovered mud flats. Normally teal are excellent to eat, except during prolonged hard weather when they are feeding on the intertidal zone and are then no longer worth eating.

GADWALL

The gadwall is slightly smaller, but very similar in shape to a mallard, the male being generally grey-brown on the head, neck and upper parts, with a barred black and white breast shield, grey flanks and white belly. The rump and under-tail coverts are black with a pale brown tail. The most characteristic feature is the white wing speculum and bright chestnut shoulders, which may be hidden at rest. The legs and toes are ochreous-yellow and the bill black.

The female is very mallard-like, but with a whitish belly and with the same characteristic wing pattern as the male, but less bright. The bill is dusky with orange-yellow sides. When the drake moults into the duck-like eclipse plumage, the bill also takes on the colour of the female. The juveniles are duller and duck-like, the drakes assuming full plumage usually by November. The call of the male is a harsh, rasping grunt and the female a series of mallard-like quacks, but softer.

Gadwall breed throughout most of the temperate zone of the Northern Hemisphere, across North America, Europe and Asia, the largest populations being found in south Russia. It is increasing in north-west Europe and has already bred as far north as Swedish Lapland. Many move further south in winter.

In Britain it breeds regularly only in south-east Scotland, Gloucestershire, Somerset, Kent and East Anglia, the latter population originating from introduced birds at the end of the last century. Those in the west country originated from the Wildfowl Trust. Home-bred birds appear to move in winter to the south of France and the Iberian peninsula. Immigrants are known to arrive from Iceland (mainly in Ireland) and from north-west Europe, both German and Polish-ringed birds having been recovered here.

Some birds ringed and released in the 1960s and 1970s in west Kent proved to be partial migrants to winter quarters on the French coast of the Bay of Biscay. This is of much interest in view of the fact that they were being released in an area not frequented by wild-bred Gadwall. One abmigrant has also been recovered in north-west Germany. These hand-reared birds began breeding regularly in the wild in west Kent.

Gadwall favour well-sheltered, tree-fringed lakes and pools, where they appear to take much of the same food as mallard, such as various seeds — alder, silver birch, sedges and bulrush. They also feed very actively on insects on the surface in summer and early autumn. Nests are in thick cover, close to water and often on islands.

They make good eating, as would be expected of a surface-feeding duck with a mainly vegetarian diet. They are, however, most confiding duck, returning again and again to a favoured feeding spot even on the same flight. For anyone wishing to establish gadwall in an area therefore, the greatest care has to be taken to avoid overshooting them. Their flight silhouette is somewhat different to a mallard, even at dusk, for they have shorter necks and narrower, more sickle-shaped wings. With their light underparts, when seen in poor visibility they are in fact more likely to be mistaken for wigeon.

GOLDENEYE

This is a medium-sized very round-headed diving duck, the full round shape of the head being due to large air sinuses in the front of the skull, the function of which is still not definitely known.

The male in full plumage has a glossy-green head with a prominent circular white spot at the base of the bill. The neck and underparts are white, the back black, with black and white scapulars overlying the wings. These are black, with white shoulders and a white speculum. The tail coverts and tail are also black, as is the bill. The legs and toes are ochreous-yellow, the webs dusky.

Both sexes have a brilliant yellow eye. The female has a rich chocolate-brown head, grey upper parts, breast band and flanks, white neck and belly. The wing pattern is as in the male, but dark grey, not black. The bill is grey with a subterminal ochreous band. Juveniles of both sexes are like females, but lack the white shoulders.

British goldeneye nest in Sweden and Finland, often in nest boxes put out for them by Laplanders. Because of this, they are increasing. Occasionally they hybridise with smews, which also nest in holes in trees and nest boxes. The wing beats are rapid and produce a loud rattling sound. An astonishing fact is that a bird with such fast wing beats can fly straight into a nesting hole! Some 16,000 are counted each year with the great majority on Loughs Neagh and Beg. For many wildfowlers their diet of molluscs and crustaceans makes them an unattractive quarry species.

WIGEON

The wigeon is a highly gregarious medium-sized dabbling duck, the very large flocks which visit our shores during the winter providing the cream of true wildfowling. Their appearance in flight, with small beaks, short necks, sickle-shaped wings and white underparts make them one of the easiest duck to identify at a distance, confirmation being provided by the high-pitched

double whistle *whee-ou* of the males and the low-pitched growl of the females.

The adult male is highly colourful, with a yellow forehead and crown, the remainder of the head and neck bright chestnut, a purplish-pink breast, occasionally with dark spots or bars, finely vermiculated grey and white upper parts and flanks, white underparts, black tail coverts and whitish tail. The shoulders are white, the speculum black and green and the scapulars (which point towards the tail) black and white.

The pure white shoulders of the adult male are not developed until the second winter, so that first year birds can be recognised by their pale brown shoulders, which gradually whiten during the first winter. In eclipse, the head, neck, flanks and upperparts become a rich dark brown, the latter with traces of grey and with darker streaking. The shoulder remains white. The bill at all times is blue-grey with a black tip and the legs and feet dark grey.

Females and young are predominantly brown, the feathers of the upperparts with paler margins, those of the adult female being more strongly marked, particularly on the shoulders. A second colour phase of adult female is predominantly grey rather than brown.

The wigeon breeds right across Eurasia from Iceland to Kamchatka, the southernmost limits of its range just reaching southern England, through Germany, Poland and Central Russia to Mongolia. In winter it migrates southwards as far as central Africa, Arabia, southern China and Japan. Birds from the extreme east also winter in small numbers in North America.

In Britain, It breeds quite widely in the Scottish islands and mainlands and in northern England, less commonly in north Wales, East Anglia and Kent. It appears to have increased as a breeding bird over the past 150 years.

Immigrants reach the British Isles from Iceland – coming mainly to Ireland, Scotland and northern England, and from the Baltic, northern and central Russia, some coming from well east of the Ural mountains up to 3,500 miles away and others from the western Caspian. The British Isles are thus at the winter end of two flyways. For Russian birds, a more southerly route may be taken on the return journey as indicated by several recoveries of British-ringed birds in late winter in Italy.

The wigeon's nest is well concealed in vegetation, often on

moorland and near water, preferably on islands. The down is rather like that of the garganey, being dark with light (but not white) centres and tips. The male more often assists in the care of the young than in other dabbling duck.

The wigeon's short, rather pointed bill with a high base is adapted for grazing and particularly for clipping off short grasses. On the intertidal zone it feeds on the green seaweeds and eel-grasses and on the saltmarshes it favours the lower level grasses, such as sea meadow grass, tending to avoid the rather coarser species. It is thus good management for wigeon to graze the salting merses with sheep and to encourage turf-cutting, for both encourage the lower level grasses to become dominant. It will also take marsh samphire and, in more brackish habitat, the seeds of sea club rush.

There seems little doubt that the wigeon moved inland as a result of the disease which decimated the eel-grass beds in the 1930s, and developed new feeding habits. This was in marked contrast to the behaviour of the brent goose, the other wildfowl species which depended on eel-grass for its main winter food. As a result, the numbers of brent, particularly the dark-bellied brent underwent a catastrophic decline but has since shown a really substantial recovery.

Great numbers of wigeon are now found inland, particularly on the Ouse Washes in East Anglia where 38,000 have recently been recorded in winter. Inland foods include various grasses and the leaves of submergent water plants including Canadian pond-weed, water crowfoot, hornwort and duck weed and the succulent roots of mare's tail. Other major coastal sites include the Ribble estuary, where up to 88,000 have been counted, Lindisfarne, Lough Foyle and the northern Scottish firths. A record 340,000 wigeon were counted over all in 1991/92, higher than the previously estimated total population.

Wigeon are normally excellent to eat, except when they have been feeding for some time exclusively on the open shore. At such times they should be gutted as soon as possible and this greatly improves them for the table.

The normal wintering population in the British Isles as moni-tored by the National Waterfowl Counts through the Wildfowl and Wetlands Trust fluctuates greatly and without as yet any apparent reason. The population was at a high level 1955/56,

1961/62 and 1968/69 and at a low level in 1951/52, 1958/59 and 1963/64. The numbers of adult drakes wintering in the British Isles has been shown by the BASC Duck Wing Survey to be disproportionately high, indicating that there is a differential migration of adult drakes to this country and particularly to the south-east, where the early flocks in late September may be made up of 80% adult drakes. It is now believed, supported by other ringing studies, that the adult females winter further south in their migratory range.

PINTAIL

The pintail is the greyhound of the duck world, sleek, tall and upright on the ground, the essence of gracefulness in flight. It is the long, slender necks and pointed tails of both sexes which are so characteristic. The 'pin' of the mature drake formed by the elongated central upper tail coverts enhance the wonderful streamlined appearance.

The male is grey on the upper parts and flanks, with a chocolate-brown head and upper neck. The front of the lower neck and underparts are white, with a narrow white line extending up the side of the neck to the head. The flanks are grey and just in front of the tail coverts there is a distinct patch of pale yellow.

The tail is white, tail coverts black. Long lanceolated scapulars of black, yellow and grey overlay the wing with a bold patch of black towards the shoulder. The latter is grey, the feathers of the first year bird outlined with the narrowest of pale buff lines. The speculum of the male is bronzy-green, with a buff line in front and a broader white line behind. The bill and legs are blue-grey, the former with brighter blue on the sides, and the webs are dusky.

The female is generally brown, with a brighter chestnut head and neck, paler underparts and much speckling and outlining of the feathers of the upper parts with pale chestnut. The wing pattern and soft parts are as in the male, but duller. In eclipse, the male is rather greyer than the female and can always be recognised by the bright wing speculum.

The juveniles are much as the female, the males rather greyer and with narrow white barring on the upper parts, the female with less pale edging on the upperparts. The call of the male is very like that of a teal, but in a lower key, and the female a rather weak quack.

The pintail breeds across the whole of northern Eurasia and in North America. In the past it has spread to Greenland, presumably from Iceland. Birds move south in winter as far as West Africa, the Indian sub-continent, the Philippines and northern South America.

Immigrant pintail reach the British Isles from Iceland, Scandinavia, the Baltic States, Russia and western Siberia, the first birds arriving in September, the majority not until November. Some are undoubtedly on passage to France and the Iberian peninsular and ringing recoveries have recently shown that they may go as far as Senegal, where large wintering concentrations have recently been discovered.

The British breeding population is small and is mainly limited to East Anglia and Kent and to Scotland, with scattered records from northern England and Ireland.

Pintail can be bred quite freely in captivity. Recoveries of released birds are as yet limited, but the species has records from Asiatic Turkey, Germany and Swedish Lapland.

The food of the pintail varies according to whether it is on freshwater or saltwater habitat, but it seems equally at home on either. In fact, the pintail population seems to vary its main haunts in Britain, so that in some years it is Morecambe Bay, the Mersey, the Dee, the Solway or the North Kent Marshes which are favoured and in other years there may be very few. The main inland haunt is the flooded Ouse Washes in Cambridgeshire, which were first 'discovered' by pintail in 1941. The north-west England estuaries including the Dee, Mersey and Morecambe Bay have become the most important sites holding up to twenty thousand birds.

The food in winter is very much like that of the mallard, but on brackish water, sea club rush seeds are particularly favoured and on the intertidal zone, the small mollusc, Laver spire shell, which is taken in large numbers.

The nest is usually well hidden in vegetation, often sited on islands and there is a tendency for social nesting.

Pintail make good eating except when they are feeding exclusively on the foreshore.

SHOVELER

The shoveler is the most highly specialised of the 'blue-winged' duck, being characterised by its disproportionately large shovel-shaped bill, with a sieve-like apparatus at the sides composed of the vertical lamellae which enable water to be filtered off and small particles of food retained and swallowed.

The drake in mature plumage is one of the most colourful of British ducks. The bill is black, the eye bright yellow, the legs, feet and webs orange. The head and neck are dark bottle-green,

breast gleaming white, belly and flanks bright chestnut with some dark barring and a white patch on the sides just in front of the black tail coverts. The tail is white with minimal brown mottling.

The upper parts are dark brown with a white lateral patch. The shoulders are blue, speculum bright green with a broad white border in front and narrow white border behind. The lanceolated long scapulars which point towards the tail are bright blue, black and white in longitudinal stripes.

Adult males assume this full plumage in November, young males often not until early spring. In eclipse, the male becomes similar to but darker than the female, particularly on the head and neck and the beak takes on the colour of the female.

Females and young are generally mottled brown with darker upper parts, a pale cheek patch and eye stripe. The bill is brown with yellowish-brown on the sides. The wing is as in the male, but duller. Juveniles are similar, but the feathers of the shoulders have broad buff margins, largely obscuring the blue.

Shoveler are mostly silent, but the male occasionally utters a low double call and the female a quiet quack. The wings of shoveler are proportionately rather thinner than other dabbling duck and the wing beats are therefore particularly rapid as the bird takes off and even if heard in the dark enable it to be identified by its pronounced rattle.

Shoveler nest over much of Europe, Asia and North America, northwards to the Arctic Circle. In winter the bird migrates southwards as far as East Africa, the Persian Gulf, Ceylon, southern China, Japan, Hawaii and northern South America.

Two populations frequent the British Isles. The breeding population, which is probably linked to that of the Low Countries, nests over much of the British Isles. These birds leave in early autumn, moving south into France and the Iberian peninsular and will probably be proved to move further south into West Africa. Other ringing recoveries are from Italy and Morocco. They are replaced by a wintering population which moves down from the Baltic States and western Russia and which mostly arrives in October and November. The population is currently some 10,000 birds.

There is a marked spring migration in March and April, which in south-east England has often been composed of up to 80% drakes. Many more pass through than remain to nest in the

British Isles and these are probably en route for western Europe, many more occurring if the winds are easterly. Females follow later.

The nests are usually concealed in long grass or nettles, somewhere near water. They can be found quite easily when the male circles round soon after dawn to attract the female off the eggs. The bills of downy young shoveler begin to take on their characteristic shape when the birds are about a week old.

Shoveler feed in shallow water, moving their bills from side to side as they collect their food on or near the surface. A high proportion of animal food is collected in this way, such as insects, crustaceans, molluscs, even tadpoles and frog spawn. Seeds and leaves of emergent vegetation are also taken.

It is probably because of the high animal content of their diet that shoveler are often rather strongly flavoured and are not really particularly good to eat. They are comparatively tame and easy to shoot and it is therefore a great pity to take big bags of them − in fact many wildfowlers do not shoot them at all, or only at the start of the season.

POCHARD

The Pochard is a medium-large diving duck, feeding in winter on waters of up to about twenty feet in depth. The bright chestnut head and neck of the male, with the black of the breast extending round to the back of the neck, pale grey body and black about the tail making it easy to distinguish. The legs, feet and beak are dark grey, the latter with a pale blue band near the tip, while the eye is red. The female is uniformly dull brown, with paler cheeks and a pale patch behind the eye and on the chin. The upper parts are very finely peppered with grey. The male in eclipse is very like the duck, but there are no pale head markings and the mantle is greyer. The juveniles are like very sombre ducks. In flight there is no white wing bar and the secondaries are grey.

Pochard have slowly spread as breeding birds throughout the whole of Britain and their numbers are greatly augmented by winter migrants originating from the Baltic states eastwards through southern Germany. Czechoslovakia and central Russia, the furthest ringing recovery being from the Sea of Okhotsk,

4,500 miles to the east. Although the bulk of winter visitors do not arrive until November, a moult migration of drakes into south-east England brings several thousand to Abberton reservoir, Essex, in late summer and smaller numbers elsewhere. The number counted in 1991/92 was around 40,000 in total, most of these now being on Loughs Neagh and Beg in Northern Ireland.

The pochard mainly frequents inland waters where it feeds largely on submergent vegetation, particular the stoneworts and curled pondweed. Some invertebrates, such as insect larvae and molluscs are also taken in much smaller amounts. Most of this food is obtained by diving, but pochard will also upend in shallows in the same way as dabbling duck. During hard weather pochard may be forced out to the estuaries, when they will feed on green seaweeds, eel grass and small saltwater molluscs. On the Thames they are taking Tubifex worms.

The nest is built up of reeds and is almost invariably very close to water, but well hidden in vegetation. Often in brackish areas, the nest is built up of sea club rushes on the surface of the water. The usual clutch is from seven to nine eggs and after the young have hatched the female often takes them to a 'nursery' water, where a number of broods may gather together with their mothers.

Being largely vegetarian, the pochard is quite the best of the diving duck as a table bird.

TUFTED DUCK

The story of the tufted duck in the British Isles this century shows it to be a particularly successful duck species. At the turn of the century, the tufted duck was rare as a breeding bird, being confined to Scotland. Now it nests regularly throughout the whole of the British Isles except for the extreme south-west, Wales and north-west Scotland.

The male tufted is unmistakably black and white, the white being restricted to the flanks and belly. There is a long pendulous crest and a bright yellow eye, while the bill is blue-grey with a black tip and the legs and feet are grey with dusky webs. Adults assume full plumage by late October, young males by January.

The females are less contrasted, chocolate-brown instead of black, with pale brown flanks and whitish bellies. Occasionally there is white around the base of the bill, but never as extensive as in a female scaup and there may be white undertail coverts, but never so prominent as in a ferruginous duck. The crest is minimal. In summer, the underparts moult to a dark brown. Juveniles are a uniform dull mousey-brown, with paler bellies. The males in eclipse loose their crests, become dark grey instead of black and develop grey flanks. In flight, a prominent white wing-bar extends on to the primaries and the females often utter a harsh *Kurr*. The males are mostly silent, but have a whistle which they utter when displaying.

Coupled with the widespread increase of the British breeding population, there has been a marked increase in the wintering immigrant population. These birds, which mainly arrive in November, originate from two distinct areas, birds from Iceland moving into Scotland and Ireland, while those from Scandinavia, the Baltic States, and north-west Russia and central Europe move to England. The total population numbers around fifty thousand.

These birds are only from the western end of the tufted's breeding range, which extends across the whole of northern Eurasia as far as Kamchatka and northern Japan. In winter, others move south into North Africa, Oman, India and the Philippines.

In spite of the large numbers of tufted which can now be found in Britain, they are still relatively insignificant compared with the many thousands wintering in Denmark, Holland and Switzerland. Certainly in Britain, the successful spread of this duck is associated with its remarkable adaptation to inland, man-made waters, such as reservoirs and gravel pits.

There is still much to be learnt about this species. There is a great deal of sexual segregation, both on migration and in winter, while the moult immigration of drakes in mid-summer still has to be evaluated. On some waters it is only during April and May that the sex ratio reaches parity.

The winter movements of the British nesting population are not well known. Probably they congregate on large waters in this country and Eire. In really severe weather, as in 1963, some undoubtedly move on further south, for two British-ringed birds were recovered in Spain at this time.

The diet of the tufted duck is largely animal, particularly freshwater molluscs, crustacea, leeches and insect larvae taken in water mainly up to ten feet deep. There is evidence to suggest that the spread of the tufted duck may have been linked with the spread of the zebra mussel, a highly popular freshwater mollusc.

201

The nest is usually close to water, often on islands in thick cover under bushes or in grass. The bird is often a colonial nester.

Feeding so extensively on animal foods, the tufted duck needs careful cooking to make it really palatable as a table bird, but with skill it can be good.

NON–QUARRY SPECIES: GEESE

The barnacle goose is one of the medium-sized 'black geese', unmistakably black, white and grey, with a prominent white face and forehead, black crown, neck and breast and a bluish-grey back with well-marked narrow black and white transverse barring. A dark rump with a broad white bar, black flight feathers and tail and white underparts complete a most attractive flight pattern. The legs, feet and beak are black and a narrow black bar runs back to the eye, which is brown.

This goose tends to fly in compact packs rather than in skeins and to feed *en masse*. The call is a short sharp bark, often repeated in quick time, when it sounds like some small dog yapping.

The barnacle occurs in three distinct geographical populations, but curiously it has not developed any geographical races, unlike the well differentiated Greenland and Siberian white-fronted geese or the light, dark and black-bellied brents.

One population breeds in east Greenland and winters in Ireland and the Western Isles, many migrating via Iceland and the Faroes. The latest survey revealed a total of 26,000. A second population nests in Spitzbergen and winters on the Solway, mainly on the Caerlaverock National Nature Reserve or at Rockcliffe, most of which make a direct flight to the Solway. At the start of this century these numbered about 6,000, but from 1939 for about fifteen years there were only a mere 300−400. Now their numbers have recovered to some 12,000, probably due both to their protection, given since the 1954 Wild Birds' Protection Act and also due to a change in breeding habits, moving away from cliff nesting sites, where many were killed for food by the mining community, to uninhabited offshore islands. An unknown wintering area may yet be discovered, possibly off the Norwegian mainland. Only very occasionally do Greenland and Spitzbergen birds meet in winter quarters in Scotland. This has been proved by the use of coloured plastic neck bands in east Greenland and white leg rings in Spitzbergen.

The third population nests on Novaya Zemblya and Vaigach in Siberian tundra and winters mainly in Holland, where some 85,000 now winter.

Although most migrants arrive in winter quarters in November, the earliest usually appear in late September and remain until late April or early May. Their favourite winter foods in Britain are the well-grazed salting grasses and clover, although they occasionally visit potato fields and inland pastures with pinkfeet or whitefronts and are sometimes to be seen grazing eel-grass or sea lettuce with the brents in south-east England. Barnacles are protected at all times.

Barnacle geese breed well in captivity and a small flock which started to breed on the Lofoten Islands, north Norway, was thought to owe its origin to a free-winged feral flock in Scotland. With a world population of only about 50,000 twenty years ago, the protection of barnacles has proved an important factor for the survival and increase of this wonderful goose.

The bean goose is the largest and brownest of the 'grey geese', darker on the back with prominent white transverse barring. The bill is black with a yellow bar, which can be so extensive that the whole bill may be yellow, except for the black nail. The legs are orange. Formerly it was thought that the yellow-billed bean goose was a distinct race, but it is now known to be only a colour variety. The few bean geese which now visit Britain are known to be all of the long-billed forest race, nesting from northern Scandinavia eastwards to the Ural mountains in the forest zone, roughly between 60°–72°N. North of this, in the Siberian tundra zone, nests the tundra race of bean goose. This is recognised by its much shorter bill, very similar in size to that of the pink-footed goose. This race winters in large numbers in Holland, and, occasionally, reaches southern England, one being shot in Sussex in 1973.

The status of the forest bean goose in Britain is somewhat of a mystery. At the beginning of this century, it was clearly much more numerous, but it has gradually decreased as a breeding bird in Scandinavia, which is presumably where our wintering birds originated from. Now it is decidedly uncommon and occurs regularly only in a few areas, one in south-west Scotland, another in central Scotland and the main one in East Anglia. Numbers fluctuate from year to year but normally only total a few hundred. It would be the greatest pity if the bean goose was to stop migrating to Britain. Every care should be taken to avoid shooting them in mistake for other grey goose species. Unfortunately when in company with pink-footed geese, as indeed they often are in Norfolk, they can be very difficult to distinguish, unless they are very well seen. Their calls are, however, characteristic − a low-pitched *ung . . . unk*. Bean geese feed mainly on grass. They are, of course, a protected species.

NON−QUARRY SPECIES: DUCK

The following species of diving duck spend much of the winter on tidal waters. All feed on molluscs and crustaceans, which give them a strong taste, quite unworthy of any table, even if they were legal quarry. All are fully protected and may not be taken or killed at any time.

The common scoter is entirely a marine diving duck the male being a uniform glossy-black, with black legs, feet and bill, the latter with a pronounced knob at its base and with an orange band across the middle of the upper mandible. The females are a

uniform dark brown, particularly on the crown, some, but not all, with paler cheeks. Juveniles always have pale cheeks and pale bellies. The total population is thought to be some 25,000.

The velvet scoter, like the common scoter, is entirely marine. It is slightly larger, being more thick-set than a mallard. The main distinguishing feature in all plumages is the uniform white wing speculum. Otherwise, the male has a small white elliptical marking under the eye and a vivid white iris. The bill is black with orange-yellow sides and has a white nail. The legs are crimson, toes yellow and webs dusky.

The females and juveniles are a uniform brown, darker above, with two pale cheek patches, the latter with pale underparts. Their bills are dark grey, legs similar to the male, but duller.

Scoters have relatively large legs and paddles, being probably the strongest underwater swimmers of all the diving duck. Unfortunately they have suffered heavy casualties from oiling at sea and both species have decreased. They are difficult to identify during counts. The total population is unknown.

The garganey is one of the group of 'blue-winged ducks', which is to say that it is more closely related to the shovelers and the American blue-winged teal and cinnamon teal than it is to our well-known European teal. Furthermore it is the only duck which is a summer visitor to the British Isles, only very rarely occurring in winter and then usually in Ireland. It is fully protected.

In size, garganey are slightly larger than teal, but otherwise are similar in shape, except that the beak is relatively slightly larger − another clue to its relationship with shoveler.

The drake does not assume its full breeding plumage often until February, so it is in full plumage for less time − only three to four months − than any of our other dabbling duck. It is then unmistakable. The most obvious feature is a broad white crescent extending from above the eye to the nape of the neck and dividing the dark crown from the purplish cheek and throat, the latter flecked with white. The upper parts are dark brown with beautiful long lanceolated white scapulars, outlined in black which overlay the wings. The breast is pale brown with dark barring, the underparts white with fine grey vermiculations and the tail coverts are pale brown with darker spots.

The shoulders are pale blue-grey and can look almost white in flight, while the speculum is bright green with broad white bars in front and behind. The bill of both sexes is dark grey, the legs are paler with dusky webs.

The female is remarkably teal-like, but with the same characteristic wing pattern, similar to, but duller than a drake garganey, and the pale stripe above the eye is more obvious than in a teal, as is a pale circular patch in the front of the cheeks. Juveniles are again similar, but duller. The male in eclipse is just like a female, but can be instantly recognised in flight by the very pale shoulders.

The call of the male is a rasping rattle and of the female a high-pitched teal-like quack, which is in fact seldom uttered.

The garganey breeds right across Eurasia northwards into southern Scandinavia and (as a rarity) in Iceland. It extends eastwards south of 60°N to Kamchatka. The southern limits of its breeding range include North Africa, the Caspian, Manchuria and northern Japan.

In winter it moves southwards as far as Nigeria, Kenya, India, Papua New Guinea and has been recorded in the Transvaal and Australia. Enormous wintering concentrations occur in the delta of the Senegal river in West Africa. Ringing has linked these birds with Italy, Yugoslavia, Russia, Poland, Holland and France and it seems highly likely that British garganey will be proved to move into this area. So far, however, our few ringing recoveries indicate a south-easterly movement to Italy, Bulgaria, Turkey and Algeria. This population has been threatened by severe drought on the wintering ground.

The British Isles are on the extreme westerly edge of the garganey's range and it is nowhere numerous, but most frequent in the south-east and has bred in the Midlands, Wales, west to the Scillies and in south-east Scotland. Some fifty pairs are thought to breed. The first arrivals in the south-east are very occasionally seen in February, the majority in late March and April. The nests are hidden in long grass, usually not far from a marshland fleet and are lined with characteristic grey down with white tips and centres.

The first returning birds of continental origin move back through the south-east from mid-June during east winds and in good years numbers up to a hundred may be seen in August in Kent. Most are gone by mid-September and only stragglers are to be seen in October. Their food is said to consist more of animal matter than in dabbling duck apart from shoveler, but further food studies are required.

The scaup is very similar to but slightly larger than a tufted duck, and decidedly uncommon on inland waters. The adult male can at once be distinguished from a tufted by its pale grey and white vermiculated back and by its lack of any crest. The bill is entirely blue-grey except for the black nail.

The female has a broad white facial band and the back is

flecked with grey. Young of both sexes are duller and lack the white face. They are difficult to distinguish from young tufted duck.

Scaup visting Britain breed in Iceland, Scandinavia and the Baltic States.

The drake **long-tailed duck** is unmistakable − a superb little 'sea pheasant', the head, neck and underparts being white, with a large dark cheek patch and a black breast band which extends over the shoulders to form a central black line along the back and rump, to join the long central black tail feathers. The scapulars and rest of the tail are white, the wings uniform black. The long-tailed duck is the only duck to have a distinct summer plumage, in which the head and neck become dark with a white patch encircling the eye. A third plumage is assumed when the bird moults into its eclipse.

The female has no long tail and is generally dark above and light below with uniformly dark wings, a white head and neck with dusky cheek patch and a dark breast band. In summer the throat goes almost black. Juveniles are duller versions of the adult duck.

In flight, they fly rapidly, swinging from side to side with their wings held downwards and then land on the water breast first. In winter they move around in massive flocks and suffer severely from oil pollution when a flock pitches on a patch of apparently smooth water, which is in fact oil. Some 24,000 are thought to occur in this country, mainly in the northern and western Scottish islands.

WADING BIRDS

Since the first edition of this book was published, only golden plover, snipe and woodcock may be legally shot. Nevertheless, the wildfowler will still want to identify the other waders, now fully protected by the Wildlife and Countryside Act, 1981.

The curlew is the largest of the wading birds, standing up to eighteen inches in height with a long, down-curving bill, up to six inches long in a male and eight inches in the bigger female. It is generally mottled brown above with a white rump and brown and

white barred tail. The pale underparts have well-marked striations. The long legs are grey, the bill dark horn, pinkish at the base. The well-known call from which it takes its name echoes across the saltings and provides the very spirit of the tidal flats in winter. Now fully protected. Nests in hill country.

The whimbrel is a summer visitor to northern Europe, by which time many have already migrated southwards and the others quickly move through.

Although very similar to a curlew, the whimbrel is only about half as large and the head pattern is characteristic, with a central pale buff line over the crown and with a broad dark line on either side. The usual call is a high-pitched, rapidly repeated whistle which is normally uttered seven times − from which it gets its local longshoreman's name 'seven whistler', sometimes also referred to as a 'half curlew'. Fully protected.

The bar-tailed godwit is a slender, medium-large wading bird, with a long, slightly upturned bill and rather short legs, which do not extend beyond the tail in flight. In winter plumage it is generally pale grey-brown above and white below with a buffish foreneck and upper breast. In summer the plumage becomes a beautiful chestnut-brown with darker mottling on the upper-parts. There is no wing bar in flight, the wings being uniformly mottled in grey-brown and white. Juveniles are like very pale summer-plumaged birds.

The chestnut plumage of summer serves as a perfect camouflage when the bird is nesting in the high Arctic, particularly when the low sun bathes the tundra nesting grounds in a warm pink suffusion.

The black-tailed godwit has recently re-established itself as a nesting bird in East Anglia and more recently in Kent. It has prominent white wing bars in flight and contrasting black lower back, white rump and black tail, while the bill is straight and the legs considerably longer, so that they protrude well beyond the tail in flight. Both godwits are fully protected.

The grey plover is a medium-sized stocky wading bird, pale grey above, with a white forehead and eye stripe, white rump, grey and white barred tail and wings with a prominent white bar. The underparts are white in winter and a characteristic black patch shows up well against the whitish undersurface of the wing in flight. The relatively short bill, legs and feet are dark grey and there is no hind toe (in contrast to the golden plover).

In summer, the underparts become black and the upper parts mottled with black and white spotting. The call is a plaintive *pleeuwi*. Grey plovers are almost entirely estuarine during the winter and may be seen still in summer on their return from east Siberian nesting tundras in September. Fully protected.

The golden plover is very slightly smaller than the grey plover and lacks any obvious white wing bar. The upper parts are generally dark with golden-yellow spotting and edging to the feathers, while the underparts are white, with a greyish-brown breast band, tinged with pale yellowish-buff.

In summer the underparts become black, those of the northern form from Iceland and Scandinavia the blackest of all, with a broad white line running from the forehead, above the eye and curving down the sides of the neck and along the flanks, while those from further south on Scottish and English moorland nesting sites have less black and no distinct white line. The call is a single

drawn-out whistle *tlui*. Golden plover tend to keep to drier fields near the coast in England during the winter, but in the Low Countries, Scotland and Ireland, may be seen on low-lying flooded pasture land in big flocks. At low tide they may flight out to the foreshore at times, but seldom for long. They are really excellent to eat and can be legally shot during the open season. Some eighty thousand were counted during the 1991/92 season.

The redshank, with its loud and frequently repeated whistling call *tu-hu-hu-hu* must be familiar to every wildfowler on the saltings. It may even have been cursed by him as it jumps in alarm, calling and frightening off some duck which were being stalked over the saltmarsh.

Redshank are about the same size as golden plover, but relatively taller and more slender, with dark brownish-grey upper parts, with a pale stripe above the eye, blackish wing tips and a broad

212

white bar along the trailing edge of the wings. The rump is white and the tail transversely barred with grey and white. The legs are orange and the bill dark with orange at the base. The underparts are white with a grey-brown suffusion on the breast with some darker streaking which extends on to the flanks. In summer, the whole plumage becomes darker with spotting. The young birds also have paler spotting on the upper parts in autumn. Now fully protected.

The snipe is smaller than a redshank and has relatively the longest bill of any of the smaller wading birds. With its rapid and twisting flight accompanied by its quiet *scape* call, the snipe provides a worthy target for anyone who shoots, from upland moors to low-lying muddy areas beside fresh, brackish or saltwater habitat, preferably associated with cattle.

The snipe is dark above with bright yellowish-brown stripes running over the crown, above the eyes and down the back. The tail is pale brown with dark transverse barring. The outer tail feathers are whiter and the remainder have broad white tips, so that the tail when spread is round and appears to be outlined with white. It is used prominently in display and the 'drumming' sound is produced by holding the two outer tail feathers widely

extended beyond the rest of the tail and causing them to vibrate very rapidly as the bird dives at great speed.

The underparts are pale with darker brown on the breast, while the neck and breast have dark streaking and the flanks dark barring. The axillary feathers under the wing are prominently barred in black and white. There is the narrowest of white lines along the inner half of the trailing edge of the wings. The bill is dark horn, legs and toes pale green.

The great snipe, which is rare, is almost a third larger, the underparts in autumn having prominent dark transverse barring, and there are twelve not fourteen tail feathers as in the snipe, the tail appearing much whiter.

All the snipe and the woodcock have their ears situated below and slightly in front of the eye.

The jack snipe or 'half snipe', with its much shorter bill, should be easily distinguished from the snipe, but this is not so, particular as it first jumps and flies silently off, when many get shot. Its small size makes it a disappointing return for a cartridge. When missed it usually quickly shuts its wings and drops down into cover again. Often within a hundred yards of where it was flushed, unlike the snipe which climbs high in the sky and goes far further. It is a legal quarry only in Northern Ireland.

When well seen, the jack snipe is decidedly darker above than a snipe with two narrow white wing bars, not extending on to the primaries. The tail shows no white, but there are fulvous longitudinal lines over the eyes and down the back, while the feathers of the mantle have purple metallic reflections. The underparts are greyish-white with darker streaking on the breast, flanks and under the tail. The bill is dark, legs and feet putty-brown. Unlike snipe, it is usually solitary.

The woodcock is a member of the wader family, but its normal habitat is more likely to bring it into the game or rough shooter's bag, than that of the wildfowler.

The woodcock's barred and chequered plumage of russet-brown, black, grey and buff forms a perfect example of protective coloration when the bird crouches in the woodland and under-growth, with dead leaves matching the plumage to perfection. In build it is a medium-sized snipe-like wader, but heavier and with rounder wings. The dark eye and broad black bars over the crown with narrow white dividing bars are the most obvious feature when the bird is seen at rest.

The bill which is about three times the length of the head is held downwards in flight. The tip of the upper mandible is soft, slightly mobile and contains delicate nerve endings, which no doubt facilitate finding earthworms, which form the bulk of its food, although insect larvae and seeds are also taken, as well as small freshwater molluscs. Its ear is unusually sited, being below the eye. This may also be an adaptation for food location.

Woodcock breed across the whole of the temperate zones of Europe and Asia to Japan, from the northern limits of the tree zone in Norway to the Pyrenees in the south. In Britain it is widespread and probably increasing as a breeding bird, favouring moist woodland with plenty of low ground cover under oak, birch, hazel, chestnut and conifer trees. Open rides, such as fire breaks cut through forestry plantations, suit it ideally for its display flights in spring, known as 'roding', when two or more may chase each other at speed through the woods uttering a rapidly repeated *pip-pip-pip* call. Part of this activity is to locate breeding females with which to mate.

The nest is often at the base of a tree, but sometimes in open grass or even in moorland and the clutches of three to six eggs

215

are pale buff, heavily blotched with dark chestnut. The downy young are as well camouflaged as their parents. The female cares for the young and will often feign injury either on the ground or by flying slowly, with her tail depressed and widely fanned out and with her legs dangling.

In 1848, Charles St John first described a woodcock flying in this attitude carrying a youngster between her thighs. This has now been seen by so many reliable witnesses that there can surely no longer be any doubt that woodcock do carry their young, but so far it has yet to be photographed. When doing so they fly in a rather more perpendicular attitude and may support the young with their beaks. It is probably true that they occasionally carry their young on their backs.

Migrant woodcock greatly swell the numbers in Britain in winter, particularly in years with persistent easterly winds in late autumn, which tend to 'drift' woodcock across the North Sea which might otherwise head south into France. Most come from Scandinavia, the Baltic States and Western Russia. Many appear as hard weather migrants.

For those who really know their woods, year after year wood-cock can be flushed from exactly the same spots. In winter, woodcock are particularly solitary birds and for this reason, as well as for their twisting and deceptive flight, a right-and-left is one of the most sought after and unusual achievements of any shooter. A spaniel is the ideal dog for finding woodcock and, of course, this was how the cocker spaniel came to be named.

SHOOTING WADERS

Tony Jackson writes:

There are now, as has been made clear above, only three legitimate wader quarry species – golden plover, woodcock and snipe (jack snipe too, if you live in Northern Ireland).

Golden plover are irregular visitors to the foreshore, flighting in large flocks from inland when the tide rolls away from the mudflats. They are delightful and among the most beautiful of the waders. Hold one to the light and admire the full, liquid eyes and glinting golden flecking. Swift, high fliers, they can often be brought within range by a random shot, the whole flock diving hard for the ground at the sound. But don't try 'browning' into the pack – the result will be a miss or one or two crippled birds.

Some of the finest sport I've had with goldies has been in Ireland. There they flight in great stands from one feeding field to another, perhaps a mile or so away, so that with guns at each end of the line, the birds are kept on the move. Bags were never large, but if we returned with a dozen goldies we were content, for the shooting had been exhilarating.

Snipe are sometimes roused on the foreshore, usually when they have been driven from their soft inland feeding by a hard frost. But they are no lovers of the mudflats, moving on at the first hint of a thaw.

Woodcock, too, though strictly speaking waders, are only seen below the sea wall when migrating in the late autumn and early winter from Scandinavia. Often, after a storm-tossed, exhausting crossing of the North Sea, they are so weary that it would be grossly unfair to take advantage of them. I've known them so tired you can pick them up!

Snipe and woodcock really come into their own inland. Snipe hold a particular fascination for me, perhaps because I shoot (or shoot at!) a considerable number every season on my marsh shoot and have, to some extent, mastered the fragile art of hitting them. They are intensely loyal to certain favoured spots, such as soggy, poached tracks round gateways and the edges of pools and gutters. Again and again, a snipe will twist up from the old familiar spot, no matter how often one shoots there. The great joy of snipe is that their presence will enliven even the most unlikely day and turn what might otherwise be a blank into an enjoyable outing.

There are several schools of thought: those who maintain that snipe should be walked upwind so that they offer a slightly less difficult shot as they rise into the wind before turning, and those who prefer to walk them downwind to take, as they claim, a simple going away shot. Personally, I shoot snipe as and how the fancy takes me, and have never applied hard and fast rules. Just occasionally, though, upwind or down, they are quite unapproachable, rising fifty or sixty yards away and giving the gunner no chance at all. I have found that the long-bills are usually in a restless, nervous mood during a wild, windy day or at the first sign of a really hard frost. The day after a full moon can produce good sport, for the snipe will have fed during the night, and will be resting and digesting their well-earned worms.

As to shooting snipe I can only suggest that you fire when the 'picture' seems right. Personally, I let the bird get out some distance before pulling the trigger: it is more likely to have straightened out after the initial jinking and the pattern will stand a better chane. No. 7 or 8 shot is usually recommended, though I invariably kill my birds with No. 6 and they are seldom if ever damaged. Snipe, like teal, do not carry shot, and one or two pellets are normally enough to knock them down.

Woodcock, too, are very much creatures of habit, consistently returning to the same spot year after year. It may be a soggy patch of scrub at one end of a covert, a bracken-choked clump of silver birches or a thicket of rhododendrons, but whatever the favoured locale, when the woodcock are 'in' one or two birds will be found there, appearing mysteriously overnight and vanishing just as promptly when the mood takes them. Many birds work their way westwards and some of the finest shooting is in Cornwall, Ireland and the Outer Hebrides.

Jack snipe. Can only legally be shot in Northern Ireland.

However, the average shot is most likely to meet them when rough shooting or during a pheasant drive. Woodcock have earned a reputation, deservedly I think, for being tricky shots. They rise silently, like owls. They tend to weave and twist in woodland, using trees for cover. Although their flight is relatively slow once in the open, they keep low, often turning back over the beaters or slipping between the two guns. Cool nerves and restraint are called for with woodcock. No bottle of liquor for that coveted right and left, or pin-feathers in your hatband are worth a moment's carelessness and someone's life endangered.

Shooting Duck Above and Below the Sea Wall

Tony Jackson

When I was a 'prentice fowler, a good many moons ago, I set foot upon the foreshore with a head stuffed with theory gleaned from a dozen works ranging from Hawker to Duncan and Thorne, all boiling down to the simple fact, as I then thought, that each evening, by Divine Decree, duck leave the sea and flight inland to feed, reversing the process at dawn. In practice, as I was soon to discover, although this pleasant rule is known and practised by a good many duck, others have their own ideas and flight patterns. Life for the fowler, inland or below the sea wall, is seldom so concise or clear cut.

The duck-shooter and wildfowler has several opportunites to get on terms with duck. He can discover their flight line and hope to ambush them. He can wait for them at their feeding ground in the evening or shoot them as they leave it in the morning. He can walk them up inland, stalk them on the foreshore, waylay them on a tide flight or take advantage of any unusual weather conditions such as gales, fog or snowstorms, when the duck may constantly be moving in a restless, aimless fashion.

But let's begin at the start of the duck season. The foreshore shooter may pick up the odd mallard or teal. But in early September, when the summer is still lingering in the warm, golden days and autumn has scarcely made its presence felt, the inland duck shooter can enjoy some splendid sport with stubbling mallard. Teal, too, for I have often known these little duck come to the stubbles, particularly favouring those which have been burnt. Mallard at this time of the year are in superb condition. For my money, a corn-fed September mallard, dripping with fat and garnished with orange sauce is unbeatable.

Obviously if you have permission to shoot there and suspect that duck may be drawn to the stubbles, it is well worthwhile spending time in reconnaissance for a fortnight before September 1. You may not have suspected their presence, for duck move at times when most folk are busying themselves about tea or television. Yet, if there are good numbers of duck in your area, perhaps based on reservoirs or rivers, then it is well worthwhile keeping an eye open for stubbles, especially on high ground. Tell-tale droppings and feathers will soon give the game away.

The major problem with stubbling duck is getting within range. Duck have a tendency to veer away from potential danger spots such as hedges and gates, preferring to feed well out in the open. If the field is very large, the only answer may be a bale hide. It should be sited so that you are in a position to deal with duck which will *invariably* land upwind. In other words the wind should be over your shoulder so that the duck are coming towards you as they land. Patience is important, for under calm conditions mallard will circle again and again until their suspicions are allayed. Risk a shot at forty yards and you will probably miss and ruin the flight.

Ideally one should choose an evening when a stiff wind is blowing. The duck will come in without hesitation and the sound of shots will be muffled. Personally, I prefer to let the first bunch settle. They will draw subsequent duck and a flight will be established. Once the light has gone, you will be able to stand in the open and shoot *provided* you keep still. I have proved time and again that duck will ignore you if there is no movement. This applies to all conditions of flighting in the evening.

You can, of course, utilise a hedge in the hope that the duck will be sufficiently low for a shot. On gusty evenings, this will probably work well, but there is always the difficulty of knowing precisely at which point along the hedge they will cross.

I have never used decoys though I understand from those who have that they work extremely well. No reason why they shouldn't, though once it is dark they are unlikely to be of much use.

How often one should shoot stubbling duck depends to some extent on when the field is to be ploughed and how much scattered grain is available. Two or three nights consecutive shooting will soon convince the duck that there are better pastures elsewhere, so be sensible and space your shooting. If you have had a good evening's sport try to ensure that your cartridge cases are picked, even if it means returning the next day. Little things like this will show the farmer that you have consideration for his land – and don't fail to drop him in a brace of duck!

FLIGHT PONDS

While duck are as fickle as most fowl – here today and gone tomorrow—some degree of consistency can be achieved by the use of flight ponds. They may be highly artificial and elaborate, and none the worse for that, or perhaps a converted farm pond or a natural fed-in splash. Invariably the key-note to success is consistent feeding, restrained shooting and good management. There is no particular difficulty about making heavy bags of mallard at the start of the season. Restraint is often necessary. September mallard, when the young are still weak on the wing and lacking discretion, can easily be drawn to vast quantities of grain. It should also be borne in mind that the duck from a wide area will come in, many of them probably hand-reared by clubs and individuals.

One of the most encouraging facets of flight pond shooting is the realisation that there are few places in this country to which duck cannot be attracted by the judicious siting of a hole in the ground. Provided there is a population of duck somewhere in the area – on a reservoir, the sea, rivers or lakes – then it is possible to obtain sport where hitherto duck have been virtually unknown.

Natural flight ponds can often be constructed from the most unpromising material – choked farm ponds, half-forgotten and near-empty pools overhung and shadowed by trees, in fact the most unlikely puddles. Often ponds which, at first glance, may appear perfect for duck have the major disadvantage of being too deep. Mallard, and especially teal, prefer soft, boggy edges leading to shallows and a depth of about eighteen inches in the centre. There should be 'loafing points' – islands or artificial rafts, securely anchored – on which the duck can preen and doze, secure from attack. It is not necessary, or even particularly desirable, to have a vast expanse of water. A small pool, provided it offers food and security, may draw duck more readily than a lake which may well be exposed, draughty, deep and with little food available. Many lakes are, of course, frequently used during the daylight hours. Here duck can sleep and rest well away from the shoreline, flighting out at dusk to those cosy ponds with their grain-lined shallows.

It is, naturally, far simpler to shoot a small pond as there will be no uncertainty regarding the flight line and the guns can be disposed to the greatest advantage. Duck do not care to force their way through a tangle of branches so the pool should be relatively clear, though, if necessary, a few alders and willows can be planted against the prevailing wind to help provide shelter.

'Instant flight ponds', can be constructed with the judicious assistance of a dragline. The cost of hiring a machine and driver is usually reasonable and the results can be gratifyingly swift. One has the immense advantage of being able to site and organise the pond to your exact requirements. Don't make it a simple square or oval but see that minor bays and creeks are excavated to provide shelter. The spoil can be dumped so that it too acts as a barrier against the wind. A word of warning! Any construction which involves alteration to natural or artificial drainage may well call for permission from the local authorities. So don't try to dam the local river!

Explosives have reached some prominence as a means of short-circuiting the drudgery of digging, but obviously this method can only be undertaken by experts operating under licence. However, if one has a suitable area such as a small marsh and is prepared to undergo the formalities, a pattern of small, shallow pools can greatly enhance its attraction to duck.

One cannot lay down hard and fast rules about hides. So much depends on the type of pond and the surrounding cover. Some pools may have a surrounding growth which cuts out the need for artificial hides, others are so sparse that some form of cover is essential. A large pond can have permanent wooden hides, incorporating seats and such refinements as cartridge shelves, duck-boards and something to which the dog can be attached if necessary. Some really luxurious ponds are equipped with sunken barrels. Whatever the type, two sets of hides will probably be needed to allow for different winds.

I am familiar with one pool, hand dug in the Norfolk Broads, which has magnificent natural butts of trained willow, fashioned into a circle with a narrow entrance. Permanent hides, however, can seldom be built near a public thoroughfare. They're too obvious. This is where portable hides of netting and stakes offer a simple solution.

Flighting at dusk certainly calls for experience. The chances are in the duck's favour. The light is failing and the birds come and go like wraiths. Nevertheless, one can take certain precautions to shorten the odds. At evening flight, face the west if possible so that duck will be silhouetted against the afterglow. You will find this particularly useful when the sky is clear. As it grows darker, duck will be virtually invisible against the deep blue sky yet can still be spotted when they cross the pallid light in the west.

Ears as well as eyes are vital for successful flighting. You may hear the off-key piping of a cock teal, the whirr of a mallard's wings or the distant *whee-oo* of wigeon long before the birds appear. Learn to distinguish the late-returning rooks and jackdaws, the rolling drunken flight of a lapwing and the tearing rush made by snipe which can sometimes be confused with teal. Above all remain constantly alert. Never relax your vigilance for a moment. If you have a dog – and you certainly should – keep half an eye on him for an experienced animal will spot or hear duck long before you. Watch for his upward head movements.

Don't fire too soon. Let the duck come right in. Your object is to kill cleanly and you can best do this when the bird is at its most vulnerable – approaching and preparing to land. Don't risk snap shots at birds circling the water at extreme range. You are likely only to prick them, even if you connect, and merely ruin the chance of a more certain shot in a moment or two. Keep an eye on any duck which you think you have hit but which carries on, for it may suddenly collapse or dive for cover. If it is too dark to see, use your ears and listen for the thud which may spell success.

The weather plays a key role in flighting. A blustery evening, with the cloud driven across the sky will keep the duck low. They will tend to flight straight in, without preliminary cautious circling. The twenty-four hours before a freeze and the period during a thaw usually show some good sport, for the duck seem to sense the arrival of bad weather or its departure and are eager to take advantage of changing conditions.

225

Remember that a half to full moon may mean the duck flight late. It is well worth waiting on past normal flight time if there has been no action. Make it a rule always to stop shooting when duck are still coming. Dawn flighting on ponds is rarely profitable and may, in fact, drive the duck away permanently. Obviously there are exceptions. Every duck situation must be assessed individually. Hard and fast rules do not apply.

The use of call-ducks – white or semi-tame mallard – needs careful consideration. Mallard are notoriously aggressive and it has frequently been noted that, far from attracting wild duck, these decoys may repel them. They've staked their territorial claims and will brook no interference.

Apart from flight ponds, pools and splashes, excellent sport can often be had when the rains of late autumn and winter spill across broad river valleys or marshes. Unfortunately for duck shooters, many Water Authorities have recently been making strenuous efforts to curtail winter flooding by dredging and embanking rivers and drainage systems. The results have sometimes been dramatic. I was familiar with a wide river valley in Sussex whose green acres were, from October onwards, a vast sheet of water – an inland sea – where literally thousands upon thousands of wigeon, teal, pintail and mallard could be seen, resting in huge rafts or racing across the skies. Now, after extensive drainage, there is seldom more than the odd splash and the duck have almost entirely deserted.

Where water meadows do still flood, decoys come into their own. Hides, permanent or portable, will normally be necessary, for much of one's shooting will be during the day. Rough, gusty weather is an advantage as the duck will be kept constantly on the move. If the flood is close to the sea wall, dirty weather will send the duck streaming in from the sea to settle on the comparatively calm fresh waters.

Decoys should not be set too close to the gunner. Duck are likely to flight over high, spot the 'coys, dropping towards them against the wind. The gunner should be between the decoys and the approaching duck, with his back obviously to the wind. He will then, we hope, have a relatively easy shot.

Be extremely cautious if you try wading a deep flood. Better by far to use some sort of craft such as a gun-punt or shallow-draft dinghy. It is too simple to fall into a forgotten gutter or ditch. If you do wade carry a pole to test the ground in front of you. Thumb-sticks are ideal. Gateways, barbed wire and hedges all offer cover and netting can easily be strung from them. If you expect a substantial bag carry a sack for the slain.

WALKING-UP

Duck can be walked up through most of the season, though September and October are the prime months. Cover is still thick and mallard and teal are inclined to haunt dykes, rides and ditches, only rising at the last moment or when a questing dog turfs them out. Their numbers are controlled by the amount of flooding locally available. In a dry winter one is more likely to find duck along the edges of rivers and ditches.

Remember, if you are walking a river that bends, to approach curves at right-angles, for duck are quite likely to be tucked under the bank, avoiding the main current. On my own marsh the river is bordered by huge banks formed as a result of dredging, so that, provided one spots them before they see you, duck can easily be approached without detection.

Occasionally a wounded duck, if it drops in water, will provide a severe test for a dog. Some animals, with age and experience, become adept at catching swimming and diving duck under water, but a youngster is likely to be quite baffled, swimming around head in air, puzzled by the abrupt disappearance of his quarry just as it seemed within his jaws. In such circumstances, make sure that the dog is out of the way, then stand back and shoot the bird the moment it appears. Diving duck, such as pochard and tufted, have an uncanny knack of being able to 'duck the flash'. I have several times seen a bird literally vanish as the shot splatters the surface, only to reappear apparently unharmed a few seconds later.

BEYOND THE SEA WALL

I have always maintained, to the irritation of some of my shooting friends, that a duck shooter can only really call himself a wildfowler if he shoots beyond the sea wall. There, in that magic world of huge skies, empty landscapes and the tangled, spicy smells of the foreshore, the fowler is very much alone. An element of danger has added a new dimension to his sport. Danger from tide, wind, fog and mud to trap the unwary and over-confident. Let's not over-emphasise this aspect of the sport − hundreds of wildfowlers go from season to season with barely a hint of drama. Much depends on the area, for some parts of the coast are inherently more dangerous than others. Nevertheless, one must never, at any time, underestimate the elements. Fog is extremely dangerous, tides may be thrust, ahead of schedule and forecast height, by an unexpected wind, while mud has a nasty habit of shifting its bad patches from season to season with the swirl and suck of the tides.

So the wildfowler must be prepared for emergencies. This does not mean that he has to set out for the foreshore festooned with the contents of an army surplus stores! First and most vital he must have a copy of the local tidetable and be able to read it. Tides vary all round the coast so the exciting knowledge that it is low water at Tower Bridge may be of less than vital interest as the water laps your waist at Mudmarsh-on-Sea! Remember that gales up-Channel can make all the difference to a tide, perhaps forcing it well above its usual height and two hours ahead of schedule. Pay careful heed to local weather forecasts. Phone the Met service if in doubt. It's not a bad thing to do, anyway.

The second line of defence is a good compass. One of the best is an ex-army one which straps to your wrist. You must know how to read a compass and to take back and forward bearings.

A compass has uses other than safety. One can, for instance, take a forward bearing on a wounded goose observed to drop on the mud half a mile away.

A rubber encased torch, a powerful model, is an obvious requirement, particularly when looking for fallen birds or negotiating a gutter after dark. Buy the type with a ring attachment so that it can be secured to your waist or bag.

Mud can be dangerous in more ways than one. There are few fowlers who have not suffered the frustration of barrels choked with the wretched stuff, probably due to a stumble or fall, and usually in the middle of the flight of the season! The answer is a cleaning rod, carried in the bag, which can be unscrewed into three or four sections. Do *not* attempt to shoot while there is the slightest trace of mud, or for that matter snow, in the barrels.

As far as bags go, I prefer an army back pack or even rucksack rather then a sidebag, especially where there is a good deal of walking and carrying involved. A sidebag has a tendency to bump your hip and can soon cause discomfort. I strongly advise you to carry your gun in a canvas slip if there is no likelihood of a shot while you are setting out for your hide. Alternatively one can have swivels fitted to barrels and stock to take a.sling, though personally I find an encumbrance such as this distracts my attention while shooting. If, like me, you like to slide your left hand well forward, you may keep catching it on the swivel.

Cartridges can be carried in a belt, or, if plastic cartridges, in the pockets. If you use a cartridge belt, be sure it has closed loops. The open ones expand with use and the cartridges become difficult to extract.

For years now I have used a wooden swivel seat to keep my bottom off the mud. It is, I believe, the ideal shooting seat and I'm surprised more people don't use one. It consists of two pieces of wood about twelve inches by eight inches, joined when in use by a short metal rod. This fits into sockets attached to the underside and top of each piece of wood. The advantages of the seat are that it literally spins as you turn for a sitting shot and can be taken apart with ease, taking up little extra room in the bag.

Final minor items of equipment should include a cartridge-extractor, whistle and a strong, sharp knife, not to forget that Thermos flask of hot soup. On dangerous estuaries, some wild-fowlers include a distress flare in their pack, but with common sense you should never need to use one.

The right clothing is vital. You've got to keep warm and dry and still be free to shoot. Today thermal underwear has virtually solved the problems associated with cold, bitter weather. In the old days we used to wear ladies' tights or pyjamas under our shooting trousers or breeks to try and create some insulation but now, thanks to modern technology, all that is past. You can even include hand and foot warmers in your list of essentials if you want to feel really pampered. Seaboot stockings and thighboots complete the bottom half and a pair of short, waterproof over-trousers will keep your behind dry. Make sure your thighboots are full length and not the 'shorty' type which come only just above the knee. Apart from any other commendation, the part above the knee is good to kneel on.

As far as the upper regions are concerned, a thermal vest,

flannel shirt and thick, heavy jersey, topped by a waterproof, waxed cotton shooting coat, will keep you warm and dry in the foulest of weather. A heavy-weight waxed cotton coat, specifically designed for 'fowling is, in my opinion, absolutely unbeatable for work below the sea wall. You're going to be plastered with mud, at one stage or another, and if you are worried about preserving the pristine condition of a state-of-the-art coat you will never be able to concentrate on the sport.

As to headgear, every 'fowler has his own ideas. I prefer a balaclava in dry weather, supplemented by a waterproof, snap-on hood for less clement days. Caps and hats will simply be blown out to sea, and you do not require headgear with a prominent peak which cuts off your overhead vision.

Gloves or mittens are again a matter of personal taste − some folk swear by them, others detest them. You can, if you wish, go the whole hog, like Colonel Hawker, and dip your hands in the icy water at the start of the day − thereafter, he swore, you did not notice the cold!

Even the newest fowler is aware of the two basic movements of duck − at dusk and dawn. In the evening, they normally flight from the sea to feed inland during the hours of darkness, returning the following morning at first light. This is putting the matter in simple terms. There are several factors which may upset the schedule, such as a full moon encouraging the duck to flight late, or a sudden gale forcing them to seek shelter behind the sea wall. Tides, too, have a major influence on duck movements.

To some extent the movement of duck, and in particular, the point where they will cross the sea wall, will be dictated by the available food supply. In the autumn, mallard fly to stubbles, then, as these are ploughed in, turn to ponds, floodwater and potato fields.

Tide flights are another feature of the foreshore, but are largely governed by weather. In calm, 'butterfly' days the duck will merely drift up and down with the tide during the day, showing little inclination to move till dusk. However, rough, stormy weather will send them seeking shelter in calmer waters and they may well move backwards and forwards along the edge of the tide, uncertain and unsettled. Teal, in particular, are inclined to follow the contours of large gutters and an ambush can often yield a useful bag as they head for the sea wall.

Although far more are now found inland, I always tend to associate wigeon with the mudflats. There is a tiny resident population in this country but the main influx comes from abroad in October and early November, numbers often being boosted when the Baltic is frozen. There was a time, before the last war, when eel or wigeon grass (*Zostera marina*) was the principal food of wigeon. But there seems to have been a disease affecting the *Zostera* throughout the North Atlantic. *Spartina*, or cord grass, introduced by man, has ousted *Zostera* throughout much of the coastline. *Spartina* is useless as a food plant. The wigeon have turned to sweet inland grass and, naturally enough, have moved to freshwater splashes and floods. The Ouse Washes in winter hold a maximum population of over 30,000.

Wigeon can still be found on the coast, but in nothing like their former numbers. On odd occasions, superb sport can be had just after the spring tides when the shallow pans and flashes on the high saltings where the grass is sweet, are flooded to a

depth of a few inches. A careful survey will show, by droppings, feathers and torn-up grass, where the wigeon are feeding. If all goes well, the sky is covered with fleecy cloud illuminated by a moon, the tide is rising and there is a strong wind, you may have the flight of a lifetime. But there are so many ifs!

Concealment on the foreshore calls for some intelligence and observation. The basic requirement is clothing which blends with the background. The ubiquitous donkey jacket, once so often seen, stands out like a polar bear in the desert against any background – even at dusk. It is equally pointless wearing an elaborately camouflaged jacket if the foreshore is sheeted in snow. A milkman's jacket and white cap are not difficult to procure and will make the difference between a full and an empty bag. Although no lover of face-nets I concede that on the fore-shore they can be a boon – nothing is more likely to turn duck than a white face peering over the edge of a gutter. You can, if you wish, smear your face and hands with mud, but it rather depends on your degree of fanaticism!

Duck are incredibly wary and it wants only the slightest move-ment to send them sheering off in alarm. If you are using a gutter for cover, try to stamp out a firm foothold. It's pointless to try to take difficult shots when you may be half slipping down a mud slide. Select a point in the gutter with a fringe of crab-grass or other vegetation and keep your head down, using your eyes and not your head. You will soon acquire the habit of glancing from side to side, a sort of lighthouse 'sweep', as you watch for duck.

There is often natural camouflage on the foreshore in the shape of tree roots, storm-tossed timber and the wreckage of boats which, with the judicious use of netting, can make adequate hides. Fowl soon become used to such objects littering the shore and tend to ignore them.

A portable hide can often come in very handy. I have in mind a roll of fine netting, and three or four light, short poles. The entire thing can be bundled up and strapped under the flap of your knapsack. Make sure the hide has a low silhouette; the foreshore is flat and a sudden protuberance will excite suspicion.

Always bear in mind the insidious, creeping menace of a rising tide. It is so easy, when the tide has dropped far away, leaving acres of mud exposed, to imagine you have all the time in the world. You haven't! Once the tide starts to move, it will gurgle into the gutters at an incredible pace, and creeks which you crossed with only an inch or so of water in the bottom are soon terrifying rivers. Never manoeuvre yourself into such a position that one or more large gutters have to be negotiated in order to reach safety; far better to follow the edge of a creek as it meanders seawards, even if it takes longer.

There is a definite art to walking on mud. I have often seen beginners trapped in mud scarcely up to their knees – trapped largely because they panic and flounder as soon as they feel themselves sinking. The secret is to keep moving at all costs and to put your feet into the mud toes first. An experienced mud-walker conveys the impression that he is almost skating across the mud. A thumbstick is a 'must'. With it you can probe ahead and retain your balance.

Goose Shooting

Arthur Cadman

No sportsman can be fully successful unless he studies in great detail the habits of the quarry which he pursues and also their exact habitat. It goes without saying that he must also be able to identify his quarry correctly – and geese can be confusing. Jeffery Harrison has written elsewhere in this book on their identification and natural history (see pages 172–205) so I will confine myself to one or two points and a useful identification chart.

The wild geese of Britain are divided into two categories: the black geese – Canadas, barnacle, brent and redbreasted: and the grey geese – greylags, bean, pinkfeet and whitefronts, which are sub-divided into European, Greenland and lesser.

Of the black geese it is legal to shoot only Canadas. Canada geese (*Branta canadensis*) were introduced to Britain 250 years ago. They became semi-domesticated and lost their migratory instinct. But many Canadas now migrate annually in June to the Beauly Firth for the moult, returning in September. They have increased enormously and become established as feral geese in a great number of localities, although there are only a few areas in Scotland where they are resident.

Canada geese frequent inland lakes – the meres of Cheshire and Shropshire are typical of thosë referred – from whence they flight to nearby pastures or stubbles to feed. There are places where they flight to the open shore to roost, but in Britain their habitat is primarily inland. They are not as wary as the grey geese and tend to fly at lower levels.

Barnacle geese (*Branta leucopsis*) are very much smaller with an average weight of $4\frac{1}{2}$lb. The barnacle has a white face, with a dark, smudgy eye streak and a black top to the head. The neck is black with a black front to the breast. The rest of the plumage is a pale grey. In flight, no other goose gives such an impression of being pale blue-grey. Their call note is a yelp, rather like a pack of yapping pekinese. Barnacle geese belong to the salt marsh and 'machair', or short turf, of the outer Isles. Occasionally the Solway barnacles flight to potato fields. They roost on tidal estuaries. They are protected, and may be viewed from the Caerlaverock Reserve, near Dumfries. Sometimes white barnacles are present.

Brent geese are now fully protected.

Brent geese (*Branta bernicla*) are protected. They are small geese and look black. Their heads and necks and upper breasts are black, with a white patch each side of the upper neck rather like that of a wood pigeon. The wings and back are dark grey. They are almost entirely sea geese and only occur inland by accident. Their feeding habits on *Zostera*, or eel grass, are controlled by the tide, half flow and half ebb being the optimum period. They do not fly in V-formations as frequently as other species. The call is a resonant honk or 'krruk'. In recent years they have been feeding inside the sea-wall on pasture and winter wheat, where they cause considerable damage. Numbers have increased to well over 100,000.

The redbreasted goose (*Branta ruficollis*) is an accidental visitor, there being some twenty records. Usually they occur with European whitefronts, having got lost on migration. They breed in West Siberia and winter in the south of the Caspian Sea and Persia. They are protected.

The grey geese are much more easily confused, but the main identification pointers can be summarised in a simple chart. For the finer points I recommend you to consult Jeffery Harrison (pages 172–205).

Identification chart for grey geese.

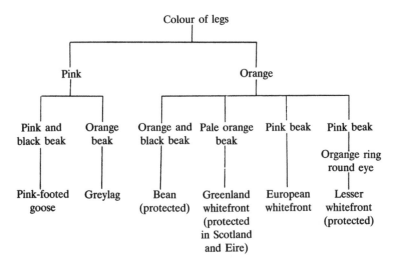

The main habitats of the grey geese vary somewhat. Greylags and pinkfeet are primarily geese of the agricultural lands. Their main feeding areas are pasture fields, stubbles, potato fields, after frost has broken down the small potatoes left on the surface, winter wheat, reseeded fields and in the spring, early corn and the 'early bite'. In very hard weather greylags will eat turnips. This is a comparatively recent habit, which pinkfeet have not yet followed. They will eat carrots. Both species will feed readily on salt marshes, when there is sufficient freedom from disturbance. Greylags have been hand-reared and released and there are now feral flocks in England and Anglesey, and parts of Scotland.

Bean geese are similar in their feeding habits, but they spend rather more time on pasture land than on arable. European whitefronts are also mainly geese of the pastures and, particularly, freshwater marshes. They also use saltings.

The Greenland whitefront has the most specialised habitat. These geese frequent acid bogs in high rainfall areas. This is because their favourite food is the root of the common cotton grass (*Eriophorum angustifolium*) and also in spring the young fresh shoots of the white beak sedge (*Rhyncosphora alba*). Both these plants grow in waterlogged peat bogs. But Greenland whitefronts also graze freely on pastures and rushy meadows. They tend to split up into smaller groups than the other grey geese, which, at times, congregate into very large flocks, sometimes numbering several thousand.

In broad terms the behaviour pattern of all the grey geese is similar. They roost at night, using the nearest estuary or open sands on the shore. Owing to pressure of shooting on the shore, geese have taken more and more to roosting on inland lakes, reservoirs or mountain lochs and, sometimes on shingle banks and the backwaters of wide rivers. Flood water is readily used, provided that the flood is not too violent. At dawn they flight from the roost to the feeding ground. If the feeding ground is a sanctuary with but little disturbance, they tend to flight earlier than they do when there is a probability of danger on the feeding areas. Thus they may flight in the half-light at duck flighting time: but usually it is broad daylight before they move. Although geese may fly considerable distances daily to their feeding area (e.g. from the Humber up to the Yorkshire wolds) the usual distance is not often much greater than five miles, and very often much less.

During fog, geese will be late flighting. If the fog is likely to lift, then they seem to sense this and they will wait for it to disperse. But if it is set in, then they are reluctant to leave the shore. They will often fly up and down the saltings and drop into the first fields they find.

During a long, black frost they tend to flight earlier in the morning and later in the evening, because they are extra hungry. But during a heavy white hoar frost, they may delay their morning flight. When they arrive on their grass feeding area, they often sit about, 'warming their toes', until the hoar frost thaws. Perhaps, like deer, they do not like eating blades of grass coated in hoar frost.

Pressure of shooting has a considerable effect upon their behaviour patterns. Where they are coming to a sanctuary, they plane down and settle on the chosen area quite quickly. But when shooting pressure is heavy, they circle high, often many times, before venturing to settle. Once geese are on the ground, other geese of the same species in the area quickly find them. A flock of sixty to two hundred geese may build up to a thousand during the course of the day. Thereafter they feed in the same area each day until the ground gets stale, food is used up or disturbance takes place.

Pinkfeet and greylags may use the same field, but, if they do, they remain in their separate flocks on different parts of the field. Usually they have their own separate feeding areas. They roost on different parts of an estuary or lake. But a single goose of any species, or even a small group, may be attracted to a large gathering of a different species, if none of its own species is within the area.

There are a number of popular fallacies about geese. It is true that geese are very strong hardy birds. They fly high and fast by nature, and adverse weather probably has less effect upon geese than on any other birds. They are keen-sighted, wary and quick to spot danger. But they are not possessed of great cunning, as some would have one believe. It is often said that when geese are feeding, a sentinel is posted to keep a look out, and that, from time to time, this sentinel is relieved by another who takes his place! This is nonsense. Every goose in the flock is a potential sentinel and each goose, from time to time, puts up its head to look for danger. As with deer, the oldest ones do this much more frequently than the young. When an old gander has spotted something which he distrusts, most of the heads in that part of the flock will soon be up. Then, the slightest movement from a hidden fowler will put all away. But none of this is the result of a specially posted sentinel.

Another fallacy is that a scout is sent out to look over the feeding ground before the main body of geese arrives. It is very easy to believe this, because often a single goose does arrive in the half light and it does fly round the field calling. The truth is that these solitary geese, which arrive early, are either young birds which have become separated from their family party, or they are one of a pair whose mate has been shot. If a careful watch is kept it will be seen that they do not mingle readily with the main flock. They are restless and very often move right away again. They also call most of the time. They are foolhardy and often provide the only good chance!

A single goose may be a 'pricked' or wounded bird. But in that case it will tend to flight *after* the main skeins have gone. Or, if it flights at the same time it will tend to fly, settle and feed somewhat apart from the rest. It is usually silent, too.

The normal morning/evening flighting routine becomes less regular during the period of the full moon. All the goose species may move to feed during the night when the moon is full, but greylags do this much less than the others. There are various factors which affect this: clear moonlight is essential; an overcast moon, even though there may be better light than during the period of the dark of the moon, will not tempt them to fly, but they may swim to the edge of a loch or float in to the saltings on the tide, and then walk onto land. A strong wind is likely to cause them to flight under the moon. This is especially so when they are roosting on tidal areas. As the tide reaches their sandbank, the choppy waves become uncomfortable and a moon flight often results. The last factor is hunger. In early October, the hours of daylight are long and the food supply is lavish and the geese are well fed. Later in the winter, days are short and food supply less plentiful. Four hours after their last feed, the geese are ready to feed again. If the moonlight is clear, they will be tempted to move to a feeding area. When flighting under the moon, they tend to move in small skeins and family parties. They fly lower and they may use fields nearer the roost than during the day. Sometimes they will remain on the feeding ground in the evening and not flight out to the roost.

Many wildfowlers have never shot a goose. There are some shooters, who are not wildfowlers, who have − by chance. Luck plays a very important part. Once I was waiting on the Solway in the teeth of a south-westerly gale. I knew the geese would come out low and I was well concealed. Just at the moment when the geese should have been flighting, a youth walked past me carrying a single-barrel gun and wearing flannel trousers and smart 'winkle pickers' on his feet. He stood upright sixty yards from me in full view. Within a matter of moments a big skein of pinks came beating into the gale, straight over his head. He put up his gun and two fell dead to his single shot. I helped him pick them up and asked him: 'Have you shot many geese this season?' 'No,' he replied, 'I've never tried before. Easy, isn't it?'

The would-be goose shooter should study the daily movements of the geese in his area. He should know where they are feeding, or at least in what direction their feeding grounds lie: and where they have been roosting. It is very important to remember that tide and wind have a very significant influence on the flight-line in the morning. In the evening they will settle in what may be called the evening roost, which is, according to the state of the tide, either sandbank or water. If the weather is flat calm, they may be in the same position in the morning. More often they will move on the night tide, sometimes floating and drifting a considerable distance with it. Often, when the tide reaches them, they flight to a different part of the shore where there is more shelter. These are things which must be studied before deciding where to go to intercept them at morning flight. Geese take off (and of course settle) into the wind, but they will wheel quickly in order to get on course for their flight-line. Usually, once airborne, they fly direct to their feeding ground, but a strong cross-wind will cause them to drift downwind somewhat. It may be necessary to make allowance for this. Where shooting pressure is high they sometimes make a wide circle to gain height.

Having decided on the probable line of flight, the next problem is to pick a position where there is a chance of reasonable concealment. The good wildfowler is not the man who scrapes down a goose at extreme range with a lucky pellet: he is the man who can conceal himself adequately, where the geese will pass within thirty-five yards. It often works out that the better the cover is for concealment, the less likely are the geese to pass directly over it. Certainly the best chances come to he who can conceal himself adequately with the minimum amount of cover. Some knowledge of camouflage is necessary. Either you must be completely concealed, so that the geese just don't see you. Or you must become part of the landscape. They see you but do not recognise you as a man! A lying position can be the most effective, but one's angle of fire is restricted to an arc from 7 o'clock to 2 o'clock. When lying, one should try to position oneself so that, where head and feet are at 6 o'clock and 12 o'clock respectively, the geese will be coming from about 10 o'clock. Whatever position you are in, whether standing in a deep ditch, kneeling, crouching or lying, it is absolutely essential that there should not be the slightest movement until the geese are within range. The slightest movement of head, or of the left hand moving up the gun barrels, is enough to catch a wary eye and cause the whole skein to veer off just out of shot. When the normal call notes change to a grunting note, you can bet that you have been spotted and subsequent skeins which hear, or see, the alarmed geese will be warned. A face mask and gloves are necessities as nothing shows up more than a pink human face and hands!

It is also true that geese can be seen coming from a great distance. Sometimes it is possible to move quickly twenty or thirty yards to a better position, when they are still a long way off. Howerer, usually, it is more prudent to remain absolutely immobile in a moderately well-concealed place, than to risk any major move to a completely effective hide.

When two or more fowlers are returning after a morning flight, or walking to their evening position, it is wise to proceed singly at about forty yard intervals. If an unexpected skein of geese, or late flight of ducks, comes, then one of them is more likely to be placed well for a shot. A bunch of shooters walking along the top of a sea wall is obvious for miles. Yet, how often one sees this stupid mistake. Always walk under the sea wall or behind whatever cover there may be. On occasions I have seen two, or even three fowlers sitting all together for a flight. What could be more foolish? By being spaced out their chances are trebled and, anyway, it is difficult enough for one fowler to find good cover on the shore, let alone three in one place.

Whether one is lying or crouching, it is easier to hide behind a perpendicular creek face. The action of the tide leaves the sides of creeks rounded. There are few places which cannot be improved by a dozen strokes with a small spade.

Shooting geese inland is easier than on the open shore − but it is much less exciting! First one must have permission to shoot on the land. It is worthwhile spending some time watching the geese and planning a foray. What natural cover is there near where the geese are feeding? When considering this point, it is very easy to fall into the mistake of selecting the best possible cover, perhaps a large clump of gorse, or a very deep overgrown ditch, or a thick hedge, just because it is the best cover available. A wire fence crossing the flight-line is better than a deep ditch at the side, even if one has to use great ingenuity to become concealed. Modern farming has made goose shooting easier. Sometimes there is unbaled and unburnt straw lying on the field. Nothing is easier than to cover oneself with this in the centre of the field. Bales of straw are useful too, especially if they are put out in time for the geese to get used to them. But it is better to lie between four bales − two each side − than to make up a super hide of the greatest comfort and degree of concealment, which the geese will avoid like the plague. This is true of all hides for goose shooting

241

− the simple, small hide is more effective than a large elaborate one. The most practical mobile hide is one of netting interlaced with branches of broom, or other local material such as reeds, and supported by three good stakes. Such a hide can be rolled up and carried by a cord tied to each end. Background is important too.

Good decoys make shooting on the fields very easy. Decoys should not be set *all* facing upwind: that makes them too symmetrical and unnatural. The general tendency should be upwind. I like to arrange them so they are not all in one group. It is most effective to have some feeding, or sitting contentedly, with three or four outliers walking towards them. It is a very broad rule with all decoying that the greater the number of decoys the more efficiently they work. Two decoys may pull in singles and even perhaps half a dozen geese. The bigger lots will ignore them. To be effective one needs ten or a dozen.

The siting of the decoys in relation to the hide is important, but depends to some extent upon the wind strength and direction, and local topography. If one places them behind one, i.e. upwind, there is much more risk of being seen. If one puts them in front (downwind) geese may drop short. Where cover and layout are suitable, I like to be slightly downwind at the side, about thirty-five yards away.

It is exciting to watch a distant skein of geese high in the sky spot the decoys, set their wings, and 'come in'. It is almost as if one is winding them in on a string! But the shooting is easy and it behoves anyone shooting such wonderful birds as geese over decoys − or anywhere else where they are easy − to limit the bag. Half a dozen should be enough for anyone. On the fields a time limit should be imposed.

What gun and what ammo? This is the most frequent question of all. 'Use the gun that you shoot best with' is the soundest advice. There is a lot of space around a goose, big though it is, and it is surprisingly easy to miss. As for ammo: as I see it, this depends on two main factors − first the skill of the man behind the gun and secondly his skill in putting himself within fair range. As with all forms of shooting, pattern is of paramount importance. The first class shot, who can regard a goose's head as a snipe, and put the centre of the pattern just there, can kill a very tall goose with number six shot with a two-and-a-half-inch chambered game gun. My skill with a gun is not in that category and therefore I like a heavier size of shot. I use number three in the right and BB, or number one, in the left, whether I use my game gun or my three-inch magnum. In theory, BB in a game gun gives rather an open pattern. In practice, over the years, very many geese have ended up in the larder as a result of the BB. $1\frac{7}{8}$ oz of BB, which is the standard three-inch load, has tremendous shocking power. However the other day I saw a first-class shot kill two pinkfeet one morning, and two greylags the next, with a twenty-bore loaded with number five shot!

Any wildfowler, and particularly goose shooter, should carry a pair of field glasses. With glasses one can tell whether the 'blobs' out on the tide line are geese or oystercatchers. After the main flight is over, one can pick out the odd lot that has not yet moved. You can watch the distant V's in the sky and make a fair estimate as to their feeding and roosting grounds. And if you have the misfortune to wound a goose, you can watch it as far as possible. A wounded goose may carry on a long way before it comes down. It is a fair rule to pick a goose as quickly as possible. If a goose falls into thick cover, even if it appears to drop dead, it should be gathered without delay. A wing broken at the shoulder will cause a goose to fall like a stone. Once on the ground it will disappear very quickly.

A winged goose is more skilful than a cock pheasant in evading capture, although on bare ground, or mud, it may be some little while before it runs off. A goose that has come down, badly hit, but without a damaged wing, should be approached with caution. It may take off again, and fly clean away. One is more likely to get near enough to finish it off by an oblique, rather than direct, approach.

To kill a wounded goose quickly and humanely, hold it by the neck with its head between two fingers and then rotate the body three or four times rapidly. The neck will be dislocated causing instant death. A lightly wing-tipped goose may be kept alive and it will become tame remarkably quickly.

I am often asked what advice I can give to enable beginners to shoot geese well. I hesitate to define this, because it is easy to cause confusion. But there are several well accepted lines of advice. Bill Powell's 'Try to miss them in front' is sound. 'Forget the body and regard the head as a snipe' is also a good recipe.

My own successes are based on Major Ruffer's advice, which is to mount the gun pointing the muzzle at the bird all the time and fire as the gun comes into the shoulder. The tallest geese I have killed have been by following this method and not one inch of conscious 'lead' was given. The worst misses have been by trying to make a conscious 'lead'! But there is one very important item. When one is crouching in a cramped hide, or muddy creek with all foot movement impossible, it is so easy to mount the gun in a sloppy manner. Practise mounting the gun with the muzzle pointing at an imaginary target and the stock well into the cheek, frequently. That advice will add to the bag, whatever the quarry.

On the open shore a fowler should carry a compass. He should *never* go out without a pull-through. It is very easy to get sand, or mud, or snow up the barrels. Thighboots, waterproof trousers, waterproof shooting jacket, hat, face-mask and gloves are all more or less essentials. Whether to take a dog or not is often a problem. If there is enough cover for him, then take him, especially if shooting near a tideway. A goose dog must be trained to lie motionless, yet to be bold and very wide ranging, when collecting a wounded goose.

Every fowler *must* have a tide table. Before he leaves home he should know precisely where he intends to position himself.

The last point of all is one of fair sportsmanship. Geese are fine birds. They are also very tough. More foolish long shots are fired at geese than at any other bird. A higher proportion of geese carry pellets than do any other birds. To wound a goose is a sad thing, and it is all too easy to misjudge range, because geese are very large birds and look nearer than they are. They inhabit wide open spaces where it is easy enough to misjudge distances, anyway. I would make a plea for restraint at all times. It is so much better to hold one's fire, than to fire stupid long shots. It is also more productive because, if the first skeins go over safely, without being shot at, a later lot may come lower, and present a fair chance. It is so much better to kill a clean right and left at fair range, than to scrape down a fluke at a ridiculous distance. Not long ago I was next to a lady who was flighting geese for the first time. Her husband was the fine shot who killed two birds with a twenty bore, standing about eighty yards from her. Some greylags came over her about five gunshots up, probably on their way to the moon. To my surprise she fired two shots.

Afterwards she said: 'I'm sorry I missed those easy ducks that came right over my head!' Nothing could illustrate more clearly how very easy it is to misjudge geese, and distances. A fair rule is: 'If in doubt, don't fire.'

Shooting geese on their roost, or on their feeding grounds too frequently, will drive them from the area. Shooting at them with a rifle will do so even more quickly.

Barnacle geese.

V
STALKING

V

Stalking

I am not a stalker though I have stalked both roe and red deer. I have shot two Highland stags, as a result of which I came to the personal but not very original conclusion that the excitement was in the stalk, not in the shot. I have crept through Thetford Chase on an early June morning with a most accomplished Polish expert only to miss my buck as he showed fleetingly among the pine trees. Richard Prior, who contributes the woodland stalking section, initiated me into some of the mysteries of roe deer control in Cranbourne Chase when we were working together on his book in the Survival series, *Living with Deer*. Though I have been fascinated and enthralled and found the outdoor world of the deer as beautiful or magnificent as any I have experienced, stalking, I have to confess, is not for me. I cannot precisely explain why. Perhaps I haven't the steady temperament and infinite patience required. When it comes to it, I would as soon not pull the trigger, though I never think twice about doing so on a bird. I number at least three 'deer nuts' among my friends. They are all stalkers and two of them are highly skilled naturalist cameramen. The problem is to persuade them to film a subject other than deer by which they seem totally obsessed. Though I do not entirely share it, I can understand their sporting obsession with these shy, enticing creatures. The late Lea MacNally in his loving profile of Highland red deer, which begins this section of the book, goes a long way towards explaining the stalker-naturalist's involvement with his quarry. For my money, Richard Prior comes somewhere close to the heart of the matter when he compares the solitary joys of stalking with those of wildfowling.

C.W.

The Rifle

Richard Prior

The stalker's rifle is a great deal more than just a precision tool. It is his fragile bridge to success; potent and a little magical. Buying one is a major and expensive step to take. If a would-be stalker asks for advice from his friends, he risks being drowned in a cauldron of jargon stirred up by conflicting and rigidly held opinions. Each expert that he consults will have his own ideas based on different experience, and if in desperation he decides to ask a gunmaker, he may be worried by the thought that anything that is brought out may either be the most expensive weapon in the shop, or one that has been gathering its dust for years, obsolete and unloved.

Here are a few basic facts which will help with the decision: the rifle should be soundly constructed and well maintained; designed for a cartridge which is easily obtainable; capable of a high degree of accuracy; and suitable for the fitting of telescopic sights without unreasonable expense. Many are the strange gas-pipes which linger in the recesses of the gunmaker's workshop, but do not be misled into investing in one of these, lured on by an apparently low price or the high quality of the original work-manship. A lot of once famous cartridges are now completely unobtainable and weapons designed for them are no more than curiosities.

Bolt action rifles are reliable and a good choice for most people. They are time- and war-proven, capable of extreme accuracy and some models are even available in reversed form for left-handed stalkers. In contrast to target rifles, sporting bolt actions have a magazine holding three to five rounds for instant reloading.

Various single-shot rifles are made, mostly based on the Far-quharson falling-block action. Some of these are hand-made, others, like the Ruger No. 1, are factory-made. They are capable of fine accuracy. In the luxury class one finds rifles made on the drop-down principle like a coventional shotgun. Many double-barrelled rifles were made in this style around the turn of the century, some in .303, others in heavier calibres for big game. New ones, mostly made abroad, are often single-barrelled and the stalker must have a second cartridge handy in case a quick follow-up shot is necessary.

There is often some confusion about triggers, which come in three types. The double pull, the single pull and the set trigger. Riflemen with army experience will probably have a preference for the double pull, that is, when the finger is tightened on the trigger there is a perceptible movement against fairly light pressure, then a heavier pressure discharges the rifle. If, on the other hand, you learned to shoot with a .22, then the single pull will be more familiar. The best of these gives the impression of snapping a piece of glass. There is no perceptible movement of the trigger but at a pre-set pressure the sear is released and the cartridge fires.

Most continental stalkers are brought up to use the set- or hair-trigger, often a source of fumbling and even danger to anyone not accustomed to it. The rifle has two triggers like a double-barrelled shotgun. If the front trigger is pulled the rifle will fire, but only after a long dragging pull. If however the rear trigger is first clicked this sets the front trigger to go off with the merest touch. In another design there is only one trigger which can be pushed forward to 'set' the hair trigger. Habit and prejudice are bound to affect one's decision on this; certainly the hair-trigger has its uses when a deliberate shot at long range has to be made, but against this, I have on many occasions seen a roe alarmed by the click of the first trigger, giving no time for the change of grip and correction of aim necessary to reach the second. Whatever one decides, it would be most inadvisable to mix the two types.

CALIBRES

Accuracy is the most important thing, not fire power, but do not be misled by the gun bugs. Ultimate accuracy is produced by a match rifle, with all the trimmings of heavy barrel, fancy stocks and so on. This accuracy is not available to the stalker if his muscles are trembling with fatigue from lugging the monster up hill. Neither is the potential power of a super-magnum any use if the proud owner flinches every time he lets it off. To put the whole thing in a nutshell, it is best to make a short list of suitable cartridges, and then look for an accurate rifle chambered for one of them.

Choice is limited by the provisions of various legal enactments. which should be studied. At the time of writing the following apply:-

Area	Minimum calibre (inches)	Minimum bullet weight (grains)	Muzzle Velocity ft/sec	Muzzle Energy ft/lb	Species
England & Wales	.240	n.a.	n.a.	1700	All
Scotland	n.a.	100	2450	1750	All
	n.a.	50	2450	1000	Roe only
N Ireland	.236	100	n.a.	1700	All
Eire	.22	55	n.a.	1700	All

In all cases a soft- or hollow-point bullet must be used.

Particular note must be taken of cartridge denominations. Many continental calibres are marked in millimetres, e.g. 8×64, the first being the calibre and the second the cartridge length. This may be followed by letters which have a very precise meaning. Cartridges for the $8 \times 57\,JR$ will not, for example, exchange with those for the $8 \times 57\,JRS$. English measurements can also be confusing, for instance, the .303 Savage, an obsolete cartridge, will not exchange with the .303 British, for years our Service cartridge. Many rifles in different actions are available for the latter, and if in good condition and otherwise suitable they should not be despised. Modern ammunition for the .303 British is perfectly suitable for deer stalking. Enthusiasts tend to make extravagant claims for the latest thing in power and pep, and one should not deny the gunbug his fun, which is all quite a legitimate part of the pleasure to be got out of stalking and gun ownership. Few stalkers can indulge their favourite hobby more than odd times in the year and a good hot argument over the respective merits of one bullet or another can make the evening fly for a party of walled-in shooters. It is sadly noticeable however that the more a man chops and changes between weapons for some theoretical advantage, the more often it happens that at the critical moment his carefully selected bullet does not connect with the selected target. In contrast a man who is lucky enough to get plenty of real stalking will tend to use one rifle until it is completely familiar to him.

Ask a few of such stalkers, whether they are professionals or not, and you will probably find that they are using bolt action rifles chambered for cartridges in the medium power range such as the .243, .270, .30/06 and .308, or in metric sizes the 7×57 (.275), 7×64 or 8×57. These are all capable of taking any British deer cleanly and humanely, and they have the advantage of being freely available in most parts of the world in a variety of bullet weights. Specialist weapons are discussed on page 254.

THE BULLET

The question of bullet design appears to be a blind spot in the minds of a surprising number of stalkers. Bullets are not all designed for the same purpose, and in making his choice a stalker must at least consider the variations available in muzzle velocity, bullet weight and expansion rate. Light bullets have high velocity and a very flat trajectory which eliminates errors in range estimation. They fly to pieces instantly on impact, eliminating danger of ricochets, but used on an animal as large as a deer the expansion will be too quick and a surface wound is created which is unlikely to be fatal. Even if the beast is killed, a large quantity of meat will be wasted by shredding. On the other hand, a really heavily jacketed bullet may slip through without expanding, particularly if a heavy bone is not touched. The stored bullet energy is not expended in the deer but it is wasted on the farther side. The dilemma of the bullet maker is to design the core and jacket in such a way that for all practical ranges and for many different targets, expansion will commence quickly but be controlled to allow penetration to the vital regions of the animal. All these characteristics vary between makes of ammunition and a certain amount of experiment is worth while to find a bullet which really suits your own style of shooting. When he finds a good one I would advise any stalker to stick to it and not change about.

After a season or two the stalker will know what he wants, and can either exchange his original purchase for one which exactly matches his needs, or buy a second rifle for some specialist work. There is a danger after a series of poor shots and perhaps a drama with a wounded beast, that he should be tempted into considering a heavier calibre or a weapon of greater power in order to correct the trouble. 'Magnumitis' is a well-recognised and deadly disease of stalkers. The sufferer attempts to get over his incompetence in shooting or stalking by using larger and larger cartridges. Unfortunately a man who is incapable of shooting a medium rifle accurately will be even less capable of using a magnum. The cure for his trouble is to use a rifle of *lesser* recoil and practise with it diligently so that the accuracy of his shooting can be improved, and the tendency to flinch ironed out.

CHOOSE YOUR WEAPON

The question of a specialist weapon for roe is restricted in England and Wales by the provisions of the Deer Act. However the choice of one of the potent .22 centre fires is still open to the Scottish stalker, provided that he is sure that he will not have occasion to use it in England. I myself used a .22 Hornet for many years before the passing of the Deer Act and found it adequate for roe in careful hands, though it is not now legal even for roe in Scotland. There is no doubt that slightly more powerful cartridges such as the .222 Remington, .22/250 and .223 are very much better.

Before taking the plunge, one should pause to consider what advantage there is in choosing an ultra-small bore for deer stalking. If safety is the paramount factor, one can obtain bullets for the bigger calibres which are just as fragile. Wastage of meat by shredding varies with bullet design more than calibre. A small cartridge does make slightly less noise but there is still a sharp and penetrating crack. Possibly the one major advantage, and it is a most important one, is that the rifle can be made very light and yet extremely accurate. Lack of recoil allows the shooter to extract every bit of potential accuracy from himself and his weapon. To balance this it is all too easy to find yourself out in the woods after roe, suddenly confronted with a fallow or even a stag. What do you do? Do you go home and fetch your heavy rifle and hope that the animal is still there, or do you take a chance and risk wounding him with the popgun? In helping to avoid such a dilemma the .243 Winchester is in a class by itself. It is a cartridge of great accuracy and little recoil. It complies with the requirements of the Deer Act, and while it has proved in every way suitable for roe, it has sufficient power for fallow and red hinds. Many professional stalkers in the Highlands now use the .243 for red deer, but the visitor would be prudent to have a bigger reserve of power to cover minor mistakes.

Nobody is likely to consider buying a rifle specially for English forest stags, but they are animals of enormous weight, anything up to four or five hundred pounds, and something firing a heavily constructed bullet with plenty of power behind it is certainly justified if such a weapon is available. Even so we come back to the 'magnumitis' problem. A set of galloping flinches will not help you to collect your giant trophy. If you have one of the general purpose rifles mentioned and are familiar with it, you will do better to rely on this. Make use of the versatility offered by the variety of bullets available; if you habitually stalk roe, and use a bullet well adapted to these small animals, then a change to something heavier is probably advisable, but you should clearly understand that, when you change over, the rifle will need re-zeroing, and again when you return to the usual load.

SIGHTS

There used to be a lot of prejudice against the use of telescopic sights, either on the grounds that they were unsporting and encouraged the stalker to take long shots, or that they were fragile and liable to get out of adjustment. The argument was often on the lines of 'Well, if you can stalk to within sixty yards, my boy, then you won't need a telescopic sight.' Those days are now largely passed and even in the Highlands you are unlikely to attract any criticism if you arrive with a scope on your rifle. It is generally acknowledged these days that scope sights allow one to shoot with greater precision, which gives quicker and more humane kills and less wastage of meat. They are reasonably robust, and particularly for woodland stalking they have the great merit of allowing one an extra half hour or so at each end of the day when poor light would make shooting with iron sights impossible.

There is no doubt that longer shots can be taken, and taken with certainty, compared with iron sights. It is up to the stalker himself to decide whether a shot is too far and therefore risky, whether this is 75 yards with open sights or 175 yards with a scope.

Fitting a scope on your rifle does increase the overall cost, and in calculating this one must include not only the price of the sight, but the mounts and any work on the rifle needed to fit them. The question of cost should not, however, prevent one from being fitted, because very reasonably priced sights can be obtained for something less than the value of two deer. This will soon be recovered by the added accuracy and versatility of the rifle. In choosing a sight it does not do to be penny-pinching. The cheapest sights are designed for use with .22 rimfire cartridges, and the comparatively heavy recoil of a stalking rifle will soon loosen the lenses. High light transmission is also important, to allow use in bad light. In practice this means a tube diameter of about one inch, with the ends enlarged to accommodate the eye-piece and object lenses. Television and the cinema have made most people familiar with the aiming device or *graticule* (US reticule) inside a scope sight on which the image of the target is superimposed. Traditionally this consists of two cross hairs, which are in practice unlikely to be cluttered with the range finding marks which fiction demands.

Cross hairs allow very precise aiming but in bad light they may disappear in the general murk, which can be very disconcerting if you are trying to shoot into a heavily shaded area. For this reason various other graticules which stand out more boldly than plain cross hairs are widely used. Usually they consist of different designs of posts, either alone or in conjunction with cross wires. Posts which taper sharply at the top tend to shoot high in poor light because one cannot see the tip. For this reason I prefer a flat-topped post, or a combination of three posts and short central cross wires. Graticules consisting of a dot, either alone or on the intersection of cross wires, are used in America, but I have not found them well adapted to shooting in bad light. Without the cross wire one is very inclined to cant the rifle and thus shoot inaccurately.

Scope tubes are made of alloy or steel. The alloy ones are lighter but will take less battering and general use before going out of adjustment. For Highland stalking at least, it is worth sacrificing the weight advantage and buying a steel-tubed scope. Adjustments for elevation and windage should be internal, controlled by two knobs on the top and the side of the tube respectively. Some older scopes were not fitted with a windage adjustment and this has to be supplied in the mount. Zeroing one of them can be a rather tedious operation for in many cases the sliding dovetail will be found to be jammed or rusted up.

ZEROING

A rifle bullet starts to drop away from the line of projection as soon as it leaves the barrel no matter how fast it is going. The curve that it describes in the air is called the *trajectory* and each load has its own individual trajectory curve. The idea of zeroing is to make the line of sight coincide with the flight path of the bullet at some convenient distance from the muzzle. As the trajectory varies between loads, *any change of ammunition must involve re-zeroing the sights*. This applies as much to iron sights as to a scope. Incidentally, it is prudent to make sure that the iron sights normally fitted to any rifle are reasonably well zeroed for the load which you use, even if you do not intend to use anything but a scope sight. In case of a fall or other mishap you have a second line of defence.

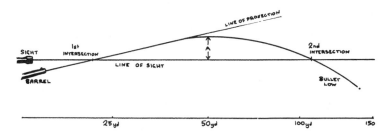

The trajectory of the bullet intersects with the line of sight through the 'scope at two points'. 'A' is the 'mid-range trajectory' often quoted in ammunition tables.

Telescopic sights have to be fitted some way above the bore, usually about one and a half inches, and reference to the diagram will show that the flight path of the bullet is intersected twice by the line of sight. Once fairly near the muzzle, and again at the set

257

distance of perhaps 100 or 120 yards. Actual trajectory figures for the ammunition you use can be obtained from the manufacturers, from which you can calculate the height of the bullet above or below the line of sight at any particular distance. It is a common mistake to sight-in rifles at far too great a distance. Most roe are shot at under 100 yards and the majority of stags under 170. If you zero your rifle to be spot on at 200 yards it will be shooting quite high, say three or four inches, at the range at which you take the majority of your shots. I find it is easier to remember to aim up a trifle on a long shot, which is bound to be deliberate, rather than to aim down for a short-range shot in the heat of the moment.

Whenever you feel the need of a zeroing session, and this should be reasonably often, it is worth following a set pattern in order to eliminate some of the variables. No rifleman should be without a set of screwdrivers which have been ground to fit the various screwheads of his weapon without burring them. Before zeroing it is worthwhile meticulously checking each screw to make certain that it is firmly home, in particular, the action screws securing the rifle to the woodwork, the screws holding the scope mounting blocks to the rifle, and the mounts themselves. If these have split rings, there are four screws which clamp the rings to the scope tube. All these should be checked carefully. The bore should then be mopped out with a piece of dry rag in order to remove any oil. This must be done before shooting in any case. An oily barrel will probably not shoot to the same point as a dry one, and surplus oil in the barrel or chamber can actually be dangerous.

Having found a safe place in which to let off a number of shots, a large sheet of paper with a small black aiming mark in the middle should be set up so that it will not flap (bulldog clips on the edge of a board are practical). Work should commence at short range, twenty-five to thirty-five yards, round about the first intersection of the trajectory with the line of sight. This will mean not only that the shots will probably hit the paper, but that errors in aiming and shooting are largely eliminated. Remove the bolt from the rifle, lay it down on what coats or boxes you may happen to have, and fiddle with it until it is possible to see the aiming mark by looking down the bore. Then without moving the rifle look through the scope sight and check that the graticule is aiming more or less at the mark. If it is, your first shot should hit the paper and ammunition will be saved accordingly. Replace the bolt and make three careful shots at this range.

If they are in a tight group you can safely go ahead to the next stage which is to lie down once more, this time looking through the scope sight, and clamp the rifle so that the graticule is resting on the aiming mark. Then keeping the rifle absolutely steady and peering through the sight, turn the adjusting knobs to move the graticule *to the group of shot holes*. Provided you are completely alone and not in a hurry, your next shot will be very near the aiming mark. If, on the other hand, there are onlookers yapping away and giving unneeded advice the result is anything but certain.

Not until the rifle is spot-on at this short range should a move be made to check it and make final corrections at the longer range you have selected. It will probably not be far off. All the shooting should be done either prone, using some sort of rest, or from a shooting bench if one is provided. One should never shoot with the rifle, barrel or woodwork resting directly on a hard surface, whether it is a rock, a tree trunk or the rail of a high seat. The natural vibrations of the weapon will be interfered with and it will probably shoot very high. Always have your hand under the rifle with a rolled-up coat underneath it or with the wrist rested against the hard object.

It is impossible to shoot consistently and accurately without meticulous attention to zeroing. Straight shooting is not the only skill needed by the stalker − far from it − but it is possibly the most important. A bad shot and a wounded beast can turn the most perfect day to misery. Not only for the stalker, but for some unfortunate beast. We all have a duty to shoot safely, thoughtfully and as accurately as science and care allow.

The Natural History of Red Deer

Lea MacNally

Highland red deer, the deer with which I have had most experience, are also the deer which most people think of when the term 'deer-stalking' is used. There is only one deer-forest, in the accepted Highland sense of the term, in England, that of Martindale, in Cumbria. There deer-stalking is carried on much as in the Highlands. Elsewhere in England where 'free-living' red deer exist, notably Exmoor, control of red numbers is by hunting or, as in the Thetford Chase area in Norfolk, by woodland techniques perhaps more akin to roe-stalking than to traditional Highland deer-stalking. In Galloway, in south-west Scotland, an area where some of the finest red deer in Scotland at present exist, some hill deer-stalking is still possible. But, here also, woodland techniques must be increasingly applied as forestry areas replace former hill ground. So it is of Highland red deer that I now write.

Our Highland red deer are to me the most rewarding of our native wild mammals. They exist on our largely treeless hills where they can be watched, from long range, using a deer-stalking 'glass', as they go about their daily business, undisturbed

by any suspicion of a human intruder. They are unique in that they are animals large enough to watch from a distance, not liable, or able, to vanish, after perhaps only a fleeting glimpse, into wooded cover, as are continental or most of the red deer in England. This doesn't mean that they are always *easy* to see, in the vast expanses of rugged hill ground. But to the skilled watcher with a knowledge of hill and red deer, they can always be found.

Highland red deer are a triumph of natural selection, of adaptation to a vastly altered environment. They were originally woodland creatures, thriving in an era when much of the now treeless Highlands was covered in forest and scrub. In the process of adaptation to a habitat of heather and rock, evolution has ensured and selected the fittest. So much so that one is tempted at times to think that a 'new' race of red deer has evolved, so different is their present day Highland habitat from that of red deer elsewhere throughout the world.

Under these vastly altered and very much less favourable conditions of food and shelter, the Highland red deer *had* to become smaller, in both body and in antlers. It also had to become hardier to combat the harsh conditions (conditions not by any means confined to winter) of their present hill habitat. Our red deer use bare high ground up to four thousand feet: above the thousand foot level is quite normal for them at all times of the year, especially in daytime. In their nightly grazing they often come quite low down into the glens simply because there is then less risk of human disturbance. Prolonged bad weather, such as snow in winter or periods of rain and gale force winds in spring, coupled with the paucity of grazing, may also drive deer temporarily lower to seek shelter and feed.

HIGHLAND VERSUS WOODLAND

To my eye, lack of size and weight, in both body and antler, is more than made up for by their grace and carriage. You see it best in the majesty of the mature stag in autumn which Landseer immortalised, if a little romantically, in his 'The Monarch of the Glen'. Their agility in movement, their ability to endure all the rigours of Highland winter, the sight of a large herd of stags high out on the hill in the tawny hues of September, or of a huge herd of hinds, dark against the purity of snowclad hills sparkling under a frosty sun, all go to put Highland deer in a class of their own.

I have seen English and Continental 'woodland habitat' red deer and have been deeply impressed by their size and weight, in body and antler. But, for me, both hinds and stags have a certain unwieldiness that is much less appealing than the compactness of the Highland animal. The woodland stags at times appear more bovine than cervine and their antlers, while vastly thicker, heavier and with more points than those of Highland red deer, so often lack the symmetry and beauty of a perfectly balanced head, in terms of evenly matched points. There's nothing to beat a good Highland 'royal', with brow, bez and trez, and a shapely cup of three evenly matched points on each top. Size, after all, is a relative thing. Shape and symmetry will always outweigh sheer bulk, at least to my eye!

The start of our human year is January, but for the red deer of the Highlands one could say that their year starts in June, when most of the calves are born. A few early calves will arrive in late May and occasional late ones throughout July, August and even as late as September. I suspect most of these latecomers will succumb before they are a year old. June, in fact, would seem to be the ideal month for the birth of red deer calves under Highland conditions. By then, the always tardy regrowth of new grazing is well established and there is sufficient time before the often early onset of the Highland winter to enable the June-born calves to grow strong enough to survive their first winter and following spring. I couple spring with winter, for it is in the spring that the real privation time comes for Highland red deer. During February, March and April, the grazing is at its poorest.

My own personal experience in typical deer-forest ground in central Inverness-shire is that one seldom finds many newborn calves before June 5. From then on the calves arrive steadily reaching a peak around mid-June and then gradually shading off so that after June 25 only the occasional late calf arrives. Red deer hinds do not, understandably, all come into season simultaneously in the main rutting month of October. In a herd of hinds held by a 'master' stag, only one or two may be in season on any one day of the 'peak' three weeks of the rut. Thus, after the eight-month gestation period, the June births are spread out also.

CALVING

Giving birth to a calf is usually accomplished with little difficulty by the hind and mortality in either mother or calf is so small as to be insignificant. I have only witnessed three cases, spread out over many years, of hinds dead with only half delivered calves. I have been reliably told of cases where either shepherd or stalker has come upon a hind so weak with a half-delivered calf that they were actually able to catch the hind and deliver the calf themselves.

I have been lucky enough to watch hinds actually calving, on a few occasions over the years, always at long range, while using my stalking glass. Most hinds seem to leave the herds to which they are normally attached, but the first hind I ever watched calving did so close to three other hinds. I first spied her at 9 am on a June morning, in a high, green corrie, just as she jumped to her feet to leave her companions, presumably impelled by the first of her birth pains. All around the wide bowl of the corrie she walked, at times kicking out jerkily with one or other hindleg, or nosing around, body doubled, with questing muzzle at her rump, until she had left the three hinds well behind. Periodically, but only for minutes at a time, she lay down. At one moment, I thought she was about to give birth as she lay; but, no, again she sprang up and this time began to retrace her way back around the corrie. Now her pace was quicker; at times she was stung into running a few yards, but still she had her periodic short rests. She worked her way right back to the group she had left and lay down only a short distance from them. A few moments after her return, she raised her head and neck skyward and gave a single mournful-sounding, bovine-like bellow, a sound which I have only heard from hinds at this time of year. It was a sound I have never seen mentioned in any red deer writings, but one which I have come personally to regard as indicative of a hind near to calving, or only recently calved. In the case of this particular hind I was inclined to regard it as indicative of pre-natal pains, but I have since heard and seen it used by hinds before calving, by hinds while actually calving, by hinds in what appeared to be smug self-satisfaction while lying beside a recently born calf or by hinds 'mourning' a dead still-born calf, a rare occurrence. Once I even heard it used by a hind standing over her dead day-old calf which I later discovered had been killed by an eagle, also by one standing over the narrow orifice of a deep peat cavern in which her calf was trapped. I was able to rescue this calf simply because the bellowing of the hind had attracted my notice, at over a mile away.

Enough of the 'calving bellow', however, I must get back to my calving hind.

As I continued to watch her, she lay extended on her side and rubbed head and neck on the grass, now and again lunging out with a hind leg. While this was going on, her three companions continued placidly to chew their cud. About 10.30 am she suddenly sprang to her feet and, as she stood broadside on, I could now *see* about six inches of two jet-black, spindly-looking legs, tipped with yellow-white hooves protruding from her. Once more she lay down, on her opposite side this time, in very obvious discomfort: now and again she bellowed, a bellow filled with painful yearning. When she jumped up once more, I could see that the birth was imminent. Yet again she lay down at full stretch, vigorously scrubbing head and neck on the short grass. Came a sudden convulsion of her body, she sprang to her feet and as she did so, the calf dropped, literally dropped, so that I winced for its hitting the ground. The newborn animal glistened perceptibly, even at that distance. The hind began immediately to tear away the envelope which partially enclosed the calf. As she lifted her head momentarily, I could see a long white streamer of this drooping from her working jaws. Some she swallowed, some she discarded. It was 11.17 am, two hours and seventeen minutes after I'd first seen her. Almost at once I could see the dark knob of the calf's head bobbing about and by 11.25 am it was struggling to rise. At 11.27 am, ten scant minutes from its birth, it was on its feet, only to fall at once. It kept struggling to regain its feet while the hind, unbelievably clumsy to my eyes, kept knocking it over in her own restless movements. By 11.45 am the calf eventually remained long enough on its feet to find the udder of the hind, only to have its still unstable legs fold up once again. Tenaciously persistent, it was up again at once and this time had a feed lasting six minutes before tottering off to one side and folding up again. It weighed 12 lb at an hour old, below the 14–15 lb which I found usual for a recently born red deer calf in that area.

MATERNAL COURAGE

A new-born calf has no apparent inborn dread of man, its over-riding instinct is to lie perfectly still to avoid detection. Obviously, in general, this works, but I have seen calves frozen in pathetically obvious places, devoid of all cover, on short heather, against the contrast of short, bright green grass, or in even greater contrast, on the jet-black surface of a wide expanse of dry peat bog. Glaringly obvious to my eyes, how much more so to the keener eyes of hunting eagle or fox, with hungry young to feed?

While both eagle and fox are predators on deer calves, the proportion they take is restricted mainly to the relatively short time when the very young calves are left lying alone in the absence of the mother, grazing far enough away to be unaware of danger to her calf. A red deer hind is a devoted, almost fearless, mother and will drive off fox or eagle in defence of her calf. While ear-tagging deer calves for study purposes, I once had the unique experience of having a red deer hind face up to my approach, audibly grinding her molars as I drew near, but with absolutely astounding maternal courage, refusing to run from that most feared of predators, man. I was near enough to touch her before she turned at last. But she soon halted and returned so that I literally had to shoo her away before I could tag her calf, feeling an absolute brute as I did so.

Though the calf may be two or three weeks old before it accompanies the mother everywhere (individual behaviour varies in deer just as in humans) the instinct to lie still lessens markedly when the calf is about two days old. Some calves of that age may still trust to immobility, others will rise and run, often emitting an ear-piercing squeal as they do so, a signal which will bring every mature hind within earshot rushing in. I have had no fewer than seven hinds, ears erect, in a questioning semi-circle around me, drawn by such a squeal.

Red deer calves retain their dappled coat for about three months when it is gradually replaced by their first dark thick winter coat.

The coats of all our red deer change twice annually, from winter to summer coat in June−July time, and from the short-lived summer coat back to winter coat, in autumn. The summer coat is a beautiful eye-catching red, a thin, single coat. The winter one is usually much darker, a very deep brown in fact (though some individual hinds may have a distinctly yellowish-brown winter coat) and it is a double coat, of wiry long outer guard hairs under which is concealed an inner coat of fluffy texture which provides much needed insulation against cold while the outer guard hairs shed rain, sleet and snow.

At the calving time most milk hinds are very shabby-looking, still in winter coat, but now bleached to a paleness approaching grey-white. In striking contrast, those hinds which are not bearing calves, either because of immaturity (Highland hinds are commonly three, sometimes four years old, before they have their first calf) or because they are 'resting' for a season after three or four successive calf-bearing years, may be sleekly beautiful in full summer red. The collective term for such non-breeding hinds in the Highlands is 'yeld'. It should be emphasised that a 'yeld' hind is *not* a completely barren hind, but is either immature or regaining condition after successive calf-bearing years.

THE RUT

While the mature hinds are bearing and rearing their fast-growing calves, the stags, summering in 'stag parties' in areas distinct from the hind herds, are growing their new antlers, having shed their old ones towards the end of March. Younger stags cast their antlers later, at times as late as May, and are consequently later in their regrowth. By mid-June, most mature stags should have their antlers well advanced and by mid-July these should be about fully formed though still encased in the covering of velvet under the protection of which the nourishment for the growing bone of the antlers circulates. By early August many of the mature stags will be shedding this velvet, a process continuing down the age groups until eventually even the youngest of the antlered stags are in 'hard antler'.

In the daytime during July and August and for perhaps some of September, the red deer, in herds of hinds, calves and yearlings interspersed with a sprinkling of young staggies still attached to the family group, will be mostly out on the highest ground available to them. There they take advantage of the grazing with its relative lack of human disturbance, also the cool breezes and freedom from flies and other winged pests. This is the peaceful, good living time.

As September wears on, the greens of grass and purples of heather change to the tawny hues of approaching autumn, a tawniness into which the coats of the deer, hitherto bright against the summer hill, merge magnificently. The hind herds, still apart from the stag herds, begin to be seen a bit lower in the corries again. A growing sexual unrest works a gradual disruption of the former amity in the herds of mature stags. Roaring starts, that matchless sound of the autumn hills, blood-tingling or spine-chilling but always insistently enthralling. The rut is beginning. In October, the month of the roaring, it really gets under way. On boggy flats one comes on peat wallows, edges fringed by scattered deer hairs and scarred by hoof-marks, but in places smoothed out by the rubbing of the wallower's body. Both stags and hinds use the wallows, stirring their peatiness to the consistency desired before luxuriating in the jet-black depths. A rutting stag freshly emerged, dripping wet and shining black from a wallow is an intimidating sight, to man if not to a similarly peat-clothed rival. The heather itself stinks, even to the inefficient scenting powers of the human nose, of the rutting stag, a heavy rank, self-sprayed odour which clings to his coat, rendering the long coarse curling hair of the belly black and moist. I have seen stags at this time lower their heads to between their straddled forelegs, slowly wag them from side to side and spray them liberally with their own urine, a silvery jet visible through my stalking glass, the long coarse hairs of the mane getting drenched also. Clumps of rushes are antler-thrashed, broken and devastated, sprayed with urine and then rolled on, low-growing branches of birch, rowan or willow are left dangling, broken, reduced to fibrous shreds, the ground below cut and trampled by the plunging hooves of rut-inflamed stags.

Possessed by this savage unrest the mature stags will not be satisfied until they have acquired hinds. For the first three weeks in October, the height of the rut, the big stags have it all their own way. Seldom do the younger stags have much chance until their older, stronger peers have had their desires assuaged, or cut short, where deemed necessary, by a human stalker. A really strong stag, having once acquired hinds (it may be twenty miles or only twenty yards from where he was born), will generally come back, year after year, to the same area where he has first had success. He may hold his herd for perhaps all of three weeks, their numbers waxing and waning as circumstances or competitors decree, and then, a travesty of the stag he was only three short weeks ago, he will have had enough. For a day or two longer he may lie on the fringes of the herd, dozing, supine in the heather he so recently rampaged through, at times unashamedly asleep, a cervine despot satiated at last, before wandering off at leisure towards his wintering ground and renewed male companionship, uneasy and irritable at first, leaving behind a jumble of younger stags fussing and fretting with adolescent roaring over the few hinds yet to come in season. Small wonder that the stags lose so rapidly the condition achieved by months of good summer grazing in the relatively short, mad spree of the rut.

THE HAREM

I firmly believe, however, that his decline is not mainly due to the actual mating with a number of hinds. It is his ceaseless frenzy in jealously guarding his hinds which gives him no rest and leaves him little desire or even time to feed. His first reaction, having acquired hinds, is to expel summarily all the 'knobbers' (young males of about fifteen months with as yet only knobs instead of antlers) forcing them to leave the family group for the first time in their lives. No males older than the calves of that year will be tolerated among his hinds. This done, he maintains a constant patrol among the hinds, throwing out anew any knobber trying to regain the family group, racing out to drive away any young stag ambitious enough to try his luck, emitting a series of enraged, coughing grunts as if explosively expelled from him every time his madly racing hooves contact the ground. Having chased him as far as prudence dictates, he is perhaps barely in time to rush frenziedly at another would-be aspirant to marital status who has taken advantage of his absence. This dealt with, perhaps at the loss of one or two hinds adroitly cut out by the sagely departing suitor, he rounds his hinds yet again, unable to be at peace or even to eat except for the occasional snatched mouthful. Singling a hind out he will pursue her through the warily side-stepping others, weaving an erratic, seemingly purposeless course through the herd. Even rutting stags tire, however, and he may be forced eventually to lie down, to doze uneasily, jerking awake the moment he hears a distant roar, answering on an almost lazy note as long as the roaring remains distant but resuming his patrolling if it approaches nearer. If a would-be challenger is of size and strength near to his own, he will let him advance just so far, returning roar for roar, until serious intent seems established on each side. The stag in possession will then advance a set distance from his herd to meet his challenger, each belligerence personified, but each, at this stage, observing a set ritual. The stag in possession turns broadside to his hinds and slowly, stiff-legged and deliberate, paces in a wide arc around them. His rival meanwhile also turns broadside, pacing alongside, head on a level with the other's shoulder, step by stiff-legged step, but *always* on the *outside* of the stag in possession. The challenged stag *may* dictate a turn, to pace on a return arc, and the challenger will make no attempt to break past him but will also observe the rules and pace back with him, still on the edge away from the hinds.

Quite often the opponents have sized each other up well before this and the challenger may decide he is over-matched. If this occurs, no false pride prevents his withdrawal. He simply turns away and stalks, still stiff-legged and in apparent arrogance, away. The challenged stag simply halts and, head thrown up, roars after him, probably in a mixture of relief and scorn. He never pursues, because this would leave his hinds vulnerable to another rival.

At other times, with a movement swift as lightning, challenger and challenged will suddenly wheel and crash into each other, clearing each other's antlers with a series of clearly audible clicks so that they can get their foreheads into contact. A frenzied, hoof-plunging, peat-spattering, pushing and heaving shoving-match ensues, each stag striving for uphill advantage and, having gained it, pushing his rival headlong downhill. Often the positions are reversed by a swiftly executed wheeling manoeuvre. Superior weight and strength dictates the winners of these contests, irrespective of antler calibre. At the extremes, a heavy hummel (antlerless stag) may defeat a lighter 'royal' or a ten-pointer. Such encounters usually last only a few minutes, so hot is the pace. I twice saw such a bout go fifteen minutes. In *both* cases the stags were so utterly exhausted that they were almost literally on their knees. I watched one of these pairs separate, as if by mutual decision, and crawl slowly away, each to opposite sides of a huge herd of hinds for which they had presumably been competing.

The actual mating act is witnessed relatively infrequently. A stag, too energy-worn as the rut progresses, may *cover* a hind several times before he actually *serves* her, propelling her forward some yards in this last act while he rears momentarily erect on his hindlegs, before dropping to all-fours again.

Most of the spectacle of the rut is over as October ends. The glens cease to resound with the savage music so much part of the October scene and hinds and stags gradually drift apart into distinct herds again, wintering apart as they summered apart.

WINTER HARDSHIPS

Highland winters can be a real test of the hardihood of the deer but they usually cope amazingly well, lying in apparent comfort in self-created oval beds of deep snow, or enduring torrential rain or horizontally driving gale force sleet, while any human watcher becomes unendurably chilled and soaked, no matter how well clad. When rain, sleet or blizzard is over, beast after beast rises to its feet and with one swift shake expels the moisture from its coat in a silvery nimbus. They then lie down again and resume rhythmic cud-chewing.

For most of the winter there is sufficient 'carry-over' of grazing to cater for the needs of the deer and they are capable of scraping down, using a flailing foreleg, through quite an appreciable depth of snow, to the grazing below. Stags, their condition lowered by the rut, endure the winter with less fortitude than the hinds. It is they who will sometimes be found to encroach on arable ground in winter, seldom the hinds.

By February, hill-grazing is depleted and of poor quality, Towards the end of this month the annual toll of natural mortality begins, weeding out the weaker beasts in two main age groups, calves still in their first year and the old beasts. Where ground is over-stocked, mortality will be higher than on ground well-managed and mortality in the old class can be reduced by judicious selection of obviously old, poor-doing beasts while stalking. Nature *is* ruthless but not needlessly so and management of deer can go a long way to counteract the lingering death of 'natural' mortality.

Towards the end of March the mature stags will begin antler-casting, a process prolonged into May in the younger stags. New growth, velvet encased, quickly begins and by mid-May, with new grass on the hill grazings, the new antlers will be well advanced.

Red deer are at their shabbiest now, the once sleek winter coat bleached and tufty with patches of loose outer hair and inner fur in it, a tawdry-looking transition stage gradually to be replaced by the svelte red coat of summer. June brings new life to the deer herds and increasing growth to the new antlers of the stags.

The old year is dead, the spring privations forgotten, and a new one begins for the red deer, who are the very essence of our Highland hills. Long may they continue to be so.

Stalking Highland Deer

Lea MacNally

Revised by Richard Prior

It is one of the paradoxes of sport that those who pursue game bird or game animal are also in the main involved in and attracted by the lives of those they pursue. This being so it is perhaps unnecessary for me to preface this section on deer-stalking with the plea to all potential deer-stalkers to remember that their target is *not* one of inanimate cardboard or wood but a living, sentient animal capable of feeling pain every bit as much as any human being, if infinitely better at enduring it. I think it was Scrope in his classic on deer-stalking who referred to the successful dénouement of a stalk as 'a kind of assassination' and while this simile may be distasteful to many there is a very great element of truth in it. In a really successful well carried out stalk, your quarry should have no suspicion or mental apprehension of danger and the well-placed shot which ends it is neither heard nor felt. In this, I personally feel, deer-stalking compares favourably with any field sport practised in the British Isles or indeed in the world.

Having said this, one is only too well aware that human beings are all too fallible and that, at times, the 'human element' can wreak havoc with the most skilfully conducted stalk, involving, at best (if one can use that term), a miss when it seemed well-nigh impossible, or, at worst, a wounded beast to follow up. To all professional stalkers this is a nightmare. They will do anything to avoid unnecessary suffering to the deer whose downfall they have been striving to encompass.

It is the duty of every stalker to ensure that his equipment, particularly his rifle, cannot be faulted. The rifle must be faultless in its accuracy, adequate in its calibre before you go deer-stalking. You must be absolutely familiar with its balance, loading, ejecting, reloading and trigger pressures.

All this may seem elementary, yet it is astonishing, as I know from a life-time of professional stalking, how many rifles are not as efficient as they should be. 'It shoots a little low' − or 'high' or 'to the left' or 'to the right' − 'but of course I always allow for it'. There is *no* excuse for this just as there is no excuse for putting a rifle away at the end of a short stalking season and never handling it again until the start of the next one. 'Allowances', for rifles shooting 'off-centre' in any way, are all too apt to be forgotten in the field. The remedy is to have sights zeroed so that the rifle shoots 'spot on' and to test this *personally* on a target at, at least, a hundred yards' range. Many rifles in use in deer-stalking today have a certain sentimental appeal to their owners because they were used by a father, or even a grandfather. Most understandable, but rifles, like ancestors, wear out. Happily, unlike one's ancestors, they can be given a new lease of life by re-zeroing, re-barrelling or re-stocking.

THE RIFLE

Familiarity with your rifle is essential. A few *seconds* may be vital at the climax of a stalk. An exciting day's stalking, engrossing and often arduous, has resulted in a chance at a stag at last. All that is needed to complete the very satisfying glow of achievement in besting the elements, terrain and the keen senses of the ever-alert quarry is the necessary culmination of a skilful stalk, an equally skilful shot. This can be distressingly muffed by unfam-iliarity with your rifle. You perhaps take an over-eager first shot, resulting in a miss. The chance of the easy second shot which, however undeservedly, is *sometimes* offered is completely lost as the now over-excited user of the rifle tries too quickly to eject and reload and jams on a half-ejected empty. Even worse is the risk that a beast which one has had the misfortune to wound may have to endure a needless period of suffering before it is finally brought to bag. Smooth ejecting and reloading should become automatic as soon as a shot is fired, no matter the apparent result; a rifle with an 'empty' in the chamber is of little use to even the most expert shot. A 'dead' stag should never be accepted as dead until one is actually performing the last rites on it. I have bitter memories, admittedly few but nonetheless distasteful, of being handed a rifle to 'finish off' a fleeing wounded stag only to lose vital seconds as the metallic click of firing pin tells me I've fired on an empty chamber.

Even if you don't get much chance of target practice, 'dry practice' in handling and aiming your rifle, and the cultivation of the ability to shoot from a variety of positions will prove invaluable when it's the real thing. The expert deer-stalker is one who can adapt himself to shoot from a thoroughly uncomfortable position though, *at all times*, ensuring that his accuracy is not affected. You may have to fire while clinging on to a steep side-brae position, or from the depths of a distinctly damp, black and odorous peat bog, with perhaps rocks intruding all too feelingly upon the tenderer parts of one's anatomy. I once had to hold on to the ankles of a redoubtable lady while she craned over into space to shoot at a stag directly below her. She made no mistake with her shot despite the 'indignity' of her position (I should, perhaps, add that she was wearing breeches).

It is the man, or woman, behind the rifle who matters more than the calibre. For red deer, in fact, a calibre of .240 is the minimum which should be considered. Rifle calibres are now regulated by law in Scotland. Specifications are given on page 252. I have personally used calibres of .240, .243, .244, .256 (or 6.5 mm), .270, 7 mm, .303 and .300 and found them all adequate. My personal preference nowadays is for the .243 with the 100 grain bullet. For many years I used an ex-army First World War .303 with the 174 grain bullet and it never let me down. This .303 had a sweetness of bolt action and a smoothness of trigger pressure which many of the modern sporting rifles appear to find difficulty in achieving. There is enough variety, in price and in makers, in the calibres mentioned to satisfy the variety in tastes and pockets of those who wish to go deer-stalking nowadays. Calibre being adequate, the choice of rifle is very much a matter of individual preference. Much the same can be said about the type of sights used. Directly postwar, open sights were still by far the most commonly used with telescopic sights almost a novelty. Nowadays they are far more common than open sights. There was at one time a prejudice among certain of the old school that 'scope sights made it too easy, a theory with which I never have agreed. Richard Prior, I note, largely agrees with my views.

SIGHTS

In my view, the shot is the essential culmination of the much more skilled and often lengthy business of getting close enough to the deer to shoot. When you make the shot surely you want your equipment to be as efficient as possible. There is no question in my mind but that the 'scope sight *is* more efficient than the open sight and thereby enables 'kills' to be made more cleanly and surely. Another criticism is that 'scope sights encourage longer range shooting. This may have some grain of truth in it, but there are very few experienced stalkers who would allow the taking of a shot at undue range, whether with 'scope or open sights. Most shots in stalking are still taken from 100 to 150 yards' range, and rarely at more than 200. There will always be individuals who will take overlong shots with a rifle just as there will be those who do the same with a shotgun. With open sights, which I used for over half my stalking career, I always preferred the aperture (or peep) sight. My next choice was the very wide, shallow V-sight, in which one could always see the bead of the foresight clearly, without the blurring liable with a narrow V, or U backsight. Where 'scope sights are concerned I have a personal preference for the 4× (four times magnification) sight with the crosshair reticule as against the 'post' type reticule. I have heard the theory often expressed by very experienced shots that the 'post' type reticule is easier seen in dim light, but I have never found it so. I prefer the crosshair under any lighting conditions.

With 'scope sights it is always advisable to re-target the rifle after any accidental jar or knock. 'Scopes are, after all, fairly delicate precision optical instruments and as such are vulnerable. It may be regarded as a counsel of perfection, or even as a vote of no confidence in the guest for the day, but I firmly believe it to be desirable for the professional stalker to have the chance of a target shot with the guest's rifle before going to the hill. In the event of the rifle having to be handed over to the stalker to administer the *coup de grâce* to a wounded stag, the stalker will at least have some idea of how he can perform with the strange rifle. It should not need to be emphasised that in the case where a wounded stag has to be dealt with, it will help immensely if the rifle is speedily passed over to the professional. The overriding consideration must be to end any suffering by the wounded beast *as quickly as possible.* A final word on the rifle; do carry plenty of ammunition, it is better to have too much than too little. Your stalker will gladly pocket that extra ten or twenty if you don't feel like carrying the little extra weight. I have been stalking all my life and I never go to the hill without at least twenty rounds, even if I am only out for one shot. Incidentally I once had a guest who was optimistic enough to come out with *five* rounds; strangely enough, he did not see a stag that day.

AIMING

Point of aim on your stag is a matter of some controversy nowadays, influenced I am afraid to some degree by the fact that venison dealers will pay a better price for venison carcases which have been 'neck shot'. The neck shot has been extolled and advocated as either a dead beast or a clean mess. This is by no means guaranteed, particularly when the neck hairs are long and shaggy as in the rutting season. It is possible to put a bullet through these long hairs, to inflict a superficial wound, or to '*nick*' the jugular vein and have your stag go off as if untouched; or, alternatively, to put a hole right through a stag's windpipe and again watch it go away as if unharmed. In both the latter cases the stag will probably die a lingering death. A well-placed neck shot, one, that is, which shatters the vertebrae *is* a certain and quick killer but it is one which I never take unless I am very close to my quarry and with a very good firing position. Nor am I too keen on the heart shot. At times a heart-shot beast may run up to two hundred yards before dropping and two hundred yards in broken ground can pose its own problems when it comes to finding the dead stag. At other times a heart shot can drop a stag instantly. I have heard the theory expressed that this apparently inexplicable difference depends on whether the heart, in its function as pump in the blood's circulation, is full or empty of blood. Even if this is true, it does not solve the problem of knowing whether the heart is full or empty when you shoot. My own preference is for the lung shot, which usually drops a beast at once or at worst within seconds without it going more than a yard or two, if at all. The point of aim for this shot is midway up the chest and *just behind* the 'elbow' joint of the foreleg. Always remember that your primary consideration is to ensure as clean and humane an end to the stalk as possible and your point of aim should be chosen with your own limitations, if any, in mind. It is also of course desirable to 'spoil' as little venison as possible with the shot, but this should always be a secondary consideration.

EQUIPMENT

On the 'open' hill with views of herds or individual deer as far as the eye can see, views changing as the day and the miles go by, an enthralling day may be spent without ever a shot being fired. It is this opportunity to see deer going about their daily existence which makes Highland red deer-stalking unique. To enjoy it to the full one must have good optical aid. The professional stalker will always carry a stalking telescope ('glass' in stalking parlance) of about 20× (magnification), but the average stalking guest will probably be better suited with binoculars. There is a wide choice nowadays, in price range and in magnifying power; 7 × 50s are good 'all-rounders', while reasonably priced 10 × 50s are available for those who want higher magnification coupled with the ease of use and wide field of view. To the professional, the glass, though slightly more difficult to use, is indispensable in *assessing* deer at a range beyond the power of binoculars and in selecting *which* stag is to be the object of the stalk. In wet weather, *soft* tissue paper hankies are invaluable for drying-off rain-soaked glass or binoculars, for 'scope sights, too. They're much better than a linen handkerchief. *Soft* toilet paper is excellent for that same purpose.

Footwear is very important. One may tramp for miles over terrain varying from peaty bog, long heather, leg-straining tussocky grass, to harsh, rock-strewn ridges. My own choice in footwear is to combine lightness and comfort with strength, and, always, 'commando type' rubber soles for the great virtue of their silence on rocky ground. The metallic far-crying 'clink' of the traditionally tacket-shod shoe has saved the life of many a stag. On a really 'wet' hill in bad weather there is much to be said for the light-weight, green-coloured 'Hunter' wellingtons.

277

PERSONAL CAMOUFLAGE

For clothing nothing beats Highland tweeds (Irish 'thornproof' tweed is also good). After all, tweeds were evolved for Highland conditions. Plus fours or knee breeches are not unduly uncomfortable even when soaking wet and tweed retains warmth even when wet and is reasonably quick to dry. Above all it does *not* rustle noisily when crawling or wriggling in the last stages of the approach. Modern synthetic fabrics are appallingly noisy and the keen ears of the deer are sensitive enough without providing them with outside help. Choose drab shades of red-brown, grey, green or a mixture of these. Avoid very dark colours or those which will become very dark when soaked with rain, and, at the other extreme, light colours such as 'off-white' windcheaters. You are, after all, going to be in view over vast expanses of hill ground, just as the deer are going to be to you, and the choice of suitable 'blending-in' clothing will save many a long detour. Carry a lightweight coat or three-quarter-length jacket of nylon or similar waterproof material in a pocket if you must but never wear rubber over-trousers unless you wish to alert your deer long before you are within shot. A willingness to accept the fact that getting wet is one of the 'occupational risks' of stalking will be an asset when it comes to crawling up a burn bed or over an expanse of black, clinging peat. I once took an indomitable lady crawling up an exceedingly wet, black and odoriferous peat drain, so wet that the jet-black water ran in at our jacket sleeves and made its way thence down and out our arm-holes. She got her stag and she certainly deserved it.

The eyes of deer are good, especially at picking up movement, so skylines must always be crossed with great care. Their sense of hearing is, as I have pointed out, even more acute. But the keenness of their scenting powers beats all other senses. It has been said before, but it is well worth repeating, that one can deceive the eyes of deer, and at times the ears of deer, but never their noses.

The first essential when stalking is to spy out the ground *thoroughly* from a viewpoint as commanding as is possible, remembering always *not* to perch on the skyline of such a viewpoint and to use the utmost economy in movement, for while you are looking for the deer, the deer which may be ahead will be readily alerted by any 'foreign body' suddenly apparent on a ridge-top, or by incautious movement while spying. It is in this preliminary spying, which will have to be repeated each time fresh ground comes into view, that the stalking glass really comes into its own. With it, one can spy deer at far greater ranges and in far greater detail than with binoculars. Having located the deer, assure yourself that there is a suitable stag among what may well be a sizeable herd (you will be stalking stags still in herds, or alone, if in the early part of the season, until around the third week in September; from October onwards, when the rut is in full swing the stags will be with the hinds). You've selected your stag, now to work out a feasible line of approach. The all-important factor here is the direction of the wind. The slightest of vagrant puffs gently chilling the back of one's neck during the approach and the beast will get your scent and make a speedy withdrawal to safer quarters.

Having established the prevailing direction of the wind, one then selects an approach that will take you as near to the deer as possible while remaining unseen. In this context it is always desirable, if possible, to come in on deer from above though this will usually involve a detour, often a lengthy one, around the end of the face on which the deer may be lying. The approach from above is desirable for two reasons; first, deer, lying peacefully chewing the cud on a hill face, will usually face downhill. Their view *uphill*, even should they turn their heads to look, is invariably much more restricted. The second reason is that it gives *you* a much better view of the deer *below you*.

THE APPROACH

The wind is the deciding factor here again. On some forests, the prevailing wind may dictate an almost inevitable approach from below. In some cases an approach along the side-slope, or contour, may be possible, often by, in stalking parlance, 'slicing' the wind, i.e. coming in with the wind blowing to one flank or the other instead of *directly* into your face. This is often preferable to an approach directly from below, though riskier as far as the tell-tale wind is concerned.

If one *has* to approach from below, this again often involves

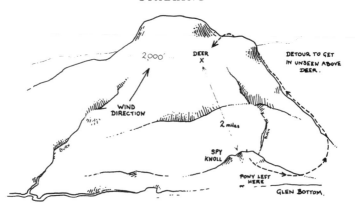

An approach from above.

a lengthy preliminary detour to get, *if possible*, below any swell of the face on which the deer are lying, before the last inevitable, nerve-tingling, upward approach. In the last stages of any stalk, over-eagerness and natural impatience *must* be guarded against. If the deer are grazing they are much easier to approach than if they are lying up placidly chewing the cud but with nose, eyes and ears ever alert. A very good guide as to whether your deer are completely unaware of your proximity is to watch the rhythmic movement of their jaws chewing the cud. If any one deer suddenly ceases chewing the cud and her ears prick up, *freeze*, no matter in what position you are caught. It is an instinctive, but fatal reaction to attempt to shrink down as near to the ground as

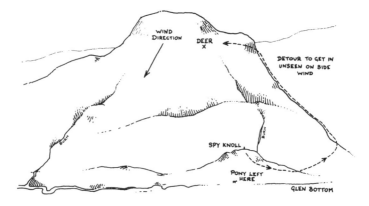

Approach by detour and in along the contour where wind precludes a direct approach from above.

possible if one fears that suspicions are aroused. The eyes of deer are much more attuned to picking up movement and *then* recognising the object responsible for it than they are to identifying a completely motionless object. If one *can* remain immobile long enough, there is every chance of a faintly suspicious deer becoming reassured sufficiently for you to resume your stalk. The slightest movement would have confirmed the suspicions aroused.

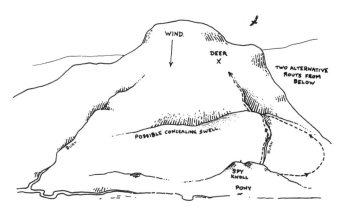

Two alternative approaches from below. Straight up a concealing burn, if there is one conveniently at hand, and if the lower reaches are not too exposed to view; or a detour to get below a concealing swell which may obscure the middle distance but not the lower part of the face. In the second instance one would be trying for the cover of a convenient burn, peat hags or undulations for the last part of the stalk.

One other very common failing, shared by professional and amateur alike, is to concentrate all one's watchfulness on the selected beast. This, after all, *is* the one you want, but it may be, and most often is, supported by the watchfulness of many other pairs of eyes and ears. Basically, deer-stalking is simply applying common sense in approaching deer so as not to alarm them by giving them your wind, letting them see you or allowing them to hear you. Experience and ground-knowledge, of course, augments this greatly and this is where the professional stalker comes in. He's not simply a guide to keep you from becoming the object of a mountain rescue exercise or trespassing on an adjacent deer forest. He's an invaluable aid to the success and enjoyment of your cherished day, or days, on the hill.

Be guided by the stalker, therefore, as the man who should

know best, how to go and where to go, on his own ground. Walk directly behind him when moving on the deer ground; this is *not* a position of inferiority but simply one which presents the smallest possible front to the ever alert eyes of the deer. Do not misinterpret the fact that the stalker may not have much to say on the way out, the time for talking is on the way home, but you can be sure that a *good* stalker will be able to point out any places or wildlife of interest and so add to the enjoyment of the day. Copy the stalker implicitly in the last stages of the stalk, keep your rump down *as well as your head* when crawling and, when wriggling flat, endeavour not to telegraph your whereabouts to the deer by waving your legs in the air while propelling yourself forward by the knees. *Drag* them instead and *draw* yourself forward by the arms. Jerky, quick movements are the ones which catch the attention of the deer while slow, studied movements can get you across ground which at first glance appears impossible. Avoid wearing 'flashy' wrist watches while stalking, they will heliograph your whereabouts on a sunny day as your jacket sleeves 'ride-up' in crawling, and there may well be forty or more pairs of eyes in the herd you are stalking, especially when the rut starts and the stags have collected a sizeable herd of hinds each as their respective 'harems'.

When, and if, the shot is successful, it will be much appreciated if you can give the stalker a hand to drag the stag to where it can be loaded on to a pony, or vehicle as the case may be. Remember that many a stag is taken in a place from which the stalker *knows* it will be difficult to extract it, simply not to disappoint the guest rifle. Dragging a stag is seldom an easy or pleasant job and in many cases on short-staffed Highland estates the stalker will be single-handed apart from the ponyman who may be some miles away waiting with the pony.

Deer-stalking was at one time regarded simply as a sport, usually restricted to those 'well endowed' with the goods of this world. The stag was the only quarry regarded as worthy of pursuit. Hind-stalking was only done by the professional estate stalkers. With the hind there was no 'trophy', only the venison, and venison was not then terribly highly regarded in culinary circles. Indeed, I know as a definite fact that even in the late 1930s, before the war, when hinds became too numerous on any one estate, simply because they were *not* then annually shot, stalkers going out to do the 'culling' in many cases simply dragged the carcases out of sight into a handy peat-bog. The situation has changed very much for the better since those days, with much being done, by the Red Deer Commission, English Nature and privately organised groups. These groups bring together a number of estates which might, in the old days, have quarrelled jealously over deer, deer which had spent part of the year on one estate only to be eventually shot, as a trophy, on an adjacent one.

THE COMMISSION

The Red Deer Commission acts as the catalyst to achieve this co-operation. It was set up under the Deer (Scotland) Act 1959 to further the conservation and control of red deer. The Deer (Amendment) (Scotland) Act 1982 extended its powers to include sika deer or such other deer as may be specified by the Secretary of State. It also promotes the management of deer and supports the work of deer management groups and, in general, keeps under review all matters relating to deer. It has a chairman and twelve members, five representing landowning, sporting and forestry interests, five from agricultural interests, one from Scottish Natural Heritage and one from the Natural Environmental Research Council. It has three deer officers and five operational staff, together with the secretary and three administrative staff based in Inverness. At the start, it was by no means regarded with favour by many deer forest owners. One of its first jobs was the highly unpopular and distasteful one of investigating complaints of marauding on agricultural land. This usually occurred where deer were too numerous or had been deprived, by other forms of land use, of former wintering grounds. I am glad to say that it has gradually become recognised that the Red Deer Commission *does* have the interests of deer very much at heart and that they are not simply killers of deer ready to be called in case of need. Their practical work in the counting of red deer, in research such as the earmarking of recently born deer calves so that their future movements and life span can be studied, and their practical down-to-earth advice on all aspects of deer management has, in my opinion, eclipsed that of any other body concerned with red deer.

Their *estimate* of red deer numbers in Scotland is about 300,000 and their opinion (which I share) is that this number is more likely to have to decrease than to increase under the present land use policy. Since *adult* deer have no natural predators, man *must* exercise the role of keeping the numbers of deer consistent with the grazing available to them. If deer-stalking was ever to be banned as a 'blood-sport', deer numbers would increase to the point where deer would be forced to encroach on agricultural ground. They would slowly, but progressively, eat out their hill habitat with increasing and distressing natural mortality each winter and spring. Another realistic reason for good central management is that venison *is* nowadays readily marketable and provides a cash crop in areas where no other crop is viable.

The estimated annual cull necessary to keep the natural increase in check and the deer population more or less static is one-sixth of each sex. The emphasis in selection, in order to maintain a healthy stock, should be to give priority to the weeding-out of stags of inferior antler quality and the unfit, poor-doing and aged of both sexes.

Hind-stalking has never enjoyed much popularity as a sport and frankly I believe it is better that way. It has been summed up neatly as 'to be endured rather than enjoyed' and as it takes place in the rigours of the Highland winter there is a large element of truth in this. Nevertheless it is a very important aspect of red deer management. I personally regard it as more skilled in the selection of beasts to be culled, than the stalking of the stags. Undeniably, however, it does lack the attraction of the antlered majesty of the quarry in stalking the stag, the often thrilling pageantry of the rut and the breathtaking beauty of the autumn hills. In selecting stags, one judges mainly by antler calibre, allowing oneself the occasional trophy where the stock is predominantly of good quality but always removing those of inferior quality, 'switches', 'hummels', one-antlered or spike-topped stags as a priority. As to hind culling, it is relatively easy to pick out the extremely aged or unfit but not nearly so simple to pick out the 'intermediates' which *should* next be selected in preference to the really thriving ones.

Facilities for deer-stalking are much more widely available nowadays. Although much ground is still in private ownership, some days or part of the season may be let by the owner either through local hotels, or through sporting agents in Scotland, London and elsewhere. The *Yellow Pages* are a useful source of information, and such publications as the *Scottish Sporting Gazette*. The Scottish Tourist Board, Revelstone Terrace, Edinburgh, may also help.

Prices vary widely according to the facilities offered, which might include the occupancy of a comfortable lodge. Hill stalking without accommodation might average £250 per day, including the services of a stalker and a ponyman to take home the beast. Some forests do still use ponies for the purpose, though unromantic but useful all-terrain vehicles have often taken their place these days. A tip to stalker and ponyman is traditional and, as hours don't matter on the hill, it can perhaps be regarded as 'overtime'. This must be left to individual decision but £20 to the stalker per outing and £10 to the ponyman is often well deserved. Good stalking!

Woodland Deer-Stalking

Richard Prior

Deer-stalking, like coastal wildfowling, is one of the last truly wild sports and has the outstanding merit in these cheek-by-jowl days that one can enjoy it alone. By tradition, stalking as a British sport has meant the pursuit of red deer on the open hill in Scotland. Only recently, in the last twenty or thirty years, has woodland stalking grown up into a recognised sport that is also something of a science.

We are all accustomed to the idea that wildlife is doomed. Most people are astonished to hear that deer thrive in the majority of British woodlands, even within the dormitory areas of our largest cities. In some places they have increased to such an extent that they are a problem to foresters and farmers, a nightmare to gardeners and too thick on the ground even for their own good health. Because of this, the stalker can perform a useful service and enjoy his sport at the same time, provided that he follows the rules and is not merely out for blood.

There are six different species of deer living wild in this country. Chinese water deer (*Hydropotes inermis*) are not often stalked because of their small numbers and restricted distribution. Muntjac (*Muntiacus reevesii*), the other small deer, are in contrast becoming very numerous and widespread. They are non-seasonal breeders, the does producing a single fawn every seven months. Of the others, the red deer (*Cervus elaphus*) is the largest; a big stag may have antlers more than three feet long, and weigh a quarter of a ton. They are basically forest animals, and have established themselves in wooded areas in many parts of the country. Some owe their origins to escapes from parks, others are descendants of the days of carted stag-hunting. Even in Scotland red deer were forest-dwellers before pressure from man and shrinkage of their natural habitat forced them to live on the open hill.

Fallow deer (*Dama dama*) originate largely from park escapes, although they, too, have been at liberty for centuries in The New Forest, Epping and elsewhere. Their success in adapting to the

Fallow buck.

hazards of life in the wild is reflected by the fact that fallow deer can be found in nearly every English county, thirteen Scottish counties, and even in some places in Wales, a country not noted for its deer population. His flattened antlers and normally spotted coat makes the fallow buck easy to identify. In October when the rut is on, he gives himself away by his *groans* (a loud pig-like grunting), but there are few animals more successful at looking after themselves than an old male fallow.

Japanese sika deer (*Cervus nippon*) probably top the noise league with their ear-splitting triple whistles, although they are a little smaller in body than fallow. They are not widespread, but exist in quite large numbers where conditions suit them. A good sika stag goes about 140 lb on the hoof, the fallow beating him by perhaps 50 lbs. Like all deer they look a great deal bigger than their weight suggests. If you meet a good fallow buck in a gloomy wood, he can look the size of a horse and a great deal more fierce.

These three species, the red, the fallow and the sika are all herding deer – the mature males separating from the rest for most of the year. Sometimes a herd is encountered which consists entirely of males. Others will be made up of females and juveniles. They feed largely by grazing, preferring grass and farm crops with heather and a small amount of leaves and twigs.

The roebuck (*Capreolus capreolus*) who weighs about as much as a small labrador, is strictly a woodland creature, preferring to browse on brambles and coppice growth and, let's face it, young trees, rather than to emerge on to cultivated ground. Roe are usually only seen out on the fields in spring, when food is short, or during the summer when they have been driven there by aggressive bucks or biting insects. In a very few places, roe live more or less permanently in the fields, but even there they seek out woody browse to supplement the soft grass.

Unlike fallow and sika, which are both introductions, roe have occupied this country for the last half million years. Through the Middle Ages the native stock was more or less eliminated in England and was reduced in range and numbers in Scotland. During this century, thanks in part to the enormous forestry programme begun after the First World War, roe have increased and spread. The northern community has pushed south through Lancashire and Yorkshire. Roe were re-introduced to various places in the south during the last century. Now all the counties bordering the English Channel carry their complement. From this base they have pushed north into Bucks, Warwickshire, and up the Welsh border. Thanks to another introduction to Norfolk in the last century, roe now occupy most of East Anglia. Recently, pioneers have succeeded in crossing the Thames into Oxford, Bucks and Gloucestershire. In the southern counties, roe have profited from the abundant food and calcareous soil. Trophies have been obtained there which are in every way comparable with the best to be found in Europe. Bucks from several areas of Scotland are not so very far behind.

The increase and spread of muntjac from their origins in Bedfordshire has been mentioned. They are even more restricted to woodland than roe, preferring thick undergrowth and brambles, though many are finding the delights of suburban gardens. Even in thick cover they tend to move about a good deal, and stalking them with a rifle is a challenge which is increasingly attracting enthusiasts.

DEER MANAGEMENT

One of the great charms of woodland stalking is that the stalker is concerned not only with shooting but with the management of deer. He carries a responsibility to see that what he does is beneficial to the deer herd and in harmony with the landowner's other interests. Safe use of a high-powered rifle entails the most meticulous liaison with everyone who is likely to be around in the wood, whether this is the forest worker, the gamekeeper or the owner's wife collecting fungi. A shot must never be taken where there is the slightest chance of the bullet travelling farther than you can see, and one must reckon not only on predictable woodland activities but on the bluebell picker, the overnight camper and the lurking courting couple. It is no good saying to yourself 'there can't be anyone there, otherwise the deer would have gone' for deer seem quick to realise if someone means them no harm.

Roebuck.

289

It is worth talking to the farmer and the forester, not only to find out where the deer are, but what problems are worrying them, and whether you can help them in one way or another. Perhaps a party of fallow are grazing a field of winter-sown corn. It is to your advantage as well as the farmer's that you should know about this. A well-executed raid may well deter them. The forester may have a young plantation where fraying damage is getting beyond tolerable limits. By shooting an argumentative buck there quickly, you may save him the heavy cost of replanting, and earn his gratitude and cooperation. Even so, it is much better not to go bald-headed at problems like these. Shooting an animal, any animal, may not be more than an immediate palliative to the problem, and with roe in particular you may actually do harm to forestry interests by shooting the wrong buck. If in doubt about the principles of deer management, there is now a reasonable selection of books and advice available from such sources as the British Deer Society, the Game Conservancy and the Forestry Commission.

LOOKING FOR DEER

Deer have interested me since my school days, but I became a deer-stalker almost instantaneously when the owner of some rabbit shooting I used to rent said one day that there were some deer 'up there', and I was welcome to shoot one if he could have a haunch. Three years later I read this burning phrase in *The Still Hunter* by Theodore Van Dyke; 'The most important part of hunting very wild deer,' he wrote, 'is to get sight of a deer at all.' Never a truer word so far as I was concerned, for after all that time I was still 'faint but pursuing'. I had armed myself with a formidable weapon, an old double hammer 'Paradox', more suitable for tiger than for roe. For two long summers I had crawled with the stealth of an Apache along well-marked deer paths. I had crouched with equal patience over many crossing places, tormented by midges but unrewarded, and I had traipsed across the woods, neglecting my rabbiting, with one solitary and distant glimpse of an antlered head in all that time. Of course I had failed to realise that deer, to avoid young men with rifles, got up earlier in the morning than they did.

It seems very simple now, but in those days there was no one to ask about the habits of deer, or how to stalk them. In the end I did begin to realise something of the daily life of the one buck who inhabited my ground, but it was not until another year had passed that he and I finally met. Even then the outcome was by no means certain, for I was expecting him to pass below me as I lay on the threshold of a badger's sett. Hearing a noise, I turned half on my back, to see the buck regarding me at fifteen yards' range from behind. It was only due to his steady nerves and not mine that I was lucky enough to put a bullet in his neck by firing off the left shoulder. His head was subsequently exhibited at the International trophy show at Düsseldorf but it did not need that to make the event memorable. By that time I had graduated to a ·22 Hornet rifle, which is illegal now, but in those days would kill roe well enough in careful hands. I had none of the equipment which makes today's roe-stalker so efficient. I was not even sure how to gralloch properly and, having no rucksack, I carried that heavy beast more than a mile on my shoulders which reduced me to a jelly, and my clothes to an indescribable state; not that that mattered in the triumph of the moment.

Looking back, I must have made all the mistakes in the book. I had been searching at hours when no self-respecting deer would be showing. By haunting the woods week in and week out, and worse still by tracking them on their own paths, instead of keeping to human passageways, I must have reduced the roe to a state of wildness which would have made more than a chance meeting quite impossible.

On new ground, a tremendous lot can be done by watching the open spaces from a reasonable distance downwind, and by passing along any rides or tracks where the deer are accustomed to seeing people. Only an occasional foray into the thickets should be made if you are not to disturb the normal habits of the deer you want to observe. No doubt my buck had watched from cover a hundred times as I trudged round, for they will let you pass without moving if you give no sign of having seen anything. The stalker should not look for a 'picture-book deer', but for anything which strikes his eye as unusual in the landscape. The flick of a fallow's tail, or an ear; an odd patch of colour, or the horizontal silhouette of a back which stands out in woodland where nearly all the lines are vertical. There is an almost irresistible urge to hurry on to the next likely place if the first quick look round a clearing does not at once reveal a deer. How the deer must laugh at the human equivalent of a cat on hot bricks; how they should fear his opposite who will sit motionless on a log for half an hour, convinced that there is just as good a chance of seeing a deer where he is, as anywhere else in the wood.

Binoculars are needed for sorting the deer from the trees, besides being essential for the identification and assessment of an animal when it is located. They should be worn around the neck for instant use and not carried in a case. When you are finally presented with the chance of a shot it is unlikely to be the deliberate prone business of the target range or the mountainside. Too often there is a screen of grass or bracken between you and the deer. If you are not forced to shoot standing, then a sitting position is all that that can be hoped for.

USE OF STICK

Shooting steadily under these conditions is terribly difficult, but a good stick does help. Well-seasoned hazel is the best, thick enough not to bend when you lean on it, shod with rubber and about the height of your eyes. Walk with it in the left hand with the rifle slung on your right shoulder, muzzle down. (Except where there is risk of getting snow or mud in the barrel.) The stick is first used to steady the binoculars as you watch the animal. When you decide to shoot, slip the rifle off your shoulder and grip the fore-end with the stick in your left hand. Practice and clean living will allow you to control the sideways wobble and get off a good shot. Shooting with a hangover or when you are very tired is unreliable. Shooting after drinking is just plain dangerous.

The direction of the wind is paramount in planning your stalking, but remember that it swirls and eddies in clearings and valleys. Deer will be coming out in the evening and many stalkers prefer to reach some commanding position, or sit in a high seat, before the deer are expected to move. In the morning they return to cover, and it is usual to walk quickly along the woodland tracks or the margins of the fields, intercepting them as they make their slow way back, lingering to catch a last mouthful of breakfast or warm themselves as the sun rises. During the rut, this routine gets interrupted and the keen stalker can spend most of the day in the woods.

There is a wide difference in the breeding habits of roe when compared with the larger deer. This is because the roe doe carries her young for nearly ten months, from the rut in late July and early August until some time in May when the fawns are born. Like seals and some of the weasel family, she displays the phenomenon of *delayed implantation*. The fertilised egg stays floating free in the uterus and does not attach itself to the wall until mid-December, after which development proceeds at a normal pace. When the female is in season she makes a squeaking noise which attracts the buck. This can be imitated to the same effect, either with a beech leaf or various types of manufactured whistle.

The roe-stalker tries to arrange his holiday for the first or second week in August, and is away to the woods with his rifle and a selection of calls, praying for the hot thundery weather which is most likely to bring results. He selects a place where he knows a buck lives and which, although wooded, is reasonably open. After allowing everything to become still he blows a series of squeaks in imitation of the doe. Sometimes it works. More often, let's be honest, it doesn't, but real experts are uncannily effective. If a doe comes, you know that your squeaks are too high and she has mistaken you for a fawn. Sometimes it is worth deliberately imitating the fawn so that the doe will come and bring the buck behind her. Of course the buck that appears may not be one on the list for shooting, and it is necessary in the heat of the moment to study him carefully through the binoculars.

THE RUT

Later in the year, the bigger species start their rut, beginning with the red deer about mid-September, followed by the sika. Fallow start a week or two later. Unlike the family set-up of the roe, dominant males of the three bigger species set up a stamping ground or *rutting stand* where they commence to roar, whistle or groan according to their kind. Often a wallow is near by, where they urinate and bathe and plaster themselves with the resulting mud. Coating yourself with black liquid is supposed to make you appear larger and stronger. Of course it is impossible to know what electrifying effect may also be produced on one's females by the smell. A number of aspiring males are likely to be found round the rutting stand. Woodland deer do not seem to go in much for rounding up the females as red deer do on the open hill in Scotland, or the other species in park conditions. The females appear to come and go across the rutting stand of their own free will. If one is in season she will be pursued and covered by the master stag or buck. Approaching a master stag in the rut can be extremely exciting, but if at all possible any shooting should be restricted to the first part of the rut, before the males become too *run* or wasted by their prolonged exertions.

Good deer management dictates that the balance between the sexes is reasonably level. Sufficient females must be shot, even if this is distasteful to many stalkers. It is a job which really sorts the men from the boys, not only because it can be extremely difficult, but being a winter job it is one which tends to be shirked by the less keen types. One legitimate way of helping things on is to *move* deer. The technique involves one beater who walks at random through the wood, not making much noise but behaving like a forest worker or a keeper about his normal affairs. This induces the deer to move away along their normal paths. The rifle waits concealed in a strategic place where he can examine them as they come slowly forward, shooting any suitable does when, as will often happen, they stop to look back. Males of the larger deer species lose their antlers in the spring, and this technique can be used throughout the doe season from November to February. Any attempt to use it for roe must be delayed until the bucks are beginning to show some velvet so that they can be readily distinguished from the females. This means that a start should not be made until the New Year.

AFTER THE SHOT

Sooner or later the golden day will dawn when the chance of a shot has finally presented itself, and you have a dead deer at your feet. Every stalker has the moral obligation to make the best possible use of what he has got, not only in the material terms of producing good venison and so on, but also by gaining knowledge which he can use to perfect his technique. Is the bullet hole more or less where you aimed? What was the reaction of the deer to a hit in this spot? Did he drop instantly to the shot, or run some way before collapsing? In this case it is worth retracing his steps to where the beast was standing at the shot and see what signs there are of a hit. Perhaps some cut hair, or a spot of blood. Blood will be a different colour according to its origin; bright, frothy pink for a lung shot, scarlet for an artery; darker for a shot in the liver.

If you cannot find the deer immediately after a shot, it is worth marking the place with a hat or some other object so that you can search diligently in circles round it, but do not do the same as a lady friend of mine who used a beautiful silk scarf for the purpose. After some considerable while her buck was recovered, but the headscarf could never be found. It is probably still there. If you can, get an experienced stalker to show you how to perform the gralloch cleanly and quickly. It can either be a neat, or an extremely distasteful and messy operation. I prefer to open the rib cage as well as the stomach cavity, by cutting down the sternum with a saw. This lets the carcase cool quickly, and also allows the stalker to study the location of the vital organs and the effect of his bullet on them. If the carcase is due to go to a game dealer he may need to have the 'red offal' for veterinary inspection. Otherwise the kidneys, heart and liver should be removed and put in a polythene bag as they are excellent eating. If you have a dog, the lungs and the wall of the rumen should be stowed in another bag for boiling when you get home. Feeding them raw tends to make dogs smelly. Turn the carcase over for a minute or two to drain, then either hang it in a bush by its hamstrings for collection or fold it up with its head in the middle and stow it in the rucksack. The best of these have a washable lining. It is essential to get a carcase back quickly to a cool, fly-proof larder.

Skinning is better left until the meat is needed because venison dries quickly and forms a hard skin when exposed to the air. The skull, on the other hand, should be prepared quickly. If only the frontal bone is needed, it is not a long or difficult job. The only tools I use are a skinning knife, a general purpose saw and an old saucepan. The head is detached from the body, either by sawing or by disjointing the vertebrae, and is roughly skinned. The skull is laid on its side on a bench and then, holding the antlers firmly with the left hand, a cut is made from the back of the ears through to the end of the nose. The actual line depends on a stalker's preference, but care must be taken that the saw emerges at the same level on the other side of the skull. This can be checked as sawing progresses. Cut out the lower jaw which is of interest for guessing the age of the beast, and put it and the skull into a saucepan of boiling water so that the antlers and coronets are clear of the water level.

If you throw in two tablespoonfuls of washing soda, the work will be quicker and easier, but care must be taken not to overboil. After anything from a quarter to three quarters of an hour, depending on the age of the animal, the flesh can be stripped away from the bone, using a pair of long-nosed pliers and a rather blunt skinning knife. This will leave you with a clean but greasy skull. To make it white and odourless, wrap it in a thin layer of cottonwool up to the coronets, then stand it in a dish and pour enough hydrogen peroxide over the cottonwool to moisten it thoroughly. Progress should be checked after four or five hours, but an old animal can safely be left overnight. After this the skull should be washed, allowed to dry and then mounted on any sort of wooden shield which the fancy of the stalker dictates.

BUTCHERING

When the meat is ready for eating, which can be as little as twenty-four hours after shooting in hot weather and up to a week or more in very cold conditions, cuts should be made down the inside of each leg to join up with the central incision and the skin should be eased away from the hocks using the knife. This will allow the animal to be suspended by its hocks from a low beam, or the branch of a tree in the garden. Start by freeing the skin from the lower ribs and work always towards the spine. Work round the haunches and try to do more by pulling rather than cutting.

When everything is clear down to the ribs, the shoulders and forelegs should be skinned carefully and the neck last of all, where probably some knife work will be necessary. Try not to get any loose hair on the meat as it will spoil the appearance. Consult the cook before starting to cut up the meat. Either there will be a preference for a saddle which is the most delicious joint in many people's opinion, or if freezer room is at a premium, you must fillet the back like a cod and produce two long cylinders of meat and a lot of dog bones. The shoulders can be detached with the knife alone by cutting the connecting tissue along the ribs. The haunches should be divided and then cut away from the backbone, using a saw. It is a good thing to lay out some polythene sheet on the table on which to put these joints as they come free. If they are not immediately needed for the kitchen, the various joints can be put in clean polythene bags, sealed as well as possible and labelled clearly. Once the joint is frozen it is difficult to see exactly what is inside the bag. It is disconcerting to find you have unfrozen a bag of dog meat when the boss is coming to dinner.

Venison is excellent, although young doe is a long sight better than rutty old stag. The meat is usually fairly fat-free, and care should be taken that it is not allowed to dry out in the cooking. In the old days there used to be great arguments about whether a roe was ever 'in pride of grease' that is, when the meat was well covered and marbled with fat, and during what month one should shoot the buck in order to achieve this desirable condition. I certainly agree to some extent with the author of *Autumns in Argyllshire* – 'My mind recoils with horror from Colquhoun's suggestion that bucks ought to be shot in the winter when they have lost their horns, because they are then better eating. For my part I would rather have one fine roe's head than a wilderness of haunches.' The point that seems to have escaped him is that one can enjoy the summer buck stalking, but change to does in the winter. This way you have the double satisfaction of doing a good job of deer management and laying down the best of the venison in your freezer.

EQUIPMENT

The choice of a stalking rifle is discussed in another chapter, but the odds and ends that go with it are almost as important. Only the basic items can be mentioned here. With experience you will acquire a collection.

Every stalking rifle should have a carrying sling. This should be made of reasonably waterproof material and must not rattle, or slip off the shoulder. There is nothing more annoying than having to hitch up your rifle constantly because it has slipped. I like the sling invented by that celebrated Scottish roe-stalker, Kenneth Macarthur, which consists of a leather rein covered with a rubber non-slip sleeve. A saddler will make one up. The ends of the rein go through sling loops on the rifle and are secured by leather thongs to prevent rattling. For stalking in the Scottish Highlands, it is necessary to have a rifle cover. These are normally far too small to accommodate a 'scope sight. Mine was made for a particularly unwieldy ·22 match rifle. With it, one is not left struggling vainly to pull the rifle out while the stag walks slowly away. Some have wool inside which protects the rifle from knocks. They should be very carefully dried to prevent rusting.

Every stalker needs a knife. It should be of good steel to hold a fine edge and if the blade folds, it should lock open to stop it shutting up unexpectedly. If your stalking involves a fair proportion of prone shots, a bipod makes shots over high grass, combine stubble and the like more steady and sure.

Most of the enjoyment to be had from stalking is not the act of shooting but in watching the deer, and the other animals and birds which may be encountered. Shooting is only the logical conclusion of a stalk, providing a climax to the excitement, and dividing the pleasure from the hard work. To get the best out of a day's stalking a good pair of binoculars is essential. In Scotland the professional stalker uses a telescope, but unless you are accustomed to using one, binoculars are a better bet. For woodland work the power should not be higher than 8, but the object lenses should be fairly large for bad light conditions. 7×50 binoculars, that is with a magnification of 7 and an object glass diameter of 50 mm, are used by many woodland stalkers. Good glasses of this specification cost less than the high-quality compact roof prism instruments of around $7 \times$ or 8×42 which are lovely to use and justify their formidable price by exceptional clarity and twilight performance.

Roe-stalkers use a frameless rucksack which is large enough to hold a buck, and this accommodates useful things like blindcord, polythene bags, a spare knife and possibly a thin nylon waterproof.

The stalker's equipment is expensive but need not be ruinous. The secret of success is to choose carefully and then to keep it really well adjusted and maintained.

VI
CLAY PIGEON
SHOOTING

VI
Clay Shooting

Clay bird shooting is a world of mystery to me. I have, of course, shot clays. Once, at the Welsh Game and County Fair in Glamorgan, I had the humiliating experience of being followed by a large crowd who had somehow got to hear that I was 'Town Gun' of the *Shooting Times*. In vain to explain to an expectant audience – expectant of a display of successful marksmanship – that writing about shooting is not the same as being a crack shot. Luckily, I managed to break enough of the damned things not to make a complete fool of myself. But that is about the limit of my expertise. I don't take to clay-busting for three, to me, good reasons. (1) You can't eat them. (2) They're an expensive pastime. (3) I can't hit them. The last reason is the most cogent. I do, however, realise that thousands of sportsmen find competitive clay shooting totally enthralling. Moreover I have come to recognise that many clay experts are excellent game, pigeon and wildfowl shots into the bargain. When I asked Derek Partridge to contribute this section I foolishly thought that the whole business could be disposed of in a dozen pages. In fact it took double that number and, though I may never shoot a clay again in anger, I find the contribution comprehensive and quite fascinating. This section has been brought up to date by Alan Jarrett (see A Note on the Contributors).

C.W.

Guns for Clays

Derek Partridge

Revised by Alan Jarrett

GUNS AND AMMO

For all practical purposes, the only gun used for competitive clays is a 12-bore. Exceptions to this are youngsters, ladies and, in America where skeet is shot with twelve, twenty, twenty-eight and .410. The gun is generally an over-and-under, as opposed to a side-by-side.

A simple test indicates the reason for this. Pick a small point in your room — like a light switch — and quickly 'aim' at it by fully extending your right arm, with the palm flat to the ground, so that your five fingers constitute the aiming apparatus. Lower your arm and then repeat the same procedure, only this time, tuck your thumb out of the way into your palm and have the palm at 90° to the ground (i.e. parallel with a wall), so that the aiming apparatus this time becomes the edge of the right index finger. The five fingers equate with the broad sighting plane of the side-by-side — and the edge of the index finger corresponds with the narrower sighting plane of the over-and-under. You will find that with the single-finger sighting plane, your 'aim' at the light switch will be more precise than with the five fingers.

As clay shooting *demands* utter precision for its comparatively small target, this is the main reason the over-and-under is the favoured gun. A secondary reason is that, as the under barrel is usually fired first and as its recoil is placed lower than on a side-by-side, it causes less disturbance to the second shot.

Given the principle of the single sighting plane, the gun can also be a single-barrel automatic, or even a pump-action, manually operated repeater. The disadvantage of the single barrel is that it only has one fixed choke, whereas for DTL, Olympic Trench and sporting, differing degrees of choke are desirable in each barrel. A partial solution to this problem is the existence of choke units, which are either individual chokes, which are screwed into the end of the barrel, or an adjustable type which can be turned on the barrel to a choice of settings. There even exist in America, choke units which automatically jump from one setting to another, activated by the firing of the first shot. The only trouble is that for most of the clay sports where a choice of choke for the two allowable shots is required, such choke units are not permitted! Which brings us back to the over-and-under.

The average clay gun, be it for the DTL/OT group or for the skeet/sporting group, is heavier than a game gun. Game guns are designed to be carried long hours, frequently over tiring terrain, and also to fire comparatively light loads − from $\frac{15}{16}$oz to $1\frac{1}{16}$oz − this of course excludes magnums. Clay guns are never carried for long, use loads which start at 1 oz and generally fire many more cartridges in a short space of time than any game gun. The added weight helps to reduce recoil and so the fatigue and potential flinching which can be induced by recoil affect. The weight also tends to make for smoother gun swinging.

Clay guns invariably have single triggers, often selective. A single trigger is fractionally faster than two triggers and also eliminates the necessity of moving the hand and finger back to the second trigger.

Raised, ventilated ribs are also almost universal. The ventilation is supposed to help disperse the heat haze which rises from barrels fired frequently in hot conditions. I have never held too much stock in the importance of this theory, as the haze only exists while the gun is stationary, prior to calling for the target. As soon as the barrels are moved to the clay, the haze is naturally left behind. However, I do prefer the very positive sighting plane offered by the raised rib. The top of these ribs is always file cut, to prevent sun reflection distracting the shooter. Some ribs are so broad that they all but overlap the edges of the top barrel. Such ribs are most applicable to the slower, deliberate sighting applicable to DTL and particularly American trapshooting. A larger fore-end than that found on a game gun is another feature of the clay gun. It is generally a semi-beavertail, a modification of the extremely broad American full beavertail − so called for its resemblance to the beaver's broad, flat tail. Clay shooters like to maintain a firm hold (*not* a stranglehold grip) on their fore-ends and also don't want to get their fingers burned from barrels heated by continuous firing.

Side-by-sides can be used for skeet and sporting, but even here the preference is for the over-and-under. One Italian friend of mine won the European Olympic Trench Championship twice, using a side-by-side – which he still uses – but he is truly an exception.

Now to specific guns for each clay sport. The prices quoted are not exact, but given only as a rough guide. They are based on 1993 prices and include Value Added Tax.

DOWN-THE-LINE GUNS

The standard DTL gun will be an over-and-under ejector and will have 30″ barrels, fitted with a metal or ivory foresight and perhaps an ivory midsight; bored three-quarter and full; a raised, ventilated rib; a single, usually selective trigger; a full pistol grip; probably a Monte Carlo comb with stock dimensions of $14\frac{1}{2}″$ length (or pull), $1\frac{3}{8}″$ drop at both ends of the Monte Carlo and $1\frac{3}{4}″-1\frac{7}{8}″$ drop at the heel; it will weigh 8 lb ($7\frac{3}{4}$ lb if 28″ barrels and $8\frac{1}{4}$ lb if 32″ barrels); it will have the semi-beavertail forearm and a rubber recoil pad with a serrated surface to grip into the shoulder once placed there; it will usually be chambered for $2\frac{3}{4}″$ cartridges; the trigger pulls are likely to be (if you're lucky) around 5 lb and 6 lb – I have come across some as heavy as 9 lb! – lastly, it is unlikely to have any cast-off, unless it is a Franchi.

Some DTL guns still come bored full and full. I feel both they and the three-quarter and full are unnecessarily over-choked for the distance of DTL targets and the very dense patterns given by modern cartridges – with or without the plastic cup wad or shot collar. A boring of half and three-quarter choke would be adequate – provided the 60% and 65% patterns are absolutely evenly distributed throughout the 30″ pattern circle and neither bunched in the centre, nor grouped patchily around the sheet.

A midsight is to allow for lateral and vertical checking of the head and eye alignment along the rib, prior to calling for the target. Eye, midsight and foresight want to be in line – you can check this at home in front of a mirror. While at the mirror you can make a rough check on the fit of your gun, by mounting it comfortably and slowly – with your eyes closed. If, when you open them, you're looking in the right place, there's not much wrong with the gun. However, it must always be remembered that all standard factory guns are designed to fit Mr Average Shooting Customer – an individual in his forties, about 5′ 10″ and let's say somewhat stockily built! If that's not you, you may need some alterations, probably more in terms of length than anything else. In any case, you will want those heavy, sometimes creepy trigger pulls adjusted by a qualified expert, as it is one of the most skilled gun modification jobs. The pulls should have about a pound difference between them, say 3 lb and 4 lb or $3\frac{1}{2}$ lb and $4\frac{1}{2}$ lb. A sometimes frightening test of trigger pull weight can be made by suspending the gun (unloaded but with a snap-cap for preference in the chamber), muzzle downwards, from the trigger. If the weight of the gun doesn't fire the trigger – that's a very heavy trigger pull!

CHOICE OF GUNS

A wide range of guns is used for clay shooting, with a corresponding divergence in price. It is perhaps a sad indictment of the state of our gun manufacturing trade that all competition guns are of foreign make! With new guns there will be something to suit all pockets, ranging from the bottom end of the market with Baikal and Rizzini, through Lanber and Laurona, Beretta, Miroku, Winchester, Browning and Perazzi. Prices range from not much more than £300 to £4,000 and beyond. The variety of guns on offer is seemingly of bewildering diversity, but on closer analysis the shooter can begin to sift his way through. How much can he afford? What sort of targets does he want to shoot? How versatile does the gun need to be? Once these questions are answered the choice soon becomes narrower.

Some of the largest manufacturers are shrewd enough to offer a variety of guns throughout the price range, although these seldom drop below the middle price range of around £500−£600. Thus Beretta offer a choice of guns from their 686 range, through the enormously popular 682, to the more expensive sidelock SO range. Beretta also offer arguably the best competition semi-automatic on the market. Browning offer their cheaper brands in the Medallist and Citori. They also have an interest in the Miroku stable of guns, and of course at the top of their range are the renown B, C and D grades. If you want the best, then a big cheque will be needed.

Made-to-measure guns are an obvious option and easily available at the upper end of the market. Modern technology also allows many and various adjustments to be made to 'off-the-shelf' guns. Once again you get what you pay for, although money spent on buying the gun you really want will be amply repaid in extra broken clays.

OLYMPIC TRENCH GUNS

All the preceding comments apply equally, with some very minor observations. Chokes want to be three-quarter and full; some trench shooters favour 28″ barrels as they feel they handle faster on the quicker trench targets − just as some DTL shots favour the 32″ barrels as they are steadier on the slower DTL targets − but the 30″ remains the favourite. The Italians, who are the unchallenged experts in this field, prefer less drop, i.e. a lower sighting plane than for a DTL gun (remember DTL targets have one constant, rising elevation, whereas trench birds vary from grass-cutters to sky-rockets). The Italians are also not fond of the Monte Carlo comb, but almost all use a straight comb, with a drop in the slope of $\frac{3}{8}″$ from nose to heel.

SKEET GUNS

Standard skeet gun specifications vary from DTL/OT guns as follows: barrel length will be 26″−28″ or even longer, choking skeet and skeet, or improved cylinder and quarter choke; stock length 14″, drop $1\frac{1}{2}″$ comb and $2\frac{1}{2}″$ heel; weight between 7 and $7\frac{1}{2}$lb; chambered for $2\frac{1}{2}″$ cartridges. The recoil pad will vary; if it's for ISU skeet, where it has to be mounted from the hip, it may be finished in wood, vulcanite or usually with a thinner (than for DTL) rubber pad, faced with leather and often with the heel rounded off to permit speedy, unhindered mounting. For optional gun position English skeet, the pad will be according to the shooter's whim of starting gun up or down.

Choice and preference of makes are again very similar. However, many modern skeet shooters seem to have very liberated ideas concerning their choice of gun. Bigger, heavier guns are commonplace, while there is a widely accepted interchange between guns in use for both skeet and sporting. The widespread advent of interchangeable choke tubes is largely responsible for this, making it less likely for the modern all-rounder to need more than one gun for each type of target. Thus an all-round trap gun, and an all-round skeet/sporting gun will suffice for all but the most fastidious of shooters.

The semi-automatic is perhaps best suited to skeet – largely because both targets can be shot with the same open choke. The Remington 1100 was always *the* skeet shooting semi-automatic. Today it has largely been replaced by Beretta and Browning, although a more recent relaunch has tried to win back lost ground.

SPORTING GUNS

About the only major difference from a skeet gun is that preferred choking is around a quarter and three-quarters. There are some preferences for 26″ barrels; weights nearer 7 than $7\frac{1}{2}$ lb and some shooters like the semi-pistol grip that used to be a feature of the Browning and is now a special order from them. If they are to be used for FITASC sporting competitions, where $1\frac{1}{4}$ oz load is permitted, they should be chambered for $2\frac{3}{4}$″ cartridges.

There is often a tendency for sporting clay shooters to do a fair bit of game shooting with the same gun. The advent of the interchangeable choke tube has been perhaps the single biggest break-through in sporting guns of modern times. Guns with this facility are now more versatile than ever before, and ought to yield more broken clays when in competent hands. However, this is not always an advantage. The wide choice of chokes is sometimes a problem for those shooters undecided which to use for the best. All the main gun makers now offer models with interchangeable choke tubes.

SECOND-HAND GUNS

These should obviously only be bought from a reputable and responsible gun dealer or, if from a friend, he should not be offended if you ask for it to be checked over by an expert first.

Berettas, Brownings and Mirokus seem to hold their value well. Automatics may not keep their value as well, as if not properly looked after, they can deteriorate far more.

CARTRIDGES

For DTL, 1 oz of No. $7\frac{1}{2}$ shot is the most popular load, although many shooters opt for No. 8 in the first barrel. No. 8, with $7\frac{1}{2}$ for the second shot if needed is an ideal choice, with that first shot offering a denser pattern at the closer ranges encountered. No. $7\frac{1}{2}$ is likely to be the first choice for the international disciplines, such as OT and ABT, as the pellets will have the required energy to break a hard fast target at extreme range. Many advocates of international trap favour coated shot which will deform less during passage along the barrel and hit harder upon contact. Of course such loads attract a premium price. Skeet shooters are almost exclusively users of No. 9 shot, for it patterns well at the close ranges encountered on the skeet layout. At such close ranges, even this small shot will be more than adequate to break the target. Sporting users may opt for a mix and match approach, using $7\frac{1}{2}$, 8 or 9 dependent on the range of the target. The sporting shooter can thus mix his shot sizes in order to maximise the likelihood of a telling shot.

As with guns, many cartridges come from abroad, with continental, American and even oriental suppliers having an impact on the market. The household names of Eley and Winchester now have to compete with a wide variety of competitors such as Express, Gamebore, Victory, Maionchi and a host of others. All have their supporters and all offer a wide range of loads from the cheap, slow load to the expensive, fast, superb competition load. Cartridge technology now means that most of the top brands are very similar in performance and are mostly very fine loads indeed. It is heartening to report that British cartridge manufacturers continue to occupy a strong niche in the market-place.

It speaks volumes for technology that the change to 1 oz loads was accomplished with no noticeable fall-off in scores. The likely change to $\frac{7}{8}$ oz before many more years are past is a further example of how advanced is this branch of our sport.

Home loads, extensively used throughout America for clay

310

sports, are not allowed by the Clay Pigeon Shooting Association for competitions under its auspices. This is probably as the CPSA doesn't feel we have reached, generally, the same proficiency and therefore, standards of safety, achieved by the Americans in this potentially dangerous field.

An excellent piece of advice given me when a youngster – and oft ignored! – is this: with very few exceptions, all guns and all cartridges are better than all shooters. So, for those who are perpetually blaming their guns and cartridges for their failures and for ever adjusting their guns – just remember that the nut that needs most adjusting is probably the one behind the gun!

Clay Shooting

Derek Partridge

Revised by Alan Jarrett

Clay pigeons are probably the only 'flying saucers' regularly using earth's airspace. From take-off to touch-down they make comparatively short flights of some fifty to sixty yards. Such flights are frequently intercepted, as shotgunners have learned to identify unerringly this particular UFO and blast it from our skies.

A clay pigeon most nearly resembles an upside down saucer, some $4\frac{1}{2}''$ in diameter. It's called a pigeon as it was designed to replace live pigeons used for competitive shooting. It's not made of clay, but normally of pitch and limestone. Usually it's black, but can be coloured white, yellow, orange or red to improve its visibility against different backgrounds. Some new shooters, unnerved after their first encounter with clays, call them 'flying aspirins', rather than saucers. There is one clay which even experienced shooters consider 'aspirins' − it's used for one form of sporting clays, called a Mini-clay and is only $2\frac{1}{4}''$ in diameter!

All clays are propelled into the air from the metal arm of a spring-loaded machine. This is called a trap, a throwback to live pigeon-shooting origins, in which the bird was placed in a box known as a trap. Apart from a version known as a hand-thrower (generally used for beginners), traps range from simple versions which will throw one angle and height, to the most common which will throw a clay fifty to sixty yards at one height, through 90° of angle − and on to the most sophisticated which are computerised, hold a magazine of 1,250 clays, are in constant motion both vertically and horizontally and will throw targets 80 to 110 yards, through 360° and to angles of up to 65°. 'Trap' is not the only term to come from live pigeon shooting. Clay targets are commonly referred to as 'birds', a hit as a 'kill' and a miss as 'lost'.

To the game or rough shooter, two major differences with clays are immediately apparent. Generally a clay shooter knows where and when his target will appear. On first sight, it is usually accelerating fast, then it gradually loses the impetus of being 'thrown' from the trap and finally drops back to earth. It is clearly easier to shoot the clay on its upward, accelerating flight, as it can be seen. Far harder is attempting to kill it on its decelerating, downward path, as the clay keeps disappearing from view beneath the barrels of the gun. To kill during the acceleration phase requires a degree of speed which can at first seem unobtainable to the beginner. It is acquired through practice and experience.

The majority of clays shot today are in competitions, ranging from village fetes through club, county, area, national, European and World Championships up to the Olympic Games. Clays are shot by game shooters as a form of practice for field shooting and are also the most effective form of training for any beginner, whether he intends to shoot game or clays.

SAFETY

For those using a shotgun for the first time, safety in gun handling is far more important than accurate gun pointing. When the beginner sees his first clay broken, it is almost like magic: the target flies upwards, a gun is swung, there is a bang and the clay disappears in a puff of smoke. How did it happen?

The instructor should place an empty cartridge box on the ground a few feet away. Firing the gun at the box will produce a two- to three-inch diameter hole in the box and a gaping rent in the earth behind it. A brief word to point out that a similar hole would appear in a human being, should dramatically and indelibly imprint in the beginner's mind the lethal effect of a shotgun and the consequent need for constant consideration of safe gun handling at all times.

REQUIREMENTS FOR SUCCESS

A successful competitive clay shooter requires a formidable combination of assets, for it's a very tough and demanding sport. The Russians, who carefully analyse all sports, term it 'the marathon of nerves' − making a specific comparison between the effect the twenty-six-mile run has on an athlete's physique and the strain on a competitor's nerves in a top shooting competition. The perfect competitor needs physical fitness, with supple muscles; excellent eyesight and fast reflexes; a driving determination to succeed (and to overcome the inevitable failures along the way); boundless self-confidence, tempered by the ability to recognise and correct faults; total concentration, rigid self-control and ruthless self-discipline. However, long before he approaches needing such an exacting array of talents, he needs the basics of good shooting technique: good stance and gun handling − and a gun to fit him. The guns for clay shooting are covered in the previous chapter, for now suffice to say that our clay shooter is generally going to be using an over-and-under, rather than the conventional game shooter's side-by-side. Gun fit is covered elsewhere in this book, but, just as you would with clothing, alter the gun to the man − not the man to the gun. The end result should be so precise a fit that when one's eye is looking at a moving clay and the gun is then mounted to the shoulder, the shotgunner must know, *without checking*, that his gun will be automatically 'looking at', and therefore shooting at, the same point.

STANCE

In any sport, good stance and the correct handling of the 'tool' for the job are subject to varying theories, based on the personal experiences of certain outstanding individuals. Many shooters perform well *in spite of* having basically bad stances and gun-mounting techniques, rather than *because of* benefiting from good ones. The success of each shot is largely determined by these two factors − before the target is even called for − so they are of vital importance. Most new shooters learn their stance and technique through untrained observation and from a muddle of conflicting advice. Some shooters are forced by physical peculiarities to adopt stances and techniques that vary considerably from any sort of 'norm'. If they reach the top, they are slavishly followed by other would-be champions − who have never thought to investigate what lies behind the maestro's idiosyncrasies. After years of studying many top shooters, I have tried to combine their basic, successful features with my

314

own belief in being as natural, simple and comfortable as possible.

Some shooters stand four square to a trap, which favours swinging to left-hand targets, while others stand at right angles to it, favouring right-hand targets. Each drastically restricts the ability to swing to the opposite side target. At any stand, you know the maximum angles through which your target can be thrown. If you place your feet, which position your body, to the centre of these two extreme angles, then the body has an equal swing to either side, instead of favouring one and hindering the other. An easy way to find this position is to hold the gun loosely between your hands, with your arms hanging down by your sides. As you gradually move your feet right or left, the muzzle of the gun will move too. When the muzzle is pointing at the midpoint between the two extreme angles, your feet (and body) are properly aligned. This will bring the feet to an angle of approximately 45° to the target exit point from any stand.

I have never found a valid reason to space the feet any wider or closer than you would naturally stand and talk to a friend. But some shooters virtually do the splits, as if digging in to take the recoil of a cannon, while others place their feet together, wobble in the slightest breeze and sway back under recoil. Some shooters raise back foot — we're not storks, designed to roost on one leg! We're better balanced with both feet on the ground, so you might as well leave them the way nature intended them.

Some shooters go into an exaggerated double knees bend at the moment of firing. Others emulate the Prussian aristocracy and march to the firing line, click their heels and remain stiff and unbending. Not suprisingly, this makes it hard for them to swing on to angle targets. Many shooters prefer to just break the lock on the front knee, so it — and therefore the body — can have fluidity of movement to swing sideways. Some then place most of the body weight forward on to the front leg. I find this can cause slight imbalance and prefer to gently incline my body forward, from both ankles, but keep my weight more evenly distributed on both feet. I feel this gives more stability in movement to targets.

Some shooters place their left hand back almost by the trigger guard, which gives wonderful fluidity of movement, but a minimum of control over the pointing of the gun. Others (the stiff Prussian aristocracy again!) fully extend the left arm, straining to reach beyond the fore-end, which gives fantastic pointing control, but makes it almost impossible to get the barrels moving at all! In conjunction with this, some wave the left elbow about their heads, while others snuggle it down into their bodies. It depends to some extent whether you favour the theory of left arm pointing or not. While the left arm can do the pointing, it can also act as a brake. I'm inclined to let the whole body do the pointing. The left arm/hand position is best determined by holding the gun between your hands, the right hand in position on the grip and trigger. *Presuming* you have a properly balanced gun, move the left hand up and down until the gun feels like it wants to tip neither forward nor back, but so that its weight feels squarely between the hands. Then shoulder it and let the left arm drop into a position that feels comfortable and natural, not too high, not too hunched in. Cradle the fore-end firmly in your palm, with the fingers wrapped round it, possibly with the index finger more or less pointing the way down the barrels. Make sure that neither thumb nor fingers touch or cover the top rib, as they will deflect your line of sight down the barrels.

The position of the right arm affects the position of the hand and therefore the important grip and placement of the trigger finger (this is also affected by the thickness and slope of the pistol grip). The trigger should be pulled from its lowest point, other-wise it becomes progressively harder to pull as the finger slides upwards − and if the right arm is too high up in the air, it is difficult to pull the trigger from the bottom. Together, the arms should look, from the front, roughly like a slightly off-centre, inverted V.

The position of the right arm is governed largely by the position of the right shoulder, and this is where slight body 'distortion' can be legitimate, especially if you have a long neck. (The long-neck problem can be overcome by increasing the drop at the heel.) If you mount the gun with your right shoulder in its natural, down position, you may find that the stock is some way from your face and you have to bend your head and neck down to it. The stock must always be brought up to the face, so, by raising the right shoulder, as you lift the gun, you bring the 'gun-backing' up and you'll find the stock then comes into your face. At the same time as you raise the shoulder, also raise the right elbow. This opens up a hollow pocket for the gun butt to fit firmly into − if you leave the elbow down, a hard bunch of muscles will defy entry to the butt. Once the butt is in position, allow the right elbow to drop into whatever position and level is comfortable and natural to it. The butt should be placed as far in from the shoulder as possible and comfortable, so as to bring the rib under the eye. If you mount the gun way out on your shoulder, your head is going to have to lean over to the stock, to get the eye behind the rib.

If you mount the gun so high that half the butt is visible from behind your shoulder, your neck will probably be strained backwards. If you mount it so low that it is almost sliding out from under your armpit, your neck, head and eyes will be strained downwards — naturally, at the first movement to the target, they will attempt to return to their normal positions, result: missed target. All strain is bad, because the affected body part will always try to revert to its natural state. A good norm is to have the top of the butt *roughly* level with the top of the shoulder.

Some heads are hunched so far back on stocks that you wonder why they bothered to have a Monte Carlo comb, others are strained so far forward that you wonder how they don't get bloody noses! Neck length, face length and the height of the shoulders all affect the distance from shoulder to eye. The short-necked shooter is the luckiest, as the gun will come naturally into place in his face and under his eye — it's the ostrich-necks that have problems. The head more forward than back is favoured, as it gives a better view down the rib and a better muzzle to target relationship. Obviously stock length is of prime importance here and a rough guide is: don't shoot a stock any longer than you have to — all that does is bring your head back along the comb and take the gun balance out of your hands and into the muzzle.

Cheek pressure to the comb should not be so great as to cause muscular strain on the neck muscles and, coincidentally, the arms, as the strain will cause the relief of pressure on moving the gun. This will lift the eye from the position it was set in and lifting the eye a quarter of an inch will alter the placing of the shot pattern some nine inches out at thirty-five to forty yards — sufficient to cause a clean miss. On the other hand, cheek-comb pressure must not be so light as to allow the stock to move away from the head when swinging to right-hand targets.

The above factors also affect eye alignment. The eyes should be able to view along the rib at as near their natural viewing level as possible. Again, the short-necked fellow wins out. For the long-neck, who has to lower his head a bit, avoid making the cheek pressure from the front of the cheek, for it causes the eyes to cant down. They must then peer up through the eyelashes and obviously try to return to normal viewing level when the target appears and the gun starts to move. Result: another lifted head and another untouched target. Don't forget to ascertain, preferably through an optician, which is your master eye. If you have frequent or even occasional equal strength vision, don't hesitate to close one eye – either before calling for the clay or, better still, after the clay has left the trap and as your eye and gun are closing on the target for the delivery of the shot. Your scores may improve considerably as otherwise the other equal-strength eye may sometimes take over the guidance system – with disastrous results.

Some shooters advocate moving from the hips, others move only their arms. I believe the body should be considered as a tank, with a turret-mounted gun: our 'tank' is our feet and our turret is the rest of the body from the ankles up. I move my whole body laterally to a target and there's also a slight forward movement – body-flow – out in the direction of the target I'm pursuing. When you swing laterally to a wide-angled target, don't lean over from the waist, but pivot on an even keel.

GUN-MOUNTING

This falls into two categories. The first comprises those clay sports where the gun is not mounted until the appearance of the target. For them, basic game shooting gun-mounting techniques are applicable and are covered elsewhere in this book. There is a slight, but important difference. Under most circumstances, a game gun is mounted from a position in which the muzzle is at low port, i.e. the barrels facing the ground and the butt therefore uppermost. With clays, knowing when and where the 'bird' is coming from and then needing to shoot quickly, it is an advantage to start with the gun at the high port. This means the barrels will be raised, with the muzzle at approximately eye level, the butt lowered and the upwards slope of the whole gun roughly approximating to the median angle of most shots.

The second category are the clay sports for which the gun is mounted prior to calling for the bird. Here, mounting the gun at an angle level with the shoulder and eyes is a good norm, but as above, it's worth considering mounting the gun angled *slightly* upwards. This insures that the gun is brought to the head and not *vice versa* and then, once head and gun are locked together in the correct position the whole body inclines forward (and possibly slightly downward) to the target exit point − depending on whether the exit point is at ground, waist or head level. Whether mounting in either category, the motion should be smooth and fluid, not jerky.

PREPARATION AND CONCENTRATION

Proper preparation for each shot is the key to its success or failure. First check that stance is correct, then take a deep breath, and exhale to ensure that the body is completely relaxed and finally mount the gun smoothly. Focus your eyes a little in front of the target exit point at a point where you can recognise the speeding target as a clay pigeon. If you look too close to the exit, the flash of high-speed movement will cause a panicky stab at the clay, instead of a smooth, controlled swing. Concentrate utterly on what you are about to do: break one clay pigeon. Get rid of all distracting thoughts − especially those connected with a previously missed target, for if you're still thinking about that, you'll be sure to miss the next one, too. When you are *sure* that you are *fully* prepared, call 'pull' − not too violently, or the violence of the call will cause tension in your body and again turn your gun movement into a jerky stab.

Above all else, keep your head down during the gun movement to the target. The relationship established between eye and rib must stay the same until the completion of the shot. Probably more targets are missed by lifting the head than any other fault. Generally the head is lifted because the shooter wants to see if he's broken the target − before he's even shot at it!

HOW TO BREAK THEM

To kill any moving target, you must shoot where it's going − not where it was. To do this, we 'lead' a target, which means that even after the brain has given the command to pull the trigger, the gun must be kept moving. This allows for the time taken for the brain's message to reach the muscles, the muscles to react, the time for the hammer to strike the firing pin, the ignition of the cartridge and the passage of the shot through the air to the target — which has obviously continued moving from the time your brain instructed the finger to pull the trigger. Lead can be given in two ways. The simplest is termed 'swinging through'. Using this method, the one normally used in England and Europe, every target can be shot in the same way.

Pick it up from behind, lock on to its flight path, catch it up and overtake it, firing at the moment of overtaking. It's like passing a car on the motorway — you come up from behind and smoothly accelerate sufficiently to overtake. You don't stop when you have passed the car, so don't stop your gun either — keeping it moving gives the necessary lead. Many Americans favour a method known as 'pointing out'. To achieve lead this way, they must calculate different distances in mid-air from twenty to forty yards away and then place their gun so many feet and inches in front of the moving target, so that the shot charge and target intercept at a chosen point. As there are many different shots in clay shooting, the calculated lead will have to be different each time — and as distances in mid-air also look different to each person, I've never understood how they manage the calculations without a slide rule!

DOWN-THE-LINE

DTL is among the most widely shot clay target in Great Britain and in the States, where it is known as 'trap-shooting', another hangover from live pigeon shooting terms. A squad of five shooters stands sixteen yards behind the trap house on five shooting positions, which form a slight semi-circle. The first man in the squad calls 'Pull!' and the clay is electrically released from the trap by a puller situated behind the shooters, pressing a button. The DTL clay travels forty-eight to fifty-two yards, at ten yards from the trap it's between nine and ten feet up and it can be thrown in an arc of 45° either side of a line drawn through the centre of the trap house.

Shooters used to be able to 'read' electric traps 100%, which

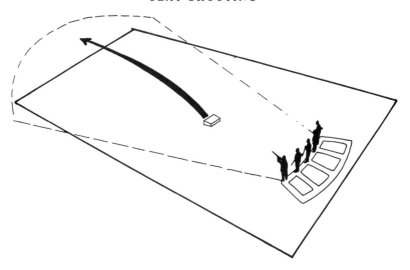

Down-the-line layout.

meant that they could calculate the automatic angling movement of the trap and know in which direction their clay would fly. This ridiculous practice resulted in equally ridiculously high scores and now electric traps are fitted with a device called an interrupter, which causes the clays to be thrown at truly random angles. To illustrate this point, at the last American Championship before the installation of interrupters, forty-four competitors went 'straight', i.e. they killed two hundred out of two hundred targets. Since interrupters, only seven to nine straights are annually registered at the same shoot. In America, they only fire one barrel at DTL, whereas we are allowed two shots, the results being scored three points for a first shot kill and two points for a second barrel. DTL is shot in 'rounds' of twenty-five targets, each shooter firing at five targets from each shooting position or 'stand' and competitions are over fifty, one hundred or two hundred targets.

Most British shooters 'sight' their guns just below the trap house roof, from one corner to the other, depending on which stand they are. This practice probably stems from the erratic exit nature of targets launched from the old manual traps, as American shooters mount their guns over the trap house roof. They know that their targets will fly an absolutely regular flight path and so place their guns very close to the actual point in the air they are going to shoot the clay. Most DTL clays are broken between thirty and thirty-three yards, just before the clay reaches its peak height. Thereafter it begins to drop, offering a somewhat slow beginner an even harder shot!

DTL VARIATIONS

A system known as Handicap is operated extensively in America and very occasionally here. The DTL shooting positions are extended backwards in one yard stages (in America by half-yard stages to twenty-seven yards). The yardage from which a competitor shoots is calculated from his past performance, and, as he wins or shoots scores over a certain level, so he works his way backwards.

Single-barrel, which, as previously mentioned, is the norm for all DTL shooting in America, is again occasionally shot here. From time to time, there are suggestions to make all British DTL shooting single barrel, too. This would be an excellent move, but is always thwarted by those whose egos prefer high scores rather than a harder test of skill.

Double-rise is when two targets are thrown simultaneously from a DTL trap, locked into one position. It is also called doubles and the two clays are thrown at fixed angles, about 45° right and left of centre. Experienced doubles shooters always take the right hand target first from positions one, two and three − and the left hander from four and five. From these stands, it is virtually a straight-away target and can be quickly killed. They then swing rapidly on to the angle bird in order to kill it while it is still rising. If they are slow, the second clay will be dropping and, as previously explained, is therefore far harder to hit. However, a balance must be found to avoid panicking too quickly on the first bird and so missing both. Doubles, like all clays, are only broken *one at a time*.

OLYMPIC TRENCH

This could be described as a highly advanced form of DTL shooting and is the only form of DTL shot by the rest of the world and the form for all European, World and Olympic Championships. Only

Great Britain, America and countries where their influence has touched shoot the true DTL. Olympic Trench is literally a twenty-four-yard long underground trench containing not one, but fifteen traps. They are adjustable, but only fire one fixed angle and height at a time. They are split into five groups of three traps, one group in front of each of the five shooting stands, and their clays exit at ground level. The clays travel around ninety mph (nearly twice as fast as DTL targets), nearly twice as far (77–87 yards), through a 90° arc, and with height variations of between 3' 6" and 13', eleven yards from the trap.

The line of shooting positions is straight, not curved, as in DTL and they are fifteen metres (16½ yards) from the traps. A squad consists of six, not five shooters, the sixth man waiting behind the number one position. Instead of firing five shots from each stand, trench shooters change positions after every shot – hence the need for six shooters, so that shooting continues uninterruptedly as the shooter from the fifth stand walks back to the first (with his gun open and unloaded). Targets are generally released by a microphone system, which is activated by the shooter's voice calling 'pull'. This eliminates any possibility of slow releases. In each group of three traps, one throws to the right, one to the left

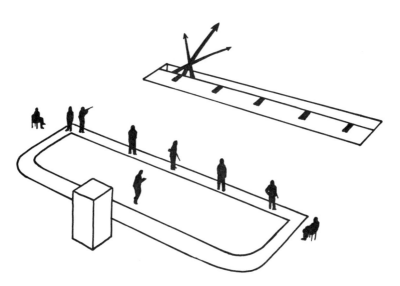

Olympic Trench; the sixth gun is waiting behind the No 1 position, until each gun moves up one place, when the No 5 man will come round behind to No 1 position.

and one more or less straight. The selection of targets is done automatically by an electric selector box. This ensures that each shooter gets very nearly the same number of lefts, rights and straights in every hundred targets, but it is virtually impossible to read the sequence, except on some outdated equipment.

As in DTL, two shots are allowed, but for trench, it's kills that count and no points system exists. Good shooters fire their first shot on average between thirty-five and thirty-eight yards, the second from forty to forty-five and even over fifty yards. Experienced trench shooters often fire the second barrel at 'bits' left from a first barrel kill. This keeps them in practice for killing with the second barrel when it's needed. In the past, $1\frac{1}{4}$oz of shot was allowed, as opposed to the $1\frac{1}{8}$oz for DTL, but now only 1oz will be allowed for trench and DTL disciplines.

Whereas DTL squads develop a certain, quite fast rhythm of one shooter following another – trench shooters take more time to prepare for each shot, as the speedier, far harder targets require much more concentration. As opposed to DTL, there is really less choice of where the gun should be held or sighted for trench. It should be held below the target exit point for if it was held above, an extreme low bird would not be seen leaving. There is a mark above the central trap of each group of three, which serves as an appropriate aiming point. The comparatively slow DTL target can be shot comparatively slowly and deliberately, but the trench target has to be shot fast. If one could find the perfect blend of instinct and deliberation, the fortunate shooter would have stumbled across something akin to the old alchemists' search for the elixir of life! A handful of top flight competitors have this rare combination, but most shooters err too much towards one extreme or the other.

UNIVERSAL TRENCH

This could be called Olympic Trench's little brother. In construction it varies from OT only in that it is a smaller trench, containing just five traps. The shooting stands, distances, angles, squads, etc., are all the same, but, instead of being faced with a choice of three targets from any one stand at OT, here you have all five

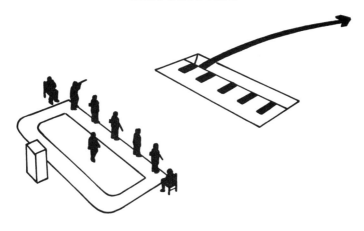

possibilities at any time. From stands one and five, this can make for some pretty sharp angles. Five trap Universal Trench was brought out to reduce the cost of a fifteen trap Olympic Trench, but has never achieved the same popularity.

AUTOMATIC BALL TRAP

Automatic Ball Trap is basically another substitute for Olympic Trench, again designed to reduce the construction, installation and running costs. It is one machine which is in constant vertical and horizontal motion. Thus it is able to duplicate all the angles and heights of OT. There are two basic versions; the first throws all targets the same distance and remains in constant motion, the clay being released at random when the shooter calls 'pull'. A more sophisticated version, which more nearly duplicates trench conditions, has an eccentric cam which allows targets to be thrown at slightly varying distances and instead of moving constantly, it is computer programmed to move to a specific position for each shot. This is to ensure, as with OT, an even distribution of lefts, rights and straights for each shooter in his hundred targets. With the constant-motion, random-throw model, it is possible for a competitor to get, purely by chance, a preponderance of one angle, as opposed to another. Shooting stands are in an arc, as for DTL, this being the only other difference from OT.

325

DOUBLE-TRAP

This is the newest of all clay pigeon disciplines and is in reality a created discipline for international competition designed specifically with television in mind. There had been assertions that Olympic Trench and ISU skeet were not exciting enough for the media. The new discipline had to be sufficiently challenging to make it worthy of competition. The guarantee of international status was enough to overcome initial reticence.

As with other trap disciplines the shooter operates around a layout consisting of five shooting stations. With Double-Trap the shooter receives five pairs of targets from each station – a fifty target course instead of the usual twenty-five. A complex scheme of targets will be received. However by the end of the round, each shooter will have received precisely the same targets as all others in the squad and in this way the discipline can be considered fair to everyone. The targets are slightly slower than in other international disciplines. However the challenge of dealing with two simultaneously launched targets is quite sufficient to retain interest!

ZZ BIRDS

These are not strictly clay pigeons, but have a white plastic centre shaped like a clay, which is fitted with red wings. It was designed (after Princess Grace of Monaco had Monte Carlo's famous live pigeon shooting banned) to replace and duplicate the flight of the live bird. Five machines are arranged in front of the shooter, in place of the semi-circle of five boxed birds. All are rotating on electric motors and when the shooter calls pull, one careers away, simulating the unpredictable zig-zag flight of a pigeon. To 'kill', the wings must separate from the body and the body *must* drop within the boundary fence for a kill to count. As with live pigeon shooting, distance handicap shooting and large money prizes apply. However, it has never begun to achieve the popularity of live pigeon shooting which is still very active in Italy, Spain, France, Portugal and the Latin American countries.

SKEET

There are two forms of skeet prevalent in Great Britain: the International Shooting Union's (ISU's) internationally recognised form, and English skeet. All skeet shots are taken far closer than any of the above clay games – from as near as only some five yards out to a maximum of about twenty-five yards. They are almost all crossing shots, as opposed to going away shots. A skeet layout is a large semi-circle comprising seven shooting positions, linking two trap houses which are forty yards apart and which, in turn, are bisected by an eighth position. One house is called the high house and releases targets from some ten feet above the ground, while the low house clays come out $3\frac{1}{2}$ feet up. Both clays fly along set flight paths and never vary in angle, so the skeet shooter knows *exactly* where every target will go. The crossing point of the high and low targets is eighteen feet out from station eight, i.e. from the centre of the two houses. All targets must be killed before they cross a line extended outwards from the front of each trap house, otherwise they are considered as lost.

Differences between ISU and English skeet are as follows: ISU targets travel seventy-one to seventy-three yards, English ones sixty yards. After calling for an ISU target, it may be released (electrically) either instantaneously or with up to three seconds delay, while English clays are released immediately. For ISU, the

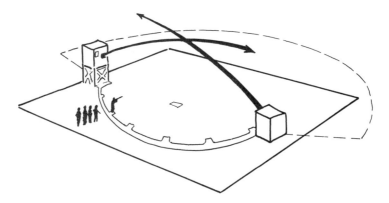

A skeet layout. The high house is on the left of the diagram and the low house on the right. The targets cross eighteen yards beyond the midpoint between the two houses.

gun must be in the down position, with the butt clearly visible below the right elbow and touching the hip — and it may not be moved until the target appears. For English, the gun can be in the shoulder or at any position below it and can be brought into the shoulder at any time the shooter chooses — this is called the optional gun position. Otherwise, the two skeet games are the same.

A squad consists of five shooters. Number one man goes to station one, loads one cartridge only and calls 'Pull' for the high house target. He then reloads and calls 'Mark' for the low house. These are known as 'singles'. Next, under a new rule known as 'speed-up' shooting (designed to reduce the time previously taken to shoot a round of skeet), he loads two cartridges and again calls 'Pull'. This time both high and low house targets are released simultaneously and are known as 'doubles'. The procedure at position two is the same, then singles only are shot from stands three, four and five, while on stands six and seven both singles and doubles are again shot. When shooting doubles, the going away target is always shot first.

Experienced shooters will break most of their targets at or around the mid-point of the range, although some of them allow the incoming target to come nearer to them. After station seven, the squad proceeds to station eight, in the middle of the range, directly between the two trap houses. They shoot a single target from the high and low house, which targets must be broken before they cross the central line. This makes a total of twenty-four targets — if a shooter has killed all of them, he then repeats the station eight low house as his twenty-fifth bird. If, however, he has missed a target along the way, he repeats his first miss and so makes the round of twenty-five birds.

There is a tendency among skeet shooters to adopt strange, crouching stances. Try to avoid them, as such awkward postures achieve nothing, except discomfort and tension. Suffice to say that anyone applying the basic principles, previously expounded, will do all right! Recall particularly smooth body movement and follow through, keeping the head down throughout the shot. For doubles, as with DTL's doubles, don't panic on the first clay, worrying about the second; that guarantees two misses. Just remember, clays are killed one at a time.

One last tip about skeet — as with the other forms already

described, don't look into the trap house exit, as the target will appear too fast and make you stab at it. Focus your eyes a short distance in front of the trap house, but it isn't necessary, if you're shooting gun down, to bring the gun all the way back to the same point. The gun has to go back in the opposite direction and you can conserve some part of the gun movement by letting your eyes do the initial tracking, while the gun is being mounted to join them on the target.

SPORTING CLAYS

Much of what applies to skeet is also applicable to English sporting. Similar guns are often used. There are national and international variations. For English sporting competitions the gun may be either mounted into the shoulder, or unmounted, prior to calling for the target. As with other domestic disciplines, it is only legal to use 1 oz loads – with shot sizes 6–9 permissible. Sporting enjoys an ever-increasing rise in popularity probably because it sets out to simulate all game and rough shooting situations and therefore has the widest appeal to shooters. The annual British Open Sporting Championship, for example, attracts entries far in excess of those attracted to other disciplines. The number of major sporting championships – many of which are large sponsored events – is increasing on an almost annual basis. The reason for this is the large amount of space required to install a sporting layout, the heavy capital outlay (in comparison to DTL or skeet) in traps and equipment – and the many people needed to run such a shoot. A description of one such ground will make the point.

It comprises:

1. A walk-up between bushes concealing thirty traps, which, between singles and doubles, throw some fifty targets at unpredictable angles and heights across or away from the shooter at distances from fifteen to forty yards. The clays are released by a puller walking behind the gun, who pulls on concealed wires connected to the traps – at the moment you least expect them and generally when you are on the wrong foot!

2. Partridges driven across a low belt of trees from concealed towers in singles and pairs, some thirty to thirty-five yards out.

3. Fur and feather — an ingenious combination where a clay disc simulating a rabbit is rolled along the ground thirty to thirty-five yards from the shooter and on the report of the gun, a 'snipe' zips back, flying low and slightly away from the shooter, in the opposite direction from which the rabbit came.

4. Rising teal — which like its feathered counterpart, when flushed from cover, stands on its tail and ascends vertically into the heavens.

5. Pheasants — that are 'driven' off a seventy-foot tower concealed in the trees, so that the singles or pairs seem to appear suddenly from nowhere overhead, or to one side of the gun.

6. Driven grouse — here the gun stands in a butt and takes one bird in front of him, swinging round to take the second behind, which has been released on the report of the first shot. In common with most targets on this course, these clays have a trajectory of seventy to seventy-five yards.

7. Pigeons, the first of which wings silently and all but invisibly through the top branches of the trees, giving the gun a clear shot as it leaves the edge of the wood, whereupon another — as if disturbed from his roost by the first shot — crashes out of the woods, bound for distant parts and, with luck is killed some forty-five yards away.

8. Rocketing pheasants — that great reducer of egos, the 120-foot tower, whose targets fairly qualify for the term 'flying aspirins'. Again thrown in singles and pairs, overhead and to either side, many targets are missed here because people talk themselves out of hitting them, believing them to be impossible. However, I have watched a fifteen-year-old, who didn't *know* they were 'impossible', calmly smashing the forty to fifty yard targets with a .410!

In FITASC sporting the gun is allowed to say 'Ready', before calling for his targets. The gun must not be mounted until the target appears. Two shots may be fired at single targets. For doubles here, the two shots must be fired at the two separate

The walk-up section of a sporting layout; the clays are released without warning

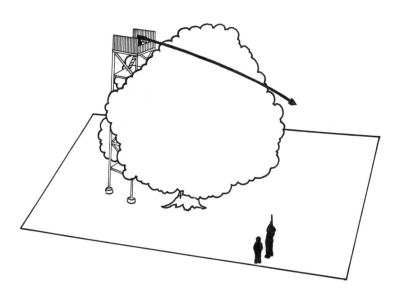

Driven pheasants, coming off a seventy-foot tower concealed by trees are one of the toughest sections of a sporting setup.

clays, while in FITASC if the first target of a double is missed, the second shot may also be fired at it. With so many and such varied targets, it is obvious that slightly different techniques are again required that we don't have space for here. Again, an application of the basic principles of good shooting is the best bet ... along with this timely reminder, applicable particularly to the high

331

tower pheasants, remember to shoot where a clay's going, not where it was: if you shoot too far in front there is still a good chance that part of the eight- or ten-foot long shot string will catch the target, but if you're one inch behind — forget it!

CLASSIFICATION

Virtually all competition shoots run in this country incorporate some form of classification system. This is to allow shooters at various stages of development or with certain levels of ability to compete among each other and so be able to win prizes which, if they always had to compete with the experts, they would have little chance of winning. Classes are generally split into AA, A, B and C, based on a shooter's performance from the previous year. If someone at a shoot has no previous record, he may well be classified, for that shoot, over his performance on the first half of the competition. For international disciplines — OT, UT, ABT, ISU skeet and FITASC sporting — classes used will be A, B, C and D. For unclassified shooters the draw system operates: for example, on a hundred-target shoot the first seventy-five targets (3×25 target rounds) are taken and a draw takes place to syphon off two rounds. Again by way of example, if rounds two and three are drawn then these are used to calculate the shooter's average and thus class for the day. In America classes continue to D and E and they also have, as we do, special classes for colts, ladies and veterans. For European, World and Olympic events, there are no classes and everyone competes on the same terms.

For any further information about clay pigeon shooting in this country, please write to the Clay Pigeon Shooting Association, 107 Epping New Road, Buckhurst Hill, Essex, IG9 5TQ. Finally, although it is of course important to each individual to become a good shot, it is more important to him — and to every member of the shooting fraternity — that he becomes a safe shot.

Shooting Law

Peter Turner

Revised by Jean Skinner, BASC

The law relating to shooting is complex and extensive, with many pitfalls for the unwary. Without the law there could be no protection of the quarry species, no means of controlling indiscriminate shooting, no means of keeping land free from disturbance, and hence no shooting. Thus, it is of vital importance that all shooting men should observe the law and see that others do so. The complexity of the law arises for reasons which are partly historical and also out of the variety and wealth of sport available in this small island. By taking pains to regulate as many aspects of the sport as possible, British legislation has succeeded in preserving the maximum of sport. This is something for which this country is greatly envied in many parts of the world. One important means of maintaining this position is to respect and enforce the law; even though, at times, this may be burdensome.

SHOTGUN CERTIFICATES

Before possessing, purchasing or acquiring any firearm, it is necessary to obtain the appropriate certificate. For this purpose a shotgun is defined as a smooth-bore gun (not being an airgun) which has a barrel not less than twenty-four inches in length and does not have any barrel with a bore exceeding two inches in diameter, either has no magazine or has a non-detachable magazine incapable of holding more than two cartridges and is not a revolver gun.

It should be noted that a gun which has been adapted to have a fixed magazine shall not be regarded as falling within that provision unless the magazine bears a mark approved by the Secretary of State denoting the fact and a certificate provided by either of the two Proof Houses or such other person as may be approved for the purpose. Any gun within this definition requires a Shotgun Certificate.

To obtain a Shotgun Certificate it is necessary to apply on a form provided by the police, to the Chief Officer of Police for the area in which the applicant resides. Four passport-type photographs of the applicant should accompany the application which has to be countersigned by someone who has known the applicant for at least two years. Such an application shall be granted unless the Chief Officer of Police has reason to believe that the applicant is a prohibited person, cannot be permitted to possess a shotgun without danger to the public safety or the peace or if he is satisfied that the applicant has no good reason for possession.

A Shotgun Certificate remains in force for three years but can be renewed by completing the appropriate application form and providing four passport-type photographs. The only conditions which can be imposed in respect of a Shotgun Certificate are those prescribed by the Secretary of State. The prescribed conditions, since introduction of the Firearms (Amendment) Act 1988, are: that the holder of the certificate must, on receipt, sign it in ink with his usual signature; that he must inform at once the Chief Officer of Police by whom it was granted of the theft or loss in Great Britain of any shotgun in his possession; that the holder must, without undue delay, inform the Chief Officer of Police by whom the certificate was granted of any change in his permanent address, and that the shotguns to which the certificate relates must at all times be stored securely so as to prevent, so far as is reasonably practicable, access to the guns by an unauthorised person.

If a shotgun is subsequently sold, let on hire, given to another certificate holder (but *not* to a registered firearms dealer), the appropriate entries should be made on the respective shotgun certificates and the police notified of the transaction within seven days, giving a description of the shotgun in question, including identification number if any. The certificate holder must state the nature of the transaction and the name and address of the other person concerned, by way of a recorded delivery or registered letter. In the case of a loan of a shotgun to another certificate holder for a period of no more than seventy-two hours, no notification is required. If the loan exceeds this time period, the previously described notification is required and will need to be repeated when the gun is returned to the lender.

If a shotgun requires repair, the repairer is under a legal obligation to examine the shotgun certificate of the person who produces it for repair.

In order to buy shotgun cartridges it is necessary to produce a valid shotgun certificate. It is possible to purchase for someone else, providing that person's certificate can be produced, together with his written authority to purchase the ammunition on his behalf.

There are some exceptions to the law which enable certain persons to have a shotgun in their possession and to use it without holding a certificate. Two are of great importance. First there is the exception which permits the use of a shotgun at a time and place approved for shooting at artificial targets by the Chief Officer of Police for the area in which that place is situated. Secondly there is an exception which permits a person to borrow a shotgun from the occupier of private premises and to *use* it in his presence on those premises. Both these exceptions are of great value in training the young and other beginners.

Except where the exemptions apply, the offence of possessing a shotgun without a certificate attracts a maximum penalty of a fine and/or a term of imprisonment.

A police constable can demand production of a Shotgun Certificate by any person whom he believes to be in possession of a shotgun. If a certificate is not produced, the constable may seize the gun and require the person failing to produce the certificate to declare his name and address.

A shotgun may only be sold or transferred lawfully to a registered firearms dealer or a person producing a certificate which enables him to purchase or acquire it.

FIREARM CERTIFICATE

Any person wishing to purchase, possess, hire, or accept as a gift a rifled weapon (other than an air weapon not declared by the Secretary of State to be specially dangerous) or ammunition therefor; or a smooth bore gun with a short barrel or a removable magazine, must be in possession of a Firearm Certificate.

Application for a Firearm Certificate must be made in much the same way as for a Shotgun Certificate. The applicant, if he is to succeed, will need to satisfy the Chief Officer of Police that he has a good reason for purchasing, possessing or acquiring the weapon, or ammunition and that he can be permitted to have it in his possession without danger to the public safety or to the peace. A certificate will not be granted to a prohibited person, nor to a person of intemperate habits or unsound mind, nor to a person whom the Chief Officer of Police believes to be for any reason unfitted to be entrusted with such a weapon.

There are four standard conditions on a Firearm Certificate but the Chief Officer of Police may impose further conditions if he considers it necessary to do so.

Possession of a rifled weapon without a certificate carries a maximum penalty of a term of imprisonment or a fine, or both when committed in aggravated form. When not so committed the maximum is a shorter term of imprisonment, or a fine or both.

A person of or over the age of seventeen may, without holding a firearm certificate, borrow a rifle from the occupier of private premises and use it on those premises in the presence either of the occupier or of a servant of the occupier if a) the occupier or servant in whose presence it is used holds a firearm certificate in respect of that rifle; and b) the borrower's possession and use of it complies with any conditions as to those matters specified in the certificate. In such circumstances the borrower may purchase or acquire ammunition for use in the rifle and have it in his possession during the period for which the rifle is borrowed, providing this complies with the authorities on the lender's certificate.

The law imposes further restrictions on the acquisition and use of all firearms by minors. Thus no firearm or ammunition may be sold or hired to a person under seventeen years of age. Furthermore it is an offence for a person under seventeen to have an air weapon with him in a public place except an air gun or an air rifle so covered with a securely fastened gun cover that it cannot be fired. There are exceptions to this rule in respect of shooting galleries and members of approved rifle clubs. Persons under fifteen may not have an assembled shotgun with them except while under the supervision of a person aged twenty-one or over, or unless it is so covered with a securely fastened gun cover that it cannot be fired. It is an offence for any person under the age of fourteen to have any air weapon or ammunition for an air weapon with him, unless he is under the supervision of a person aged twenty-one or over and the weapon is not used to fire a missile beyond the premises on which it is being used.

GAME LICENCES

Anybody intending to shoot game requires a Game Licence in addition to a Shotgun or Firearm Certificate. Game for this purpose is defined as pheasants, partridges, grouse, blackgame, moorgame, hares, snipe, woodcock, rabbits and deer.

In the case of rabbits and deer there are many exceptions and in practice a licence can usually be dispensed with. For example, a licence is not required when rabbits or deer are killed on enclosed land by permission or order of the owner; nor is a licence required by a person lawfully exercising his rights under the Ground Game Acts.

The production of a Game Licence can be demanded by the owner or occupier of land, a police officer or a person who himself holds a Game Licence, a gamekeeper or an officer of a Local Authority. Failure to produce the licence and to give one's name and address is an offence punishable by a fine.

A Game Licence is obtainable as of right at any main Post Office on payment of the duty. In the case of an annual licence this is £6 for the period August 1 to July 31 next following. For a licence from August 1 to October 31 the duty is £4 and from November 1 to July 31 £4. A licence for any continuous period of fourteen days costs £2.

Even though a person has a Game Licence and has land on which he may lawfully shoot he must only do so in the open seasons. These are as follows (all dates inclusive):

Pheasant	October 1 to February 1
Partridge	September 1 to February 1
Grouse	August 12 to December 10
Ptarmigan (Scotland only)	August 12 to December 10
Blackgame	August 20 to December 10

Hares and Rabbits	Throughout the year
Snipe	August 12 to January 31
Woodcock in England	October 1 to January 31
Woodcock in Scotland	September 1 to January 3
Capercaillie	October 1 to January 31
	All birds listed in Schedule 2 part 1 of the Wildlife and Countryside Act, 1981 not specifically mentioned on previous page (including listed ducks and geese above the high water mark of ordinary spring tides): September 1 to January 31.
	Geese and ducks listed in Schedule 2 part 1 of the Wildlife and Countryside Act, 1981 below the high water mark of ordinary spring tides: September 1 to February 20

It should be firmly understood that, even though all the necessary certificates and licences have been obtained, they do not in themselves confer any right to shoot. Unless he has parted with them, the shooting rights are vested in the owner of the freehold estate in the land. Even though the freeholder may have let his land to an agricultural tenant, he may have reserved the sporting rights to himself. These he can either exercise himself or alternatively he may let them to a sporting tenant. Sometimes the sporting tenant may also be the agricultural tenant but this is not very usual. Only the person in whom the sporting rights are vested can authorise others to shoot.

ARMED TRESPASS

Anybody who shoots on land without the permission of the owner of the sporting rights is a trespasser; even if he has no intention of shooting game. As such he renders himself liable to

338

prosecution under section 20(2) of the Firearms Act 1968 which provides that 'a person commits an offence if while he has a firearm with him, he enters or is on any land as a trespasser and without reasonable excuse (the proof whereof lies on him)'. For the purposes of this offence, land includes land covered with water. The maximum penalty is a term of imprisonment or a fine or both.

In England and Wales it is well established law that the *only* public rights over the foreshore are of navigation and of fishing. There is no right to shoot on the foreshore and such a right cannot be acquired by long usage even though the owner may not have objected to the public shooting there for as long as anyone can remember. Because there is no right to shoot on the foreshore anybody who attempts to do so without permission is a trespasser and renders himself liable to prosecution. In England, Wales and Northern Ireland the British Association for Shooting and Conservation has an agreement with the Crown Estate Commissioners (and the Duchy of Lancaster) whereby its members have been granted authority to be on foreshore controlled by the Crown or Duchy of Lancaster with a shotgun and therefore they have a sound defence should a prosecution be brought against them for armed trespass. Elsewhere, it must be stressed, permission is required to shoot on private foreshore; and the onus is on the wildfowler to establish whether the foreshore is private. Access and egress must be by public right of way unless otherwise authorised, preferably in writing.

In Scotland the position is different. First, the public has a right to resort to the foreshore for the purpose of recreation, which is considered to include wildfowling and, therefore, to go wildfowling on the foreshore in Scotland is not a trespass. Secondly, even where the ownership of foreshore is vested in a private individual, the Crown retains certain rights (including the right to make recreational use of the foreshore) in trust for the public.

It should not be forgotten that access to the foreshore, or indeed any other shooting ground, can only lawfully be obtained over a right of way. Further, a right of way is precisely what it says and nothing more. To shoot from a right of way, without permission, is a trespass.

Those who trespass in pursuit of game, woodcock, rabbits or snipe run a further risk of prosecution under section 30 of the

Game Act 1831. It should be remembered that under this section it is not necessary to show that game has been taken, merely that the person concerned intended to do so. The maximum penalty for this offence is a fine and confiscation of the gun. The Game (Scotland) Act is very similar but applies additionally to wild duck and deer in addition to the species covered by the English Statute.

POACHING

The Night Poaching Acts make it an offence to take or destroy any game or rabbits unlawfully by night on any land, open or enclosed, or on any road or path, or unlawfully to enter by night on any land with any gun, net, engine or other instrument in order to take game.

The Poaching Prevention Act, 1862, is another important legal weapon in the war against poachers. This act enables any constable, having good cause to suspect a person of coming from land in possession of poached game, to stop and search him and his vehicle in any public road or place. Any game, guns or poaching equipment found can be seized. The maximum penalty under this Act is a fine and confiscation of the gun, game and equipment.

PROTECTED BIRDS

Game birds are protected in the main by the Game Acts, which also regulate the open seasons. The shooting of other birds, which provide many people with the bulk of their sport, is controlled by the Wildlife and Countryside Act, 1981. This Act makes it unlawful to kill or take or to attempt to kill or take any wild bird. The Act does contain exceptions however, which reduce the degree of protection afforded to various species. This is done by providing Schedules which contain lists of birds which can be killed, but only in accordance with the rules relating to the Schedule in which they are listed. A change to the Wildlife and Countryside Act 1981 has removed thirteen species of pest bird from Schedule 2 Part II. These pest species are now covered by an annual general licence issued for their year-round control by authorised persons. An authorised person is the owner or occupier or the person having the sporting rights over the land on which the authorised action is taken, or a person authorised by him, or a person authorised in writing by the Local Authority or certain statutory bodies.

Schedule 2 part I lists birds which can only be killed in the open season. They are:

> capercaillie, coot, moorhen, golden plover, common snipe, pochard, gadwall, mallard, pintail, shoveler, teal, tufted duck, wigeon, Canada goose, greylag goose, pink-footed goose, white-fronted goose (in England and Wales only), woodcock.

The following methods (relating to the use of shotguns) of killing or taking both wild birds and game birds are prohibited:

1. By using any automatic or semi-automatic weapon. 'Automatic weapon' and 'semi-automatic weapon' do not include any weapon the magazine of which is incapable of holding more than two rounds.

2. Any shotgun of which the barrel has an internal diameter at the muzzle of more than one and three-quarter inches.

3. The use of any device for illuminating a target.

4. The use of any form of artificial lighting or any mirror or other dazzling device.

5. The use as a decoy of any sound recording, or any live bird, or animal which is tethered, or which is secured by means of braces or other similar appliances, or which is blind, maimed or injured.

6. The use of any mechanically propelled vehicle in immediate pursuit of a wild bird for the purpose of killing or taking the bird.

In Scotland the Act prohibits shooting on Christmas Day and on Sundays. In England and Wales, Sunday shooting of game is prohibited; and also of the Schedule 3 birds in the following counties:

> Anglesey, Brecknock, Caernarvon, Cardigan, Carmarthen, Cornwall, Denbigh, Devon, Doncaster (County Borough), Glamorgan, Great Yarmouth (County Borough), Isle of Ely, Leeds (County Borough), Merioneth, Montgomery, Norfolk, Pembroke, Somerset, Yorkshire − North Riding and West Riding.

The Counties and County Boroughs referred to are those which existed prior to Local Government reorganisation in the mid 1970s.

INSURANCE

Each year brings with it a tragic crop of accidents involving firearms. The law imposes on everybody in connection with all activities a duty to take care for the safety of others. Any person who neglects that duty runs the risk of a claim for damages being made against him if somebody is injured as a result of that negligence. A high standard of care is rightly demanded by the law from users of firearms. Similarly a parent who negligently allows a child to have access to firearms or who permits a child to use a firearm negligently is liable for injuries inflicted by the child. Even though all efforts should be made to avoid accidents, nobody who shoots or allows his child to shoot should fail to insure against liability to third parties. Not only does such a failure create a risk of financial disaster to the negligent person, it also demonstrates an inexcusable irresponsibility unless that person is so wealthy as to be able to meet all potential claims without recourse to insurance. Membership of the BASC automatically carries third party liability insurance up to £2 million in respect of any one incident arising out of shooting or conservation activity (for example, gamekeeping).

Those who need more detailed guidance should consult the statutes and case law themselves. Furthermore it should not be forgotten that the law can, and does, change. The law in this chapter is stated as at June 1993. Above all it must be remembered that although on occasion the law can be made to look an ass, it is the foundation of all our liberties, including the right to shoot. Even so, the law is no substitute for commonsense, good manners and good sportsmanship.

Appendix

FIELD SPORTS ORGANISATIONS

The British Association for Shooting and Conservation (BASC)
Marford Mill
Rossett
Wrexham
Clwyd
LL12 0HL
Tel: 0244 570881   Fax: 0244 571678

BASC represents the shooter in all aspects of the sport and not, as some guns seem to imagine, just wildfowling. Membership ensures insurance for injury to self or third party. BASC carries out research and represents the shooter in matters of legislation at Westminster, Brussels and with the police.

The Game Conservancy Trust
Fordingbridge
Hants
SP6 1EF

The Game Conservancy carries out research into all aspects of game and wildfowl conservation, and farming and conservation practices as they affect shooting. It runs an advisory service for shoots and shooters and employs the best practical scientists available.

The British Field Sports Society
59 Kennington Road
London
SE1 7PZ

The Society represents and campaigns for all field sports, including shooting.

Index

345

APR X 1996